D1606709

Computer-aided Techniques
for the Design
of Multilayer Filters

Computer-aided Techniques for the Design of Multilayer Filters

Heather M Liddell

Queen Mary College, London

Consultant Editor, H G Jerrard

Foreword by H A Macleod

Adam Hilger Ltd, Bristol

© 1981 H M Liddell

All rights reserved. No part of this publication may be reproduced, stored in a retrieval system or transmitted in any form or by any means, electronic, mechanical, photocopying, recording or otherwise, without the prior permission of the publisher.

British Library Cataloguing in Publication Data

Liddell, Heather Mary
Computer-aided techniques for the design of multilayer filters
1. Light filters — Data processing
I. Title
681′.4   TS513

ISBN 0-85274-233-9

Published by Adam Hilger Ltd,
Techno House, Redcliffe Way, Bristol BS1 6NX

The Adam Hilger book-publishing imprint is owned by
The Institute of Physics

Set in 11/12 pt Press Roman by DJS Spools Ltd, Horsham, Sussex
Printed in Great Britain by J W Arrowsmith Ltd, Bristol

Contents

Foreword   ix

Preface   xi

1 **Basic Theory and Notation for Multilayer Filter Calculations**

    1.1   Notation for multilayer calculations   2
    1.2   Reflectance and transmittance at an interface   3
    1.3   Single film calculations   6
    1.4   Multilayer calculations   9
    1.5   Alternative formulation for multilayer calculations   12
    1.6   Periodic multilayers and the classical stack   14
    1.7   Effect of reflection from the back surface of the substrate   19
    1.8   Graphical methods of calculation   24
    1.9   Calculation of field intensities inside a multilayer   25

2 **Design of Filters by Analytical Techniques**

    2.1   Classification of the most important types of filter   30
    2.2   Achromatised designs for antireflection coatings (Liddell
           1966) – an illustration of the graphical method   34
    2.3   The 'two effective interface' method   40
    2.4   Design of broad band high-reflectance coatings   46
    2.5   Use of equivalent index techniques in multilayer design   50

3 **Application of Electrical Filter Design Techniques**

    3.1   Basic notation and definition of terms used in network
           synthesis   55
    3.2   Young's synthesis of antireflection coatings (1961)   57
    3.3   Seeley's synthesis of interference filters   61
    3.4   The multilayer circuit analogy method   64
    3.5   Chen's iteration for the circuit analogy method   71

4 The Use of Merit Function Techniques in Multilayer Design

4.1	Baumeister's successive approximations method	75
4.2	Automatic design methods	78
4.3	The least squares method of Heavens and Liddell	80
4.4	Dobrowolski's method for completely automatic synthesis of thin-film systems	87
4.5	Multilayer synthesis method of Pelletier, Klapisch and Giacomo	94
4.6	Chen's turning value method	98
4.7	Reduction of polarisation effects in designs	102

5 Fourier Transform Methods of Synthesis

5.1	The approximate vector method	109
5.2	The exact synthesis method	111
5.3	The thin-film synthesis program of Dobrowolski and Lowe	113

6 Theoretical Determination of Optical Constants of Thin Films

6.1	Formulae for reflectance and transmittance of a single absorbing film on a transparent substrate	119
6.2	Use of the Hadley–Dennison curves for determining n and k	121
6.3	Bennett and Booty's method	122
6.4	Abelès and Thèye's method	123
6.5	Calculation of optical constants and thickness by Ward et al	124
6.6	Other single wavelength methods	125
6.7	Hansen's theory for optical characterisation	125
6.8	Kramers Kronig analysis method	127
6.9	Determination of optical constants of weakly absorbing thin films	130
6.10	Use of dispersion formulae	133

7 Thickness Monitoring Techniques and Methods for Analysing Errors in Monitoring

7.1	Computer simulation of errors in monitoring	143
7.2	Baumeister's sensitivity analysis method (1962)	145
7.3	Ritchie's analysis of random errors in narrow band filters	149
7.4	Investigation of errors in the turning value monitoring method	149

7.5   'Dynamic' errors in monitoring   156
7.6   Monitoring systems which employ two or more wave-
      lengths   161
7.7   Filters containing layers with unequal optical thicknesses   164

**Appendix 1 A Brief Summary of Optimisation Techniques Useful for a
Multilayer Filter Designer**

A1.1   Introduction   168
A1.2   Methods for unconstrained optimisation   168
A1.3   Methods for minimising sums of squares of non-
       linear functions   170
A1.4   Methods for constrained optimisation   172
A1.5   Use and availability of optimisation routines in program
       libraries   173

Appendix 2 Computer Programs

A2.1   Program for calculating reflectance and transmittance of a
       non-absorbing, non-dispersive film   175
A2.2   Specification of the N^2 scan automatic design program NSQ2   180

References   183

Index   189

Foreword

It gives me enormous pleasure to write the foreword for this book especially as I have known Heather Liddell ever since she began working with thin films as a PhD student in Oliver Heavens' research group. At that time I had just entered the field myself, working in a small scientific instrument company situated fairly close by, and was a frequent visitor to the Heavens laboratory, bringing my latest problems with me. Heather Liddell was deeply involved in design calculations of multilayer coatings. Computers then were much less common and much less powerful than they are now, and she was making, I remember, frequent journeys of 100 miles or so to a place on the south coast of England where Oliver Heavens had somehow succeeded in arranging the use of a computer for her. So she learned about thin-film calculations and design in demanding circumstances which left no room for program development short of perfect and when computer time was scarce and precious. I quickly formed a high opinion of her work and have continued to have a very high regard for it ever since. She is, of course, a mathematician — a real one — and a specialist in computing and this, in combination with her years of experience in optical thin films, makes her the ideal person to write this book.

Provided the optical properties of the materials are well known, then the calculation of the optical properties of a given multilayer is nowadays a fairly straightforward task, which can even be performed on a programmable calculator of modest capacity. In contrast, the problem of finding a design which should have certain specified optical properties is much more difficult, and there is no unique solution. Traditionally, the thin-film coating designer has relied heavily on a library of standard building blocks with well known properties, such as quarter-wave stacks, which, by using a mixture of experience and instinct aided by some computing, can be coupled together to yield a wide range of filter characteristics. Computer refinement is frequently used to trim designs to have improved performance, but without a reasonably good initial design computer refinement is less useful. Techniques for design synthesis in the absence of a good starting design do exist, but they still tend to be used only by a few pioneers.

Optical coating design has been described in the past, with certain justification, as being as much an art as a science. Of course, as with the products of all creative abilities, there is a real sense of beauty associated with a good design, but this is not really what is meant by the phrase. Rather it is that there is some deficiency in our knowledge of the subject which we can sometimes remedy without our being able to define precisely how or why, and it is certainly not desirable that this aspect of the subject should be preserved. Undoubtedly great progress has been made in eliminating this feature. Design techniques are constantly improving and, especially in the area of computers and computing, there are enormously powerful tools available now which were unheard of a decade ago. In fact the literature has long passed the stage where it can be mastered without expert guidance.

Powerful methods frequently imply a certain remoteness from the calculations, which carries with it the danger of losing an element of sensitivity to what is really going on, and it then becomes of even greater importance than normal that the limitations of the technique are very well understood. As a simple example, it is all too easy to find computer solutions to an ill conditioned set of equations when hand calculations would have made the situation very clear.

All of us who work in optical thin films use mathematical techniques daily, but some, perhaps even many, of us will admit to an approach to the use of mathematical analysis which is, at times, possibly just a little too cheerful and optimistic, avoiding some of the rigour of the formal mathematician and, although this allows us to move more quickly, we occasionally fall down a hole which we did not know was there. The original literature is not always the best place to track down the existence of these traps.

For all these reasons it is particularly useful that the author of this book should be a specialist in mathematics and computing for whom their application in optical thin-film analysis and design has always been a major activity. I have seen the book in various stages of preparation and know something of the enormous effort which has gone into it. It is based on many years of experience.

There is a real need for this book, to guide the optical thin-film designer through the array of available methods, warning against the many pitfalls which exist, and helping to make the field still less of an art and more of a science.

Angus Macleod
July 1980

Preface

Throughout the writing of this book, my aim was to present the subject from the point of view of the thin-film designer. I have concentrated on computer methods rather than analytical techniques because my own experience as a designer has been concentrated on the former aspect. One result of this is that the division into chapters is based upon the type of method applied to the design rather than the type of filter to be designed. The book is intended to complement books such as H A Macleod's 'Thin-Film Optical Filters' and O S Heavens' 'Thin-Film Physics' and should be used in conjunction with them. There are certain omissions, because some subject areas are not relevant to the title I have chosen, for example some of the early methods of design for antireflection coatings, where the computer played no part. Although I have attempted to keep the book up to date with respect to current publications in the subject, inevitably some of the most recent results have been omitted, and I apologise to any authors who feel their work should have been included.

My earliest introduction to thin-film optics came as a research student working under the stimulating guidance of Oliver Heavens; following on from that work, I was fortunate to be associated with John Seeley and S D (Des) Smith, and later with Tony Fawcett and Bill Gray at Rank Optics. Others with whom I have had valuable discussions from time to time include Brian Bates, Jean Bennett, Peter Clapham, Verne Costich, J Dobrowolski, Roy F Miller, Emil Pelletier, M J D Powell and Alan Thetford.

My thanks and acknowledgments are due to the following journals, publishers and authors who provided and gave permission for the reproduction of material:

Journal of the Optical Society of America (The Optical Society of America)
Applied Optics (The Optical Society of America)
Optica Acta (Taylor and Francis Ltd)
Optical Spectra (The Optical Publishing Company Inc)
Nouvelle Revue d'Optique Appliquee
Le Vide
Progress in Optics (North-Holland Publishing Co Ltd)
E Delano and R J Pegis
J A Dobrowolski
O S Heavens
H A Macleod
E Pelletier
J S Seeley

I would like to thank Neville Goodman of Adam Hilger Ltd and several colleagues — in particular H A (Angus) Macleod, who read the manuscript and made valuable comments — without whose constant support and encouragement this work would never have reached completion. I am also extremely grateful to Helen Cowie who was most painstaking in her editing of the work and to Anne Pigott who helped type the manuscript.

Finally I want to thank my husband, Alan Poole, for his help and patience during the long period of writing and revision involved in the production of this book.

Heather M Liddell
July 1980

1 Basic Theory and Notation for Multilayer Filter Calculations

Thin-film optics deals with the propagation of light waves through single films and multilayers; a multilayer is a combination of a number of thin films. Mathematically, a 'thin' film is one whose thickness is of the order of the wavelength of light and whose extent is infinite compared to its thickness; we assume it is bounded by semi-infinite planes. The film is characterised by its refractive index, its absorption coefficient and its thickness (assumed to be uniform). For the most part, we shall be concerned only with homogeneous isotropic films, although some discussion of the effects of inhomogeneity will be included in chapter 6. For many applications the films are considered to be non-absorbing, although many of the design techniques may be extended easily to include absorbing films. A thin-film multilayer has the property of being able to reflect some wavelengths and transmit others, and the particular wavelengths or range of wavelengths for which it is highly reflecting or transmitting may be altered by changing the characteristics of the component films, so it may be used as an optical filter. Thin-film multilayers may be used in the ultraviolet, visible and infrared regions of the spectrum, covering a total spectral range from about $100\,\text{nm}$ to $100\,\mu\text{m}$, although most of the materials used tend to be strongly absorbing towards the limits of this range and in particular regions throughout the infrared.

This book will not deal with the problems of manufacture of thin-film systems, but only with design aspects of the subject; two books by Heavens (1955) and Macleod (1969) have been written which adequately cover the former and the subject of thin-film physics has also been covered by Heavens (1970) who includes a chapter on inhomogeneous and non-isotropic films. Other books and review articles have been written by Vašiček (1960), Knittl (1976), Baumeister (1963) and Heavens (1960), and many useful articles appear in a series of books on thin-film physics, edited by Hass (1960–). However, many of these books deal only briefly with computer-aided design techniques; this is a subject which has been developing rapidly over the past two decades and this book is an attempt to cover this particular aspect of thin-film technology. For the sake both of completeness and for comparison purposes, some of the earlier analytical methods of design will also be included in the text. Nowadays, most designers use both analytical and computer-aided techniques as complementary tools.

There are two basic problems in thin-film optics: the first is that of *analysis* involving the computation of the spectral characteristics of a multilayer whose optical constants and thicknesses are known. Its solution is

1

fairly straightforward, although the equations involved can be rather cumbersome; with the aid of a digital computer, one can obtain results with no particular difficulty; the second problem is vastly more complicated and consists of determining the optical constants and thicknesses of a multilayer to give some specified spectral response — this is the problem of *synthesis*. The problem is further complicated by the fact that only a limited number of materials are available for use in filters, although the development of co-evaporation techniques leads one to hope that the resulting constraint on refractive index values may be relaxed in the not too distant future. However, most of the techniques for dealing with the design problem include the analysis of particular multilayer configurations as a sub-problem, so we must start by defining the notation and basic equations to be used in this work.

1.1   Notation for multilayer calculations

Various systems of notation have been devised for multilayer calculations; the one used here is similar to that used by Heavens (1955), following Abelès (1948a). The electric and magnetic vectors of the positive going EM wave in the mth layer are denoted by $\mathbf{E}_m^+$ and $\mathbf{H}_m^+$, and those of the negative going wave by $\mathbf{E}_m^-$ and $\mathbf{H}_m^-$ respectively. Alternatively, the tangential fields $\mathbf{E}_m^+$ and $\mathbf{E}_m^-$ may be expressed in terms of $\mathbf{E}$ and $\mathbf{H}$ the electric and magnetic vectors:

$$\mathbf{E}_m^+ = \mathbf{E}_m^+ + \mathbf{E}_m^-,$$
$$\mathbf{H}_m = \mu_m(\mathbf{E}_m^+ - \mathbf{E}_m^-),$$

(1.1)

where $\mathbf{E}_m$ and $\mathbf{H}_m$ represent the resultant tangential fields. At normal incidence $\mu_m = n_m$, the refractive index of the mth layer, and at an angle of incidence,

$$\mu_m = n_m/\cos\theta_m, \qquad \text{for the } p\text{-component of polarisation,}$$
$$\mu_m = n_m \cos\theta_m, \qquad \text{for the } s\text{-component of polarisation.}$$

θ_m is the angle of incidence in the mth layer, which is related to the angles incidence in the medium of incidence (θ_0) and in the substrate (θ_{sub}) by Snell's law. The phase change of the beam of electromagnetic radiation on traversing the mth layer is given by

$$\delta_m = \frac{2\pi n_m d_m \cos\theta_m}{\lambda},$$

(1.2)

where λ is the wavelength of the radiation, d_m is the physical thickness of the mth layer, $n_m d_m$ is a quantity known as the 'optical thickness' and δ_m is sometimes called the 'phase thickness' of the layer. Figure 1.1 illustrates the configuration; the refractive indices of the medium of incidence and the substrate are n_0 and n_{sub} respectively. If any of the media are absorbing, n_m is replaced by the complex quantity $n_m = n_m - \mathrm{i}k_m$, where i is the square root of -1 and k_m is the absorption coefficient which is a measure of the energy

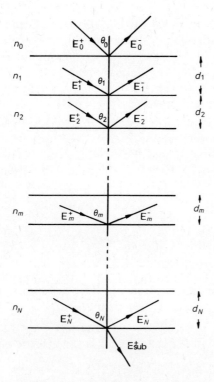

Figure 1.1   Multilayer notation.

absorption; the attenuation of the amplitude of the wave in a path of one vacuum wavelength is $\exp(-2\pi k_m)$ – i.e. the intensity of the wave drops by $\exp(-4\pi k_m)$ in one wavelength. The reflectance $\mathscr{R}$ and transmittance $\mathscr{T}$ of a multilayer are defined as the ratio of reflected and transmitted energies respectively to the incident energy. The *amplitudes* of the reflected and transmitted waves are complex quantities whose arguments represent phase change on reflection or transmission by the filter.

1.2   Reflectance and transmittance at an interface

We start by considering the simplest case – reflectance and transmittance at a single boundary between two homogeneous media. Physically, one observes the energy associated with the wave. The *Poynting vector*, $\mathbf{S}$, represents the instantaneous power flow per unit area; this is given by

$$\mathbf{S} = \frac{c}{4\pi}\,(\mathbf{E} \times \mathbf{H}),\tag{1.3}$$

(cgs units are used; $\mathbf{E}$ is measured in electrostatic units, $\mathbf{H}$ in electromagnetic units). For a full description of the electromagnetic field equations, the reader should consult Born and Wolf (1959). If **E** and **H** are complex, real parts should be used in evaluating the above expression. In practice, because of limitations in detecting instruments, one measures a time-averaged quantity $\bar{S}$. For real n,

$$\bar{S} = \left(\frac{c}{8\pi} \text{ Re } (EH^*) \right) \cdot \mathbf{r}, \tag{1.4}$$

where E, H represent vector amplitudes, **r** is a unit vector in the direction of propagation of the EM wave and the asterisk denotes complex conjugate. For a medium of index n, $n(\mathbf{r} \times \mathbf{E}) = \mathbf{H}$, so (1.3) and (1.4) may be expressed as

$$\mathbf{S} = \frac{c}{4\pi} n |\mathbf{E}|^2 \mathbf{r}, \tag{1.5}$$

$$\bar{\mathbf{S}} = \frac{c}{8\pi} n |\mathbf{E}|^2 \mathbf{r}. \tag{1.6}$$

The light reflected or transmitted at the boundary may be determined by applying the boundary conditions to the solutions of Maxwell's equations; for wave propagation in a non-conducting medium these equations are

$$\frac{\epsilon\mu}{c^2} \frac{\partial^2 \mathbf{E}}{\partial t^2} = \nabla^2 \mathbf{E},$$

$$\frac{\epsilon\mu}{c^2} \frac{\partial^2 \mathbf{H}}{\partial t^2} = \nabla^2 \mathbf{H}. \tag{1.7}$$

The boundary conditions require that the tangential components of both the electric and magnetic field vectors be continuous across the boundary. The situation is illustrated in figure 1.2: a plane wave is incident on the boundary defined by $z = 0$ between the medium of incidence (index n_0) and the second medium (index n_1); the amplitudes of the electric vectors of the wave approaching the boundary are E_{0p}^+, E_{0s}^+, those of the reflected wave are E_{0p}^-, E_{0s}^+ and those of the transmitted wave are E_{1p}^+, E_{1s}^+ (subscripts p and s denote the p- and s-components of polarisation respectively). The phase factors associated with these waves are

$$\exp \left[i \left(\omega t - \frac{2\pi n_0}{\lambda} (x \sin \theta_0 + z \cos \theta_0) \right) \right], \qquad \text{incident wave,}$$

$$\exp \left[i \left(\omega t - \frac{2\pi n_0}{\lambda} (x \sin \theta_0 - z \cos \theta_0) \right) \right], \qquad \text{reflected wave,}$$

$$\exp \left[i \left(\omega t - \frac{2\pi n_1}{\lambda} (x \sin \theta_1 + z \cos \theta_1) \right) \right], \qquad \text{transmitted wave.}$$

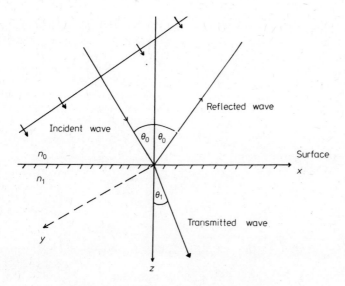

Figure 1.2 Reflection at an interface.

The sign convention followed is the one favoured by Heavens and Macleod, namely that in which the direction of the incident light is positive. This is different from that used by Born and Wolf, who prefer the cartesian sign convention. Applying the boundary conditions at $z = 0$ we obtain

$$
\begin{aligned}
E_{0x} &= (E_{0p}^+ + E_{0p}^-) \cos \theta_0 = E_{1x} = E_{1p}^+ \cos \theta_1, \\
E_{0y} &= E_{0s}^+ + E_{0s}^- = E_{1y} = E_{1s}^+, \\
H_{0x} &= n_0(-E_{0s}^+ + E_{0s}^-) \cos \theta_0 = H_{1x} = -n_1 E_{1s}^+ \cos \theta_1, \\
H_{0y} &= n_0(E_{0p}^+ - E_{0p}^-) = H_{1y} = n_1 E_{1p}^+.
\end{aligned}
\tag{1.8}
$$

These may be solved to give the ratios of the transmitted and reflected amplitudes to the incident amplitude for each component of polarisation, thus leading to expressions for the *Fresnel coefficients of reflection and transmission*:

$$
\begin{aligned}
r_{1p} &= \frac{E_{0p}^-}{E_{0p}^+} = \frac{n_0 \cos \theta_1 - n_1 \cos \theta_0}{n_0 \cos \theta_1 + n_1 \cos \theta_0}, \\[2mm]
r_{1s} &= \frac{E_{0s}^-}{E_{0s}} = \frac{n_0 \cos \theta_0 - n_1 \cos \theta_1}{n_0 \cos \theta_0 + n_1 \cos \theta_1}, \\[2mm]
t_{1p} &= \frac{E_{1p}^+}{E_{0p}^+} = \frac{2n_0 \cos \theta_0}{n_0 \cos \theta_1 + n_1 \cos \theta_0}, \\[2mm]
t_{1s} &= \frac{E_{1s}^+}{E_{0s}^+} = \frac{2n_0 \cos \theta_0}{n_0 \cos \theta_0 + n_1 \cos \theta_1}.
\end{aligned}
\tag{1.9}
$$

The energy reflection coefficients or *reflectances* obtained using equation (1·5) are

$$\mathcal{R}_p = \frac{(E_{0p}^-)^2}{(E_{0p}^+)^2} = r_{1p}^2,$$

$$\mathcal{R}_s = \frac{(E_{0s}^-)^2}{(E_{0s}^+)^2} = r_{1s}^2,$$

(1.10)

and the energy transmission coefficients or *transmittances* are

$$\mathcal{T}_s = \frac{n_1 \cos \theta_1 (E_{1s}^+)^2}{n_0 \cos \theta_0 (E_{0s}^+)^2} = \frac{n_1 \cos \theta_1}{n_0 \cos \theta_0} t_{1s}^2,$$

$$\mathcal{T}_p = \frac{n_1 \cos \theta_1 (E_{1p}^+)^2}{n_0 \cos \theta_0 (E_{0p}^+)^2} = \frac{n_1 \cos \theta_1}{n_0 \cos \theta_0} t_{1p}^2.$$

(1.11)

For *normal incidence,* these expressions become

$$\mathcal{R}_p = \mathcal{R}_s = \left| \frac{n_0 - n_1}{n_0 + n_1} \right|^2,$$

(1.12)

$$\mathcal{T}_p = \mathcal{T}_s = \frac{4 n_0 n_1}{(n_0 + n_1)^2},$$

(1.13)

provided n_0 and n_1 are real.

Note. There are two ways of considering reflectance and transmittance definitions which only really affect the transmittance. Either one may consider the intensity of the transmitted beam measured with the detector placed normally to the beam, or one may consider the flow of energy normal to the boundary, with the intensity measured normal to the boundary (i.e. the detector is placed parallel to the boundary). At a boundary this second method ensures $\mathcal{R} + \mathcal{T} = 1$, whereas the first does not. Thus the second convention is the one adopted here. This is only important in a multi-layer system when the exit medium is of a different index from the entrance medium.

1.3   Single film calculations

We have seen that the reflectance and transmittance of light at a single surface may be expressed in terms of the Fresnel coefficients, r_m and t_m respectively; for an absorbing film, these are complex (see chapter 6). The Fresnel coefficients are polarisation dependent; for non-absorbing media and the p-component of polarisation of light incident from the $(m-1)$th medium to the

mth medium we have

$$r_{mp} = \frac{n_{m-1}\cos\theta_m - n_m\cos\theta_{m-1}}{n_{m-1}\cos\theta_m + n_m\cos\theta_{m-1}}\,,$$

$$t_{mp} = \frac{2n_{m-1}\cos\theta_{m-1}}{n_{m-1}\cos\theta_m + n_m\cos\theta_{m-1}}\,.$$

(1.14)

The corresponding Fresnel coefficients for the s-component are

$$r_{ms} = \frac{n_{m-1}\cos\theta_{m-1} - n_m\cos\theta_m}{n_{m-1}\cos\theta_{m-1} + n_m\cos\theta_m}\,,$$

$$t_{ms} = \frac{2n_{m-1}\cos\theta_{m-1}}{n_{m-1}\cos\theta_{m-1} + n_m\cos\theta_m}\,.$$

(1.15)

In order to find a formula for the reflectance and transmittance of a single film illuminated by a parallel beam of light of unit amplitude at wavelength λ, we must consider the multiple reflections of light at each surface of the film and perform a multiple beam summation (see figure 1.3). Thus the total reflected amplitude is given by

$$R = \frac{r_1 + r_2\exp(-2i\delta_1)}{1 + r_1 r_2\exp(-2i\delta_1)}\,,$$

(1.16)

where

$$\delta_1 = \frac{2\pi n_1 d_1\cos\theta_1}{\lambda}\,,$$

(1.17)

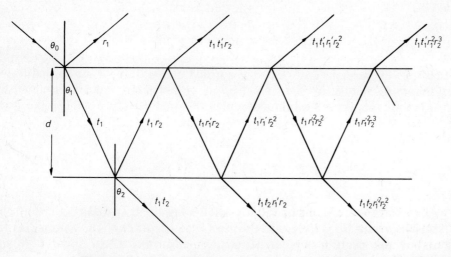

Figure 1.3 Multiple beam summation for a single film.

and the total transmitted amplitude is

$$T = \frac{t_1 t_2 \exp(-i\delta_1)}{1 + r_1 r_2 \exp(-2i\delta_1)} . \tag{1.18}$$

In these equations, the p and s subscripts have been dropped; the appropriate values for r, t should be inserted as required. The subscripts 1 and 2 refer to the first and second surface of the film. The film is assumed to be plane and parallel sided of thickness d_1 and refractive index n_1 and is bounded by semi-infinite layers of indices n_0 and n_2. The energies of the reflected and transmitted beams are $n_0 RR^*/2$ and $n_2 TT^*/2$ (the asterisk denotes complex conjugate), so the energy reflectance and transmittance are given by

$$\mathscr{R} = \frac{r_1^2 + 2r_1 r_2 \cos 2\delta_1 + r_2^2}{1 + 2r_1 r_2 \cos 2\delta_1 + r_1^2 r_2^2}, \tag{1.19}$$

$$\mathscr{T} = \frac{n_2}{n_0} \frac{t_1^2 t_2^2}{1 + 2r_1 r_2 \cos 2\delta_1 + r_1^2 r_2^2} . \tag{1.20}$$

For non-absorbing media, since energy is conserved,

$$\mathscr{R} + \mathscr{T} = 1. \tag{1.21}$$

We have already noted that the *amplitude* reflection and transmission are complex quantities whose arguments ψ and γ are the phase changes on reflection and transmission; these are given by

$$\tan \psi = \frac{-r_2(1 - r_1^2) \sin 2\delta_1}{r_1(1 + r_2^2) + r_2(1 + r_1^2) \cos 2\delta_1}, \tag{1.22}$$

$$\tan \gamma = \frac{-(1 - r_1 r_2) \tan \delta_1}{1 + r_1 r_2} . \tag{1.23}$$

The above expressions are for non-absorbing media; the corresponding forms for absorbing media are very much more complicated and are obtained by substituting the corresponding complex Fresnel coefficients for the ones given by equations (1.14) and (1.15) in equations (1.19) to (1.23). In this case, Snell's law becomes

$$\sin \theta_1 = \frac{n_0 \sin \theta_0}{n_1 - ik_1}, \tag{1.24}$$

so θ_1 is complex. A discussion of Snell's law of refraction as applied to absorbing media is given by Ditchburn (1963). The explicit expressions for $\mathscr{R}$ and $\mathscr{T}$ are given in chapter 6 and are based on the analysis of Born and Wolf (1959).

1.4 Multilayer calculations

Various methods have been developed for extending the single-film analysis to the multilayer; the most convenient method for use on a digital computer is the matrix method (Abelès 1948a, Heavens 1960). Application of the appropriate boundary conditions requiring that the tangential components of **E** and **H** be continuous across any boundary to the equations of wave propagation at the interface between the $(m-1)$th and mth layers gives

$$E_{m-1}^+ = \frac{1}{t_m} [E_m^+ \exp(i\delta_m) + r_m E_m^- \exp(-i\delta_m)],$$

$$E_{m-1}^- = \frac{1}{t_m} [r_m E_m^+ \exp(i\delta_m) + E_m^- \exp(-i\delta_m)]. \tag{1.25}$$

An alternative recurrence relation may be obtained by using equations (1.1), namely

$$\begin{pmatrix} E_{m-1} \\ H_{m-1} \end{pmatrix} = \begin{bmatrix} \cos \delta_m & \dfrac{i}{\mu_m} \sin \delta_m \\ i\mu_m \sin \delta_m & \cos \delta_m \end{bmatrix} \begin{pmatrix} E_m \\ H_m \end{pmatrix}. \tag{1.26}$$

Thus for an N-layer filter

$$\begin{pmatrix} E_0 \\ H_0 \end{pmatrix} = \prod_{m=1}^{N} \mathbf{M}_m \begin{pmatrix} E_N \\ H_N \end{pmatrix}, \tag{1.27}$$

where

$$\mathbf{M}_m = \begin{bmatrix} \cos \delta_m & \dfrac{i}{\mu_m} \sin \delta_m \\ i\mu_m \sin \delta_m & \cos \delta_m \end{bmatrix}$$

and

$$\begin{pmatrix} E_N \\ H_N \end{pmatrix} = \begin{pmatrix} 1 \\ \mu_{\text{sub}} \end{pmatrix} E_{\text{sub}}^+.$$

The reflectance, transmittance and phase changes on reflection and transmission are then given by

$$\mathcal{R} = \left| \frac{\mu_0 E_0 - H_0}{\mu_0 E_0 + H_0} \right|^2, \tag{1.28}$$

$$\mathcal{T} = \frac{4\mu_0 \mu_{\text{sub}} |E_{\text{sub}}^+|^2}{|\mu_0 E_0 + H_0|^2}, \tag{1.29}$$

$$\psi = \arg\left(\frac{\mu_0 E_0 - H_0}{\mu_0 E_0 + H_0}\right), \tag{1.30}$$

$$\gamma = \arg\left(\frac{2\mu_0 E_{\text{sub}}}{\mu_0 E_0 + H_0}\right). \tag{1.31}$$

There are two advantages in using equation (1.26) rather than (1.25); the matrix in equation (1.26) is characteristic of one layer only, whereas the matrix in (1.25) is characteristic of the *interface* between layers; if it is desired to change the characteristics of a layer, the calculation is much easier. Secondly, the matrix in equation (1.26) has unity determinant, and this provides a check on the calculation. It also enables us to use simple closed formulae for 'periodic' multilayer calulations — this process will be described in section 1.6. However, there are situations where a calculation based on (1.25) is useful, so this method of calculation will be considered in the next section. Before doing this it is appropriate to study equations (1.28) and (1.29) in more detail, including some special cases.

For non-absorbing films we may write the matrix product $\Pi_m^N \mathbf{M}_m$ as

$$\begin{bmatrix} A & iB \\ iC & D \end{bmatrix}$$

where A, B, C and D are real quantities. Then

$$\begin{pmatrix} E_0 \\ H_0 \end{pmatrix} = \begin{bmatrix} A & iB \\ iC & D \end{bmatrix} \begin{pmatrix} 1 \\ \mu_{\text{sub}} \end{pmatrix} E_{\text{sub}}^+, \tag{1.32}$$

and

$$\mathcal{R} = \left|\frac{\mu_0 E_0 - H_0}{\mu_0 E_0 - H_0}\right|^2 = \frac{(\mu_0 A - \mu_{\text{sub}} D)^2 + (\mu_0 \mu_{\text{sub}} B - C)^2}{(\mu_0 A + \mu_{\text{sub}} D)^2 + (\mu_0 \mu_{\text{sub}} B + C)^2}, \tag{1.33}$$

and

$$\mathcal{T} = \frac{4\mu_0 \mu_{\text{sub}}}{(\mu_0 A + \mu_{\text{sub}} D)^2 + (\mu_0 \mu_{\text{sub}} B + C)^2}. \tag{1.34}$$

The ratio (H_0/E_0) is sometimes called the *admittance*, Y, of the multilayer. In terms of this quantity,

$$\mathcal{R} = \left|\frac{\mu_0 - Y}{\mu_0 + Y}\right|^2. \tag{1.35}$$

The characteristic matrix $\mathbf{M}_m$ takes a particularly simple form if the phase thickness of the layer is an integral number, k, of quarter waves, i.e.

$$\delta = k\pi/4 \qquad k = 0, 1, 2, \ldots. \tag{1.36}$$

For k even, $\cos \delta = \pm 1$, $\sin \delta = 0$ and

$$\mathbf{M}_m = \pm \begin{bmatrix} 1 & 0 \\ 0 & 1 \end{bmatrix}.$$

The characteristic matrix is therefore a unity matrix and has no effect on the overall reflectance or transmittance of the multilayer. Such a layer is said to be 'absentee' (note that this is only true for the wavelengths for which (1.36) holds when k is even). When k is odd, $\sin \delta = \pm 1$, $\cos \delta = 0$ so

$$\mathbf{M}_m = \pm \begin{bmatrix} 0 & i/\mu_m \\ i\mu_m & 0 \end{bmatrix}.$$

For a system of N successive quarter-wave layers (where N is odd), the admittance is given by

$$Y = \frac{\mu_1^2 \mu_3^2 \cdots \mu_N^2}{\mu_2^2 \mu_4^2 \cdots \mu_{N-1}^2 \mu_{\text{sub}}} \tag{1.37}$$

and for N even

$$Y = \frac{\mu_1^2 \mu_3^2 \cdots \mu_{N-1}^2 \mu_{\text{sub}}}{\mu_2^2 \mu_4^2 \cdots \mu_N^2}. \tag{1.38}$$

An example of a program for multilayer analysis based on the above formulae (i.e. (1.32)–(1.34)) is given in appendix 2. A simplified version of the algorithm is the following:

(1) Read in values of refractive index for the medium of incidence and the substrate (n_0, n_{sub}).
(2) Read in the number of layers in the filter (N).
(3) For each layer i, $i = 1, 2, \ldots, N$, read in refractive index (n_i), and phase thickness (δ_i), in degrees, at normal incidence at a reference wavelength λ_0.
(4) Read in the total number of wavelengths (M) at which calculations are to be performed.
(5) Read in values of the reference wavelength, (λ_0), the lowest wavelength (λ_{min}) and the incremental wavelength (λ_{inc}) for the calculations. The actual values of wavelength to be used are

$$\lambda_j = \lambda_{\text{min}} + (j-1)\lambda_{\text{inc}} \qquad j = 1, 2, \ldots, M.$$

(Alternatively, one may read in the values of the wavelengths used directly, i.e. $\lambda_j, j = 1, 2, \ldots, M$.)
(6) Read in the value of the angle of incidence (measured in the medium of incidence).
(7) Evaluate the angles of incidence in the substrate and in each layer in the filter, using Snell's law:

$$n_0 \sin \theta_0 = n_i \sin \theta_i = n_{\text{sub}} \sin \theta_{\text{sub}}, \qquad i = 1, 2, \ldots, N.$$

(8)   Evaluate the effective phase thickness (as defined by equation (1.2)) for each layer in the filter.

The following steps (9)–(12) must be performed for each component of polarisation:

(9)   The effective indices μ_0, μ_{sub}, μ_i, $i = 1, 2, \ldots, N$, are evaluated for the particular component of polarisation.

(10) The matrix product elements are set equal to the values of the first layer in the filter, i.e.

$$A = \cos \delta_1, \quad B = (\sin \delta_1)/\mu_1, \quad C = \mu_1 \sin \delta_1, \quad D = \cos \delta_1$$

(11) If $N = 1$, go to step (12), else, for $i = 2, 3, \ldots, N$, postmultiply the current matrix product by the characteristic matrix for the ith layer.

(12) Evaluate $\mathcal{R}$, $\mathcal{T}$ for the particular component of polarisation.

(13) Calculate the average values of $\mathcal{R}$ and $\mathcal{T}$ for both components of polarisation, i.e.

$$\mathcal{R}_{av} = 0 \cdot 5(\mathcal{R}_s + \mathcal{R}_p),$$
$$\mathcal{T}_{av} = 0 \cdot 5(\mathcal{T}_s + \mathcal{T}_p). \tag{1.39}$$

(14) Print out the filter input data, including values of the reference wavelength, the refractive indices in the medium of incidence and the substrate, refractive indices and thicknesses of the layers and the angle of incidence.

(15) Print out the computed values of λ, $\mathcal{R}_{av}$, $\mathcal{R}_p$, $\mathcal{R}_s$, $\mathcal{T}_{av}$, $\mathcal{T}_p$ and $\mathcal{T}_s$ for the M specified wavelengths.

(16) If further multilayers are to be computed, return to step (1), else stop.

The program given in appendix 2 uses a 'control index' system of data input, so that after the initial configuration has been computed, only *changes* of data are input and some of steps (1) to (6) may be omitted. Allowance is made for data error, for the case where total internal reflection occurs and for the case where no film is present ($N = 0$); in the latter event, the reflectance and transmittance at the interface between the medium of incidence and the substrate are computed.

1.5   Alternative formulation for multilayer calculations

For certain applications, it is useful to treat the multilayer in terms of the interfaces between the layers, rather than in terms of the layers themselves. Following the analysis given by Delano and Pegis (1969), we let T_j and R_j represent the amplitude transmission and reflection coefficients for the $(N - j)$ layers lying between the jth medium and the substrate. Thus

$$T_j = \frac{E_{sub}^+}{E_j^+} \quad \text{and} \quad R_j = \frac{E_j^-}{E_j^+} \tag{1.40}$$

and an extension of (1.18) yields

$$\left.\begin{aligned} T_{j-1} &= \frac{t_j T_j \exp(-i\delta_j)}{1 + r_j R_j \exp(-2i\delta_j)} \\ R_{j-1} &= \frac{r_j + R_j \exp(-2i\delta_j)}{1 + r_j R_j \exp(-2i\delta_j)} \end{aligned}\right\} \quad j = 1, 2, \ldots, N+1. \qquad (1.41)$$

(In this analysis, we use the subscript $N+1$ for the substrate, in place of 'sub'.) The amplitude transmission and reflection coefficients for the entire multilayer are

$$T = \frac{E_{N+1}^+}{E_0^+}, \qquad R = \frac{E_0^-}{E_0^+} \qquad (1.42)$$

and the expressions for intensity reflectance and transmittance (cf corresponding formulae (1.11) for a single interface) are

$$\mathscr{T} = \frac{n_{N+1}}{n_0}|T|^2, \qquad \mathscr{R} = |R|^2. \qquad (1.43)$$

If we now define new variables

$$\begin{aligned} \tau_j &= (n_j/n_{N+1})^{1/2} \, E_j^+ \exp(-i\Delta_{j+1}), \\ \rho_j &= (n_j/n_{N+1})^{1/2} \, E_j^- \exp(-i\Delta_{j+1}), \end{aligned} \qquad (1.44)$$

where

$$\Delta_j = \sum_{k=j}^{N} \delta_k, \qquad j = 1, 2, \ldots, N$$

and

$$\Delta_{N+1} = 0,$$

then a recurrence relation for τ_j, ρ_j is obtained by replacing E_j^+ and E_j^- in equation (1.25):

$$\begin{aligned} \tau_{j-1} &= \frac{n_{j-1} + n_j}{2(n_{j-1}n_j)^{1/2}} \, [\tau_j + r_j\rho_j \, \exp(-2i\delta_j)], \\ \rho_{j-1} &= \frac{n_{j-1} + n_j}{2(n_{j-1}n_j)^{1/2}} \, [r_j\tau_j + \rho_j \, \exp(-2i\delta_j)], \end{aligned} \qquad (1.45)$$

and $\tau_{N+1} = 1$, $\rho_{N+1} = 0$. Thus if τ, ρ denote the values for the complete multilayer

$$\frac{1}{\mathscr{T}} = |\tau|^2, \qquad \frac{\mathscr{R}}{\mathscr{T}} = |\rho|^2. \qquad (1.46)$$

The quantity $1/\mathscr{T}$ is called the *optical opacity* of the multilayer.

1.6 Periodic multilayers and the classical stack

A 'periodic' multilayer is one in which a sequence of films is repeated twice or more. According to Herpin (1947a), any sequence of films may be represented by a fictitious bi-layer $\mathbf{M}_a\mathbf{M}_b$. If this sequence occurs q times

$$\begin{pmatrix} E_0 \\ H_0 \end{pmatrix} = (\mathbf{M}_a\mathbf{M}_b)^q \begin{pmatrix} 1 \\ \mu_{sub} \end{pmatrix} E^+_{sub}. \tag{1.47}$$

Sometimes one considers a periodic multilayer of the form

$$\begin{pmatrix} E_0 \\ H_0 \end{pmatrix} = (\mathbf{M}_a\mathbf{M}_b)^q \, \mathbf{M}_a \begin{pmatrix} 1 \\ \mu_{sub} \end{pmatrix} E^+_{sub}. \tag{1.48}$$

The basic matrix $\mathbf{M}_a\mathbf{M}_b$ is represented by

$$\mathbf{M}_a\mathbf{M}_b = \begin{pmatrix} a_{11} & a_{12} \\ a_{21} & a_{22} \end{pmatrix}. \tag{1.49}$$

Herpin (1947b) showed that the product $(\mathbf{M}_a\mathbf{M}_b)^q$ may be expressed in terms of Lucas polynomials, and Abelès (1948b) observed these may be reduced to Tschebysheff polynomials of the second kind since the basic matrix is of unity determinant. Mielenz (1959) extended the analysis as follows: let

$$X = a_{11} + a_{22}, \tag{1.50}$$

then

$$(\mathbf{M}_a\mathbf{M}_b)^q = S_{q-1}(X)(\mathbf{M}_a\mathbf{M}_b) - S_{q-2}(X)\,\mathbf{I}. \tag{1.51}$$

$\mathbf{I}$ is the unit matrix and the Tschebysheff polynomials $S_q(X)$ are defined by

$$S_q(X) = X\,S_{q-1}(X) - S_{q-2}(X),$$
$$S_0(X) = 1, \tag{1.52}$$
$$S_1(X) = X.$$

This method can be useful for computing the properties of classical quarter-wave stacks, consisting of alternating high- and low-index layers (indices n_H, n_L) of equal optical thickness $\lambda_0/4$ (λ_0 is some reference wavelength). Then $\mathbf{M}_a$, $\mathbf{M}_b$ represent individual layers, so if the films are non-absorbing, the quantity X defined above will be real. For light normally incident on such a stack

$$\mu_a = n_H,$$
$$\mu_b = n_L,$$
$$\delta_a = \delta_b = \beta = \tfrac{1}{2}\pi\lambda_0/\lambda, \tag{1.53}$$
$$X = 2\cos^2\beta - \frac{(n_H + n_L)^2}{n_H n_L}\sin^2\beta.$$

At the wavelength λ_0, the beams reflected from the various interfaces will all be in phase, so the reflectance obtained is a maximum. Using the above formulae, it can be shown that this maximum reflectance may be expressed as[†]

$$\mathscr{R}_{2q+1} = \left(\frac{(n_H/n_L)^{2q} - (n_0 n_{sub}/n_H^2)}{(n_H/n_L)^{2q} + (n_0 n_{sub}/n_H^2)} \right)^2, \qquad (1.54)$$

for a filter with an odd number of layers $(2q + 1)$ overall, or

$$\mathscr{R}_{2q} = \left(\frac{(n_H/n_L)^{2q} - (n_{sub}/n_0)}{(n_H/n_L)^{2q} + (n_{sub}/n_0)} \right)^2, \qquad (1.55)$$

for an even number of layers $(2q)$. In both cases we assume an H layer next to the substrate. Figure 1.4 shows the computed reflectance against

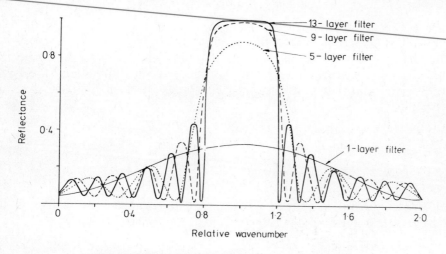

Figure 1.4   1-, 5-, 9- and 13-layer classical stacks.

relative wavenumber of 1-, 5-, 9- and 13-layer stacks of $CeO_2(n_H = 2\cdot36)$ and $MgF_2(n_L = 1\cdot39)$. It is more convenient in this instance to work in terms of relative wavenumber rather than wavelength as the spectral curves are symmetrical about $\sigma/\sigma_0 = 1\cdot0)$. It should be noted that although the maximum reflectance at $\sigma_0 = 1/\lambda_0$ increases with the number of layers in the filter, the total width of the high-reflectance band remains substantially constant. Table 1.1 gives numerical results for the maximum reflectance of the stacks illustrated above at normal incidence and at $10°$ angle of incidence. Following the analysis of Weinstein (1954), we see that for a classical stack,

[†] For this particular (central) wavelength, the formulae for maximum reflectance may be derived more simply using (1.37) and (1.38).

Table 1.1 Numerical results for the maximum reflectance of the stacks in figure 1.4.

| | | 10° angle of incidence | |
Number of layers	Normal incidence $\mathscr{R}$ (%)	$\mathscr{R}s$(%)	$\mathscr{R}p$(%)
1	32·375	33·004	31·745
3	68·226	68·914	67·514
7	95·517	95·714	95·299
11	99·450	99·504	99·410
13	99·810	99·825	99·793
17	99·978	99·981	99·974

(1.51) becomes

$$\mathbf{A}^m = S_{m-1}(X)\mathbf{A} - S_{m-2}(X)\mathbf{I},\tag{1.56}$$

where

$$\mathbf{A} = \begin{bmatrix} \cos\beta & \dfrac{i}{n_H}\sin\beta \\ in_H\sin\beta & \cos\beta \end{bmatrix} \begin{bmatrix} \cos\beta & \dfrac{i}{n_L}\sin\beta \\ in_L\sin\beta & \cos\beta \end{bmatrix}$$

$$= \tfrac{1}{2} \begin{bmatrix} \left(1 + \dfrac{n_H}{n_L}\right)\cos 2\beta + \left(1 - \dfrac{n_H}{n_L}\right) & i\left(\dfrac{1}{n_H} + \dfrac{1}{n_L}\right)\sin 2\beta \\ i(n_H + n_L)\sin 2\beta & \left(1 + \dfrac{n_L}{n_H}\right)\cos 2\beta + \left(1 - \dfrac{n_L}{n_H}\right) \end{bmatrix}$$

and X and β are given in (1.53) above. The formulae for evaluating the Tschebysheff polynomials (1.52) may alternatively be expressed as

$$S_m(X) = \begin{cases} \dfrac{\sin(m+1)\Theta}{\sin\Theta}, & X = 2\cos\Theta, & \text{for } |X| < 2, \\[2mm] \dfrac{\sinh(m+1)\Phi}{\sinh\Phi}, & X = 2\cosh\Phi, & \text{for } |X| \geqslant 2. \end{cases}\tag{1.57}$$

We see from this formulation that for wavenumbers such that $|X| > 2$, the reflectance increases steadily as m increases and tends to unity as m tends to infinity. Such a zone is called a 'stopping' zone or 'high-reflectance' zone. The limit $\sigma_{\lim}$ of this zone is given by $|X| = 2$, i.e.

$$\left| \cos^2\beta - \frac{n_H^2 + n_L^2}{2n_H n_L}\sin^2\beta \right| = 1,$$

$$\frac{\pi\sigma_{\lim}}{2\sigma_0} = \sin^{-1}\left(\frac{2(n_H n_L)^{1/2}}{n_H + n_L}\right).\tag{1.58}$$

The expression for the 'halfwidth' of this zone (i.e. the distance from the centre, $\sigma = \sigma_0$, to the edge $\sigma = \sigma_{\lim}$) is then

$$\frac{\Delta\sigma}{\sigma_0} = \frac{2}{\pi} \sin^{-1}\left(\frac{n_H - n_L}{n_H + n_L}\right). \tag{1.59}$$

The total 'limiting width' for the multilayer stack is therefore

$$\frac{4}{\pi} \sin^{-1}\left(\frac{n_H - n_L}{n_H + n_L}\right). \tag{1.60}$$

In practice, this expression may be used to give an approximate value of stop bandwidth for any classical stack of nine or more layers.

The analysis may be extended to the case of non-normal incidence (Liddell and Fawcett 1969) and the results used to give an approximation for the splitting between the *s*- and *p*-components of polarisation. In this case, the phase thicknesses β_H, β_L of the high- and low-index layers are not equal but are given by

$$\beta_H = \frac{\pi}{2} \frac{\sigma}{\sigma_0} \cos\theta_H,$$

$$\beta_L = \frac{\pi}{2} \frac{\sigma}{\sigma_0} \cos\theta_L, \tag{1.61}$$

where θ_H, θ_L are the angles of incidence in the high- and low-index media. For small values of θ_H, θ_L we may make the following approximations, neglecting second order terms and above,

$$\beta_H - \beta_L \sim O(\theta_H^2), \quad \cos(\beta_H - \beta_L) = 1, \quad \sin(\beta_H - \beta_L) = 0. \tag{1.62}$$

The basic period is given by

$$|\mathbf{M}_H \mathbf{M}_L| = \begin{bmatrix} \cos\beta_H & \dfrac{i}{\mu_H}\sin\beta_H \\ i\mu_H \sin\beta_H & \cos\beta_H \end{bmatrix} \begin{bmatrix} \cos\beta_L & \dfrac{i}{\mu_L}\sin\beta_L \\ i\mu_L \sin\beta_L & \cos\beta_L \end{bmatrix}. \tag{1.63}$$

Using the approximations given by (1.62), this becomes

$$|\mathbf{M}_H \mathbf{M}_L| =$$

$$\begin{bmatrix} \left(1 + \dfrac{\mu_H}{\mu_L}\right)\cos(\beta_H + \beta_L) + \left(1 - \dfrac{\mu_H}{\mu_L}\right) & i\left(\dfrac{1}{\mu_H} + \dfrac{1}{\mu_L}\right)\sin(\beta_H + \beta_L) \\[3ex] i(\mu_H + \mu_L)\sin(\beta_H + \beta_L) & \left(1 + \dfrac{\mu_L}{\mu_H}\right)\cos(\beta_H + \beta_L) + \left(1 - \dfrac{\mu_L}{\mu_H}\right) \end{bmatrix}$$

$$\tag{1.64}$$

Comparing this formula with (1.56), we see that the system is approximately equivalent to a normal incidence stack of high- and low-index materials of index μ_H and μ_L where each layer has phase thickness β, given by

$$\beta = \frac{(\beta_H + \beta_L)}{2}.$$

The limiting width of such a stack is then given by

$$\frac{\Delta\sigma}{\sigma_0} = \frac{4}{\pi} \frac{1}{\cos\theta_H + \cos\theta_L} \sin^{-1}\left(\frac{\mu_H - \mu_L}{\mu_H + \mu_L}\right). \tag{1.65}$$

On substituting the values of μ_H and μ_L for each component of polarisation in turn, the edge position of the stack may be estimated in each case, and a quantitative value of the splitting obtained from the difference between these two values. For non-normal incidence, it is seen from (1.65) that the position of the centre of the stack has shifted to σ_c, where

$$\frac{\sigma_c}{\sigma_0} = \frac{2}{\cos\theta_H + \cos\theta_L}. \tag{1.66}$$

Also, the formulae for maximum reflectance now become

$$\mathscr{R}_{2q+1} = \left(\frac{(\mu_H/\mu_L)^{2q} - \mu_0\mu_{sub}/\mu_H^2}{(\mu_H/\mu_L)^{2q} + \mu_0\mu_{sub}/\mu_H^2}\right)^2,$$

$$\mathscr{R}_{2q} = \left(\frac{(\mu_H/\mu_L)^{2q} - \mu_{sub}/\mu_0}{(\mu_H/\mu_L)^{2q} + \mu_{sub}/\mu_0}\right)^2. \tag{1.67}$$

The accuracy to be expected from these formulae may be seen from table 1.2, which shows the results for two 12-layer stacks, one for use in the visible region (A), ($n_H = 2\cdot36$, $n_L = 1\cdot39$, $n_{sub} = 1\cdot53$ and $n_0 = 1\cdot00$) and the other B, for use in the infrared ($n_H = 5\cdot1$, $n_L = 2\cdot2$, $n_{sub} = 4\cdot0$ and $n_0 = 1\cdot0$).

Table 1.2 Comparison of results obtained from formulae (1.50)–(1.52) with actual (computed) values.

Filter	Angle of incidence in air (deg)	Splitting between s- and p- components (nm) ($\lambda_0 = 500$ nm)		Maximum reflectance			
				Formula		Computed	
		Formula	Actual	s	p	s	p
A	45	42·1	42	0·9961	0·9712	0·9961	0·9711
A	20	6·1	6·2	0·9914	0·9869	0·9915	0·9870
B	45	14·5	14·7	0·99946	0·99918	0·99946	0·99918

1.7 Effect of reflection from the back surface of the substrate

The formulae derived above are based on the assumption that the substrate on which the filter is deposited is semi-infinite in extent; in practice, although the substrate is thick compared to the films themselves, it is possible to have reflections from the back surface of the substrate which can affect one's results. There are two ways of overcoming this — either one can 'wedge' or antireflect the back surface so that these unwanted reflectances have no effect, or one may modify equations (1.28)–(1.31) to take account of this back substrate reflection.

If an incoherent source is used, the energy reflectances from the front and back surfaces of the substrate must be summed (see figure 1.5). Subscripts 1, 2 and sub will be used to characterise the front and back surfaces of the film and the substrate back surface respectively. Thus the total reflected energy, $\mathcal{R}_{tot}$ is given by

$$\mathcal{R}_{tot} = \mathcal{R}_1 + \mathcal{T}_1 \mathcal{T}_2 \mathcal{R}_{sub} + \mathcal{T}_1 \mathcal{T}_2 \mathcal{R}_{sub}(\mathcal{R}_2 \mathcal{R}_{sub})$$
$$+ \mathcal{T}_1 \mathcal{T}_2 \mathcal{R}_{sub}(\mathcal{R}_2 \mathcal{R}_{sub})^2 + \dots,$$

i.e.

$$\mathcal{R}_{tot} = \mathcal{R}_1 + \frac{\mathcal{T}_1 \mathcal{T}_2 \mathcal{R}_{sub}}{1 - \mathcal{R}_2 \mathcal{R}_{sub}}. \tag{1.68}$$

The total transmitted energy is given by

$$\mathcal{T}_{tot} = \mathcal{T}_1 \mathcal{T}_{sub} + \mathcal{T}_1 \mathcal{T}_{sub}(\mathcal{R}_2 \mathcal{R}_{sub}) + \mathcal{T}_1 \mathcal{T}_{sub}(\mathcal{R}_2 \mathcal{R}_{sub})^2 + \dots.$$

Thus

$$\mathcal{T}_{tot} = \frac{\mathcal{T}_1 \mathcal{T}_{sub}}{1 - \mathcal{R}_2 \mathcal{R}_{sub}}. \tag{1.69}$$

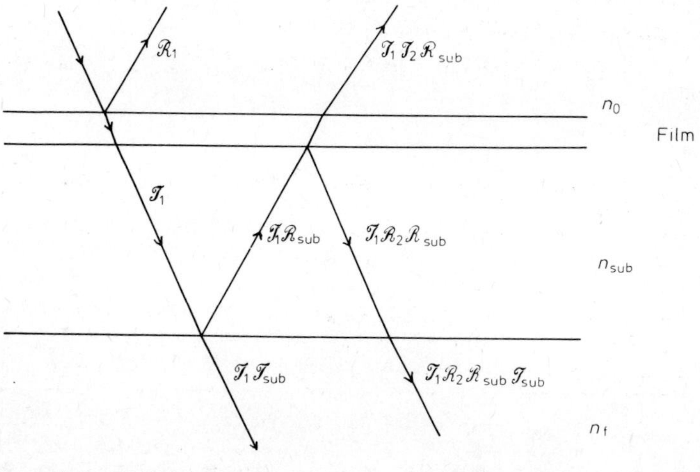

Figure 1.5   Reflection from the back surface of the substrate.

If the incident and reflected light is coherent, well collimated and if also the the aperture of the detector is sufficiently small to be able to observe interference effects between the front and back surfaces of the substrate, then *amplitude* reflectances should be summed instead of energies. In this case the phase differences of the beams in the summation must also be taken into account, so the total amplitude reflectance is given by

$$R_{tot} = R_1 + T_1 T_2 R_{sub} \exp(-2i\delta_{sub}) + T_1 T_2 R_{sub}(R_2 R_{sub}) \exp(-4i\delta_{sub})$$
$$+ T_1 T_2 R_{sub}(R_2 R_{sub})^2 \exp(-6i\delta_{sub}) + \ldots$$

and the total amplitude transmittance by

$$T_{tot} = T_1 T_{sub} + T_1 T_{sub} R_2 R_{sub} \exp(-2i\delta_{sub})$$
$$+ T_1 T_{sub}(R_2 R_{sub})^2 \exp(-4i\delta_{sub}) + \ldots.$$

R_1, R_2, T_1 and T_2 represent the (complex) amplitude and transmission coefficients from the front and back surfaces of the film; R_{sub} and T_{sub} are the corresponding reflection and transmission coefficients from the back surface of the substrate; we shall assume this is uncoated, so that R_{sub} and T_{sub} are real quantities. We may write

$$R_1 = r_1 \exp(i\psi_1), \qquad R_2 = r_2 \exp(i\psi_2),$$
$$T_1 = t_1 \exp(i\gamma_1), \qquad T_2 = t_2 \exp(i\gamma_2),$$

where r_1, r_2, t_1 and t_2 are real quantities; γ_1, γ_2 are the phase changes on transmission from the front and back surfaces of the film; ψ_1, ψ_2 are the corresponding phase changes on reflection. The total amplitude transmission may be expressed as

$$T_{tot} = \frac{T_1 T_{sub}}{1 - R_2 R_{sub} \exp(-2i\delta_{sub})}. \tag{1.70}$$

Thus the energy transmittance is

$$\mathscr{T}_{tot} = \frac{n_f}{n_0}$$

$$\times \frac{t_1^2 T_{sub}^2 \exp(i\gamma_1) \exp(-i\gamma_1)}{1 - r_2 R_{sub} \exp(-2i\delta_{sub}) \exp(i\psi_2)}$$

$$\times \frac{1}{1 - r_2 R_{sub} \exp(2i\delta_{sub}) \exp(-i\psi_2)}$$

$$= \frac{n_f}{n_0} \frac{t_1^2 T_{sub}^2}{1 + r_2^2 R_{sub}^2 - 2 r_2 R_{sub} \cos(2\delta_{sub} - \psi_2)},$$

where n_f is the refractive index of the final medium, which may be different from the medium of incidence. However, $\mathcal{T}_1 = (n_{sub}/n_0)\, t_1^2$ and $\mathcal{T}_{sub} = (n_f/n_{sub})\, T_{sub}^2$, hence

$$\mathcal{T}_{tot} = \frac{\mathcal{T}_1\, \mathcal{T}_{sub}}{1 + \mathcal{R}_2\, \mathcal{R}_{sub} - 2\, \mathcal{R}_2^{1/2} \mathcal{R}_{sub}^{1/2}\, \cos\,(2\delta_{sub} - \psi_2)}. \qquad (1.71)$$

The total amplitude reflectance is

$$R_{tot} = R_1 + \frac{T_1 T_2 R_{sub}\, \exp(-2i\delta_{sub})}{1 - R_2 R_{sub}\, \exp(-2i\delta_{sub})},$$

i.e.

$$R = r_1 \exp(i\psi_1) + \frac{t_1 t_2 R_{sub}\, \exp[i(\gamma_1 + \gamma_2 - 2\delta_{sub})]}{1 - r_2 R_{sub}\, \exp[i(\psi_2 - 2\delta_{sub})]}. \qquad (1.72)$$

Thus the energy reflectance (the intensity reflectance) is (Macleod 1976, private communication)

$$\mathcal{R}_{tot} = r_1^2 + \frac{t_1^2 t_2^2 R_{sub}^2}{1 + r_2^2 R_{sub}^2 - 2 r_2 R_{sub}\, \cos\,(2\delta_{sub} - \psi_2)}$$

$$+ \frac{2 r_1 R_{sub} t_1 t_2 [\cos\,(\gamma_1 + \gamma_2 - \psi_1 - 2\delta_{sub}) - r_2 R_{sub}\, \cos\,(\gamma_1 + \gamma_2 - \psi_1 - \psi_2)]}{1 + r_2^2 R_{sub}^2 - 2 r_2 R_{sub}\, \cos\,(2\delta_{sub} - \psi_2)}.$$

Since

$$t_1^2 t_2^2 = \frac{n_{sub}}{n_0}\, t_1^2 \cdot \frac{n_0}{n_{sub}}\, t_2^2 = \mathcal{T}_1\, \mathcal{T}_2,$$

$$\mathcal{R}_{tot} = \mathcal{R}_1 + \frac{\mathcal{T}_1\, \mathcal{T}_2\, \mathcal{R}_{sub}}{1 + \mathcal{R}_2\, \mathcal{R}_{sub} - 2(\mathcal{R}_2\, \mathcal{R}_{sub})^{1/2}\, \cos\,(2\delta_{sub} - \psi_2)}$$

$$+ \frac{2(\mathcal{R}_1\, \mathcal{R}_{sub}\, \mathcal{T}_1\, \mathcal{T}_2)^{1/2}\, [\cos\,(\gamma_1 + \gamma_2 - \psi_1 - 2\delta_{sub}) - (\mathcal{R}_2\, \mathcal{R}_{sub})^{1/2}\, \cos\,(\gamma_1 + \gamma_2 - \psi_1 - \psi_2)]}{1 + \mathcal{R}_2\, \mathcal{R}_{sub} - 2(\mathcal{R}_2\, \mathcal{R}_{sub})^{1/2}\, \cos\,(2\delta_{sub} - \psi_2)}.$$

$$(1.73)$$

This analysis is similar to that developed by Smith (1958) for his 'two effective interface' method, which will be described further in chapter 2. If the back surface of the substrate is coated, Smith's analysis can be applied directly.

The values given in equations (1.71) and (1.73) are mean values with respect to time (see earlier comments about the Poynting vector and equations

(1.3) and (1.4)) for a monochromatic line, so if one has an infinitely narrow band of wavelengths, perfectly collimated, falling on a substrate with perfectly plane parallel surfaces, this is the behaviour one would expect. In practice, one may approach this situation when using a well-collimated laser beam illuminating a very small part of the substrate so that any irregularities over the illuminated area are small. This would be one extreme. More often in practice the illumination conditions are less ideal; in order to estimate the total effect one should integrate (1.71) and (1.73) over the possible range of thickness variation in the substrate, and over the range of wavelengths and angles of incidence in the incident light, with appropriate weights — this would be a very complicated problem to solve. We may simplify the situation by assuming that the terms $\cos(2\delta_{sub} - \psi_2)$ etc vary very rapidly compared with all other terms, so the other effects (including weights) remain substantially constant. Provided the range of integration is sufficiently large to contain an appreciable number of cycles, it will be indistinguishable from the mean value; this gives the incoherent case, which is the other extreme (Macleod 1976, private communication).

Taking the mean of (1.71) over one cycle

$$\mathcal{T}_{tot} = \frac{1}{\pi} \int_{-\pi/2}^{+\pi/2} \frac{\mathcal{T}_1 \, \mathcal{T}_{sub} \, d\delta_{sub}}{1 + \mathcal{R}_2 \, \mathcal{R}_{sub} - 2(\mathcal{R}_2 \, \mathcal{R}_{sub})^{1/2} \cos 2\delta_{sub}}, \qquad (1.74)$$

$$= \frac{1}{\pi} \frac{\mathcal{T}_1 \, \mathcal{T}_{sub}}{1 + \mathcal{R}_2 \, \mathcal{R}_{sub}} \int_{-\pi/2}^{+\pi/2} \frac{d\delta_{sub}}{1 - \alpha \cos 2\delta_{sub}},$$

where

$$\alpha = \frac{2(\mathcal{R}_2 \, \mathcal{R}_{sub})^{1/2}}{1 + \mathcal{R}_2 \, \mathcal{R}_{sub}}. \qquad (1.75)$$

If we make the substitution $t = \tan \delta_{sub}$

$$\int_{-\pi/2}^{+\pi/2} \frac{d\delta_{sub}}{1 - \alpha \cos 2\delta_{sub}} = \int_{-\infty}^{+\infty} \frac{dt}{(1 + t^2) - \alpha(1 - t^2)} = \frac{\pi}{(1 - \alpha^2)^{1/2}},$$

$$(1.76)$$

i.e.

$$\mathcal{T}_{tot} = \frac{1}{\pi} \frac{\mathcal{T}_1 \, \mathcal{T}_{sub}}{1 + \mathcal{R}_2 \, \mathcal{R}_{sub}} \frac{\pi}{[1 - 4\mathcal{R}_2 \, \mathcal{R}_{sub}/(1 + \mathcal{R}_2 \, \mathcal{R}_{sub})^2]^{1/2}},$$

$$= \frac{\mathcal{T}_1 \, \mathcal{T}_{sub}}{1 - \mathcal{R}_2 \, \mathcal{R}_{sub}}, \qquad (1.77)$$

which agrees with equation (1.69), obtained for the incoherent case.

Now we consider (1.73) and again take, the mean value over one cycle

$$\mathcal{R}_{tot} = \frac{1}{\pi}\int_{-\pi/2}^{+\pi/2} \left(\mathcal{R}_1 + \frac{\mathcal{T}_1 \mathcal{T}_2 \mathcal{R}_{sub}}{1 + \mathcal{R}_2 \mathcal{R}_{sub} - 2(\mathcal{R}_2 \mathcal{R}_{sub})^{1/2} \cos 2\delta_{sub}} \right.$$

$$\left. + \frac{2(\mathcal{R}_1 \mathcal{R}_{sub} \mathcal{T}_1 \mathcal{T}_2)^{1/2}[\cos 2\delta_{sub} - (\mathcal{R}_2 \mathcal{R}_{sub})^{1/2}]}{1 + \mathcal{R}_2 \mathcal{R}_{sub} - 2(\mathcal{R}_2 \mathcal{R}_{sub})^{1/2} \cos 2\delta_{sub}} \right) d\delta_{sub},$$

$$= \mathcal{R}_1 + \frac{\mathcal{T}_1 \mathcal{T}_2 \mathcal{R}_{sub}}{1 - \mathcal{R}_2 \mathcal{R}_{sub}}$$

$$+ \frac{1}{\pi}\int_{-\pi/2}^{+\pi/2} \frac{2(\mathcal{R}_1 \mathcal{R}_{sub} \mathcal{T}_1 \mathcal{T}_2)^{1/2}[\cos 2\delta_{sub} - (\mathcal{R}_2 \mathcal{R}_{sub})^{1/2}]d\delta_{sub}}{1 + \mathcal{R}_2 \mathcal{R}_{sub} - 2(\mathcal{R}_2 \mathcal{R}_{sub})^{1/2} \cos 2\delta_{sub}},$$

$$(1.78)$$

using the results (1.74) and (1.77) above, multiplied by the (constant) factor $\mathcal{T}_2 \mathcal{R}_{sub}/\mathcal{T}_{sub}$. Consider now the remaining integrand; this may be expressed

$$\frac{2(\mathcal{R}_1 \mathcal{R}_{sub} \mathcal{T}_1 \mathcal{T}_2)^{1/2}}{\pi(1 + \mathcal{R}_2 \mathcal{R}_{sub})}\int_{-\pi/2}^{-\pi/2} \frac{\cos 2\delta_{sub} d\delta_{sub}}{1 - \alpha \cos 2\delta_{sub}} - \frac{2(\mathcal{R}_1 \mathcal{R}_2 \mathcal{T}_1 \mathcal{T}_2)^{1/2} \mathcal{R}_{sub}}{1 - \mathcal{R}_2 \mathcal{R}_{sub}},$$

$$(1.79)$$

again using (1.74) and (1.77) above, with α defined by (1.75)

$$\int_{-\pi/2}^{+\pi/2} \frac{\cos 2\delta_{sub} d\delta_{sub}}{1 - \alpha \cos 2\delta_{sub}} = -\frac{1}{\alpha} + \int_{-\pi/2}^{+\pi/2} \frac{\alpha^{-1} d\delta_{sub}}{1 - \alpha \cos 2\delta_{sub}},$$

so expression (1.79) now becomes

$$-\left(\frac{\mathcal{R}_1 \mathcal{T}_1 \mathcal{T}_2}{\mathcal{R}_2}\right)^{1/2} + \left(\frac{\mathcal{R}_1 \mathcal{T}_1 \mathcal{T}_2}{\mathcal{R}_2}\right)^{1/2}\left(\frac{1 + \mathcal{R}_2 \mathcal{R}_{sub}}{1 - \mathcal{R}_2 \mathcal{R}_{sub}}\right)$$

$$- \frac{2(\mathcal{R}_1 \mathcal{R}_2 \mathcal{T}_1 \mathcal{T}_2)^{1/2} \mathcal{R}_{sub}}{1 - \mathcal{R}_2 \mathcal{R}_{sub}},$$

which is zero. Thus, returning to (1.78), we see

$$\mathcal{R}_{tot} = \mathcal{R}_1 + \frac{\mathcal{T}_1 \mathcal{T}_2 \mathcal{R}_{sub}}{1 - \mathcal{R}_2 \mathcal{R}_{sub}}, \qquad (1.80)$$

which again agrees with the incoherent result given by (1.68).

Under what circumstances should the coherent expressions be used? In most practical cases, unless one has very narrow bandwidths and highly collimated light with parallel sided substrates, the incoherent expressions are appropriate. As an example, we may take the case of mica substrates in the

infrared; if the spectrometer has a narrow bandwidth one often sees interference fringes superimposed on the filter characteristic. However, as the slits
are opened, these fringes disappear and then, provided the filter characteristic is very much broader, this incoherent case is the mean of the coherent
case; expressions (1.71) and (1.73) are the mathematical representation of
the filter characteristic + substrate fringes, while the incoherent formulae
(1.68) and (1.69) do not show the latter. Provided the substrate is very much
thicker than the films, one may either use the incoherent formula and take
the mean of the filter characteristic (over just a few fringes), or one may use
the more complicated coherent equations in which the substrate fringes are
included. If the substrate is very thin, so that the period of the fringes is
of the same order of magnitude as the film characteristic, then it would be
more correct to use the coherent formulation; basically, we are then treating
the substrate as an additional layer added to the stack of layers forming the
actual coating (Macleod 1976, private communication).

The difference between the corrected and uncorrected values ($\mathscr{R}_{tot}$, $\mathscr{T}_{tot}$
and $\mathscr{R}$, $\mathscr{T}$) can be significant in certain cases; two examples are the computation of spectral characteristics of antireflection coatings and the determination of optical constants of a single film from photometric measurements
of $\mathscr{R}$ and $\mathscr{T}$; the latter topic will be discussed in detail in chapter 6.

1.8 Graphical methods of calculation

For a single film whose reflectance is small, we may approximate (1.16) by

$$\mathscr{R} \simeq r_1^2 + 2r_1r_2 \cos 2\delta_1 + r_2^2. \tag{1.81}$$

Physically, this means we are neglecting multiple reflections and considering
only 'two beam interference'. The corresponding amplitude reflectance is
given by the vector sum of r_1 and r_2, namely

$$R = r_1 + r_2 \exp(-2i\delta_1), \tag{1.82}$$

or in terms of the quantity ρ, defined by (1.44),

$$\rho = r_1 + \rho_1 \exp(-2i\delta_1). \tag{1.83}$$

For two films, the corresponding approximation is

$$R = r_1 + r_2 \exp(-2i\delta_1) + r_3 \exp[-2i(\delta_1 + \delta_2)], \tag{1.84}$$

i.e. R is again determined by the vector sum of the Fresnel coefficients.
This process may be extended to any number of films, provided $r_1, r_2, \ldots,$
r_{N+1} are all small compared with unity. This technique can be useful in the
design of antireflection coatings.

Several exact graphical methods have also been developed for calculating
the reflectance of a multilayer. The one most often used is the Smith chart,

named after its originator P H Smith. This is a device which is widely used in electrical transmission line theory and is based on the continuity of optical admittance (defined by equation (1.35)) across any interface. The amplitude reflectance of a multilayer whose optical admittance in the medium of incidence is Y can be expressed

$$R = \frac{\mu_0 - Y}{\mu_0 + Y} = \frac{1 - Y/\mu_0}{1 + Y/\mu_0}, \tag{1.85}$$

where μ_0 is the admittance of the medium of incidence, and is equivalent to the complex refractive index n. The Smith chart is a map of the conformal transformation

$$Z = \frac{1 - X}{1 + X}. \tag{1.86}$$

X is plotted in polar coordinates and the real and imaginary parts of Z may be read off from sets of orthogonal circles. Fuller details of this device are given by Macleod (1969).

The Kard calculator is another convenient device; it is a mapping of the conformal transformation

$$Z = \tanh(\omega/2) \tag{1.87}$$

and enables R_{m+1} to be calculated from known values of r_{m+1}, R_m and δ_m.

In recent years, these graphical devices have tended to be used less frequently than formerly; this is largely due to the growing availability of direct access to a digital computer, giving a rapid and accurate answer to multilayer analysis problems from an appropriate pre-stored program. In addition, there are a large number of cheap pocket-size programmable calculators on the market, which can easily cope with the kind of calculation involved.

1.9 Calculation of field intensities inside a multilayer

The use of multilayer dielectric coatings as the reflecting elements of high-power laser systems has given rise to interest in the determination of the electric field intensity distribution within the multilayer. This problem was discussed first by Veremei and Minkov (1972); two other useful papers describing the basic theory have been produced by Miller (1975) and Apfel (1976).

We have seen that at each film interface within the multilayer the light is divided into a series of reflected and transmitted beams. At any point within the multilayer, the amplitude of the resultant electric field is obtained from the superposition of the reflected and transmitted beams. For non-normal incidence the two components of polarisation must be treated independently. The light intensity distribution may be expressed in terms of the

26

time average of the square of the electric field. At any point z within the jth layer

$$I(z) = \tfrac{1}{2}E_j(z) \, E_j^*(z), \qquad (1.88)$$

where $E_j^*(z)$ is the complex conjugate of the field within the jth layer. Normally when presenting intensity distribution profiles, the field intensity relative to the maximum value in free space is used. The peak standing wave intensity for a 'perfect' reflector is

$$\tfrac{1}{2}E_0E_0^* = \tfrac{1}{2}(2)^2 = 2.$$

Hence the relative field intensity is given by

$$I(z) = \tfrac{1}{4}E_j(z) \, E_j^*(z). \qquad (1.89)$$

Note that in the previous descriptions of calculations of reflectance and transmittance the reference field is that in the substrate, but in this section the field in the medium of incidence is used as reference.

Various studies have been made of the damage to multilayer coatings caused by intense pulsed laser radiation (National Bureau of Standards). From these results it appears that damage will occur when the field intensity reaches some critical value in the coating material in which damage is most likely to occur. The *absorption* of radiation at any point is directly proportional to the field intensity at the point, so in order to minimise the likelihood of damage, those layers which are likely to exhibit high field intensity must be carefully prepared so that possible sources of absorption are reduced as far as possible. Buchman (1975) and Apfel (1977) have proposed methods of design for thin-film polarisers and high-reflecting multilayers so that peak electric field intensity is reduced. In order to do this, one must be able to calculate the field intensity for any given design.

The notation used for this analysis is illustrated in figure 1.6. The positive and negative going EM waves at some point z, $(z_j \leqslant z \leqslant z_{j+1})$ in the jth layer

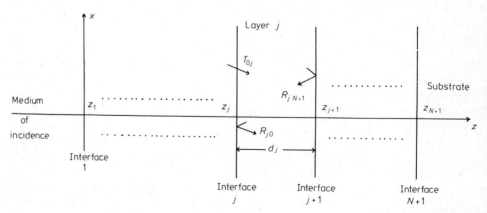

Figure 1.6   Notation for field intensity calculations.

are related to the amplitude reflection and transmission coefficients at the interfaces of that layer by

$$E_j^+(z) = \frac{T_{0j} \exp \{[-2\pi i n_j(z - z_j) \cos\theta_j]/\lambda\}}{1 - R_{j0}R_{j,N+1} \exp [(-4\pi i n_j d_j \cos\theta_j)/\lambda]} ,$$

$$E_j^-(z) = \frac{R_{j,N+1}T_{0j} \exp \{[2\pi i n_j(z - z_j - d_j) \cos\theta_j]/\lambda\}}{1 - R_{j0}R_{j,N+1} \exp [(-4\pi i n_j d_j \cos\theta_j)/\lambda]} ,$$

$$(1.90)$$

where T_{0j} is the amplitude transmission coefficient for radiation of wavelength λ travelling from the medium of incidence to the jth layer, measured in the jth layer at the jth interface; R_{j0} is the amplitude reflection coefficient for layers 1 to $j-1$, measured in the jth layer at the jth interface; $R_{j,N+1}$ is the amplitude reflection coefficient for layers $j + 1$ to the substrate measured at the $(j + 1)$th interface inside the jth layer. We have seen that the relative field intensity at z is given by

$$I(z) = \tfrac{1}{4} \quad E_j(z) E_j{}^*(z)$$

$$= \tfrac{1}{4}| E_j^+(z) + E_j^-(z)|^2$$

for the s-component of polarisation

$$(1.91)$$

$$= \tfrac{1}{4}| E_j^+(z) + E_j^-(z)|^2 | \cos^2\theta_j|$$

$$+| E_j^+(z) - E_j^-(z)|^2| \sin^2\theta_j|$$

for the p-component of polarisation.

Note that the time dependence of E_j^+ and E_j^- is eliminated by the time averaging and the denominators in (1.90) become equal to unity for both the medium of incidence and for the substrate. The above expressions only apply for non-absorbing layers; in laser-damage studies the residual absorption would be very weak, so this is usually a reasonable assumption.

We may summarise the computational procedure for the calculation as follows:

(1) at each interface, j, calculate the reflectance into the $(j-1)$th medium. the reflectance into the jth medium and the transmittance across the interface (these are needed to compute amplitude transmission and reflection coefficients on moving from interface j to interface $j + 1$);
(2) calculate the field intensity in the medium of incidence (up to the first interface);
(3) for each layer in the filter, compute the field intensity from interface j to interface $j + 1$;
(4) calculate the field intensity in the substrate (beyond interface $N + 1$).

28

Figure 1.7 shows a block diagram indicating the structure of a computer program, written by the author, for calculating field intensities: The MAIN program consists of data input (using a 'control index' method) followed by a call of subroutine CALCFI; control is returned to the main program after the field intensity profile has been calculated, so that the results may be printed.

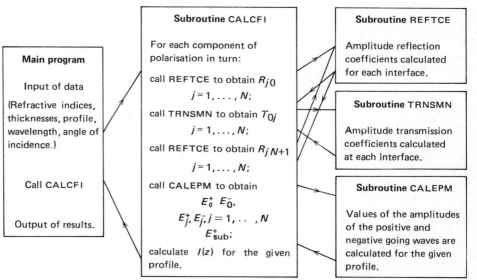

Figure 1.7   Block diagram for a field intensity calculation program.

CALCFI is the subroutine in which values of the field intensities $I(z)$ for each component of polarisation are obtained. For each component, subroutines REFTCE and TRNSMN are called in order to obtain the values T_{0j}, R_{j0} and $R_{j,N+1}$ for each $j = 1, 2, \ldots, N$. These values are used as arguments in the call of subroutine CALEPM. After $I(z)$ has been calculated for the medium of incidence, each layer and for the substrate, control is returned to the main program. In subroutine CALEPM, the amplitudes of the positive and negative going EM waves, E_j^+ and E_j^- are calculated at points z, specifying the multilayer profile (equation (1.90) is used).

This program has been tested using some of the examples given by Miller (1975) and identical results were obtained. Figure 1.8 shows Miller's results for a high-reflection coating designed for use at $\lambda_0 = 1 \cdot 064 \, \mu m$. (Most layers are quarter waves at this wavelength, except for the layer next to the substrate which is a half-wave layer.) In this design $n_{sub} = n_L = 1 \cdot 45$, $n_H = 2.3$ and $n_0 = 1 \cdot 00$. The values of field intensity at two wavelengths have been computed; the full curve is for $\lambda_0 = 1 \cdot 064 \, \mu m$, the dotted curve shows the result for $532 \, nm$, where all layers are 'absentee' (half-wave or full-wave optical thickness). The second example (figure 1.9) shows the field intensity

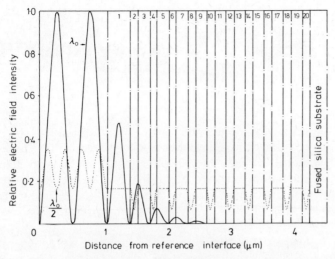

Figure 1.8 Theoretical electric field intensity distribution for the laser reflector Sub |(HL)⁹HL²| Air. Full curve, $\lambda_0 = 1.064$ m; dotted curve, $\lambda_0 = 532$ nm (from Miller 1975).

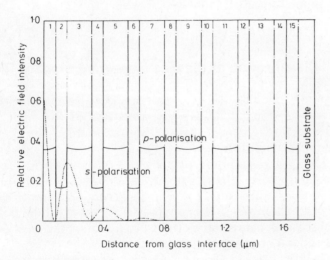

Figure 1.9 Relative electric field intensity distribution of *s*- and *p*-components of polarisation in a MacNeille type polarising beam splitter Glass|(0·5L H 0·5L)⁷|Glass (from Miller 1975).

distribution at non-normal incidence (the *s*- and *p*-components of polarisation are shown separately) of a MacNeille type polarising beam splitter (Apfel 1977). This coating was designed so that $\mathcal{R}_p = 0$, $\mathcal{T}_s = 99.99\%$ at the argon laser wavelength, 514·5 nm. The light is incident at 45° in a glass cube, refractive index 1·62. In this case $n_H = 2.04$, $n_L = 1.385$. The thicknesses are quarter-wave for the *s*-component at this angle of incidence.

2 Design of Filters by Analytical Techniques

This book is primarily concerned with 'computer-aided' techniques for multilayer design; however, a designer must be aware that there are a large number of well known and useful 'analytical' methods available for use, which are not dependent on the availability of a digital computer, although they may be used in conjunction with a computer refinement technique. The purpose of this chapter is to give an introduction to some of these methods.

In many books on thin-film optics, the material is divided into chapters according to the filter application; here we are attempting to present the designer's point of view, so the division is according to the design method employed. For completeness, however, we begin with a brief description of the most common types of filter design which the designer may be called upon to produce.

2.1 Classification of the most important types of filter

Although in theory one may design a multilayer to give any specified spectral response, in practice many designs fall into one of five main categories; namely, antireflection coatings, high-reflection coatings, band pass filters, edge filters and beam splitters.

Macleod (1969) gives an interesting account of the historical development of multilayer filters; from this viewpoint, the two most important categories are antireflection coatings and the Fabry—Perot interference filter — the latter is a special example of a band pass filter, and will be considered in detail in a subsequent paragraph as its structure forms the basis of a method of analysis of general multilayer coatings.

An antireflection coating (figure 2.1) has a spectral response giving high transmittance (low reflectance) over a specified spectral range. The application of such a coating to the components of an optical system is of great technological importance, and even today it is probable that more anti-reflection coatings are produced than any other type of multilayer filter. Many nineteenth century optical physicists including Fraunhofer, Rayleigh and Taylor were well aware that tarnishing of glass produced an increased transparency. However, no significant developments were made in the subject until the advent of vacuum deposition processes in the 1930s. Since that time much effort has been put into producing suitable designs for this

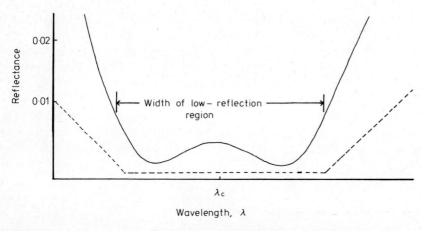

Figure 2.1   Spectral characteristics of an antireflection coating. The broken
curve denotes design specifications.

type of coating; some will be discussed in this chapter, but for a fuller
account of earlier methods, the reader is referred to the review by Cox and
Hass (1964).

At the other end of the (reflectance) scale, we have the high-reflectance
coating (figure 2.2) which has a spectral response consisting of low transmittance (high reflectance) over a specified spectral range. Two types of
reflector are available – a metallic reflector can give the desired effect, but
if it is desirable also to have low absorption, a multilayer all-dielectric
coating should be used. In chapter 1, the classical stack filter was discussed

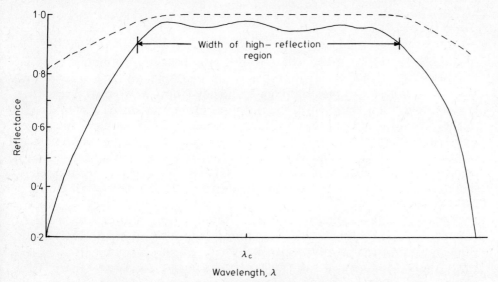

Figure 2.2   Characteristics of a high-reflectance coating.

32

and it was seen that if enough layers are used, one may obtain very high reflectance over the bandwidth of the stack. However, increasing the number of layers does not necessarily increase the bandwidth — special techniques are needed to provide broad band high reflectance; some of these techniques will be discussed in this chapter, consideration of others is more appropriately postponed until chapter 4.

Edge filters (figure 2.3) are characterised by a region of high transmittance terminated by a sharp 'cut off' edge, followed by a region of rejection (high reflectance). The overall transmittance in the 'passing' region, the steepness

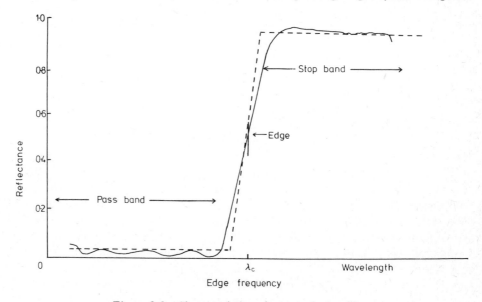

Figure 2.3 Characteristics of a typical edge filter.

of cut-off on the edge and the rejection power in the 'stopping' zone are important for this type of filter. There are two kinds of edge filter — low-frequency (long-wave) pass and high-frequency (short-wave) pass. The earliest type of edge filter relied on the absorption properties of the materials used in the filter, but at the present time it is often better to design a multilayer interference edge filter, which is either a variation of the quarter-wave stack design (Epstein (1952) and Baumeister (1963)) or which has been designed using a special purpose method such as that of Seeley (1965). Seeley's method will be discussed fully in chapter 3 as it is based on an electrical filter design technique.

A band pass filter (figure 2.4) has a region of transmittance bounded by regions of rejection on either side. Broad band pass filters (bandwidths of 20% or more) are usually designed by considering a combination of two edge filters — namely, a low-(long-wave) pass and a high-pass filter. These components are usually deposited on either side of the substrate, although it is

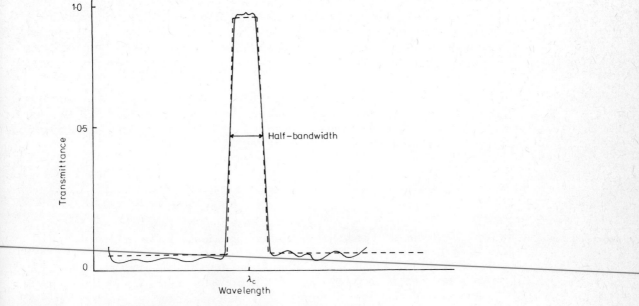

Figure 2.4 Characteristics of a band pass filter.

possible to deposit them on the same side (Epstein (1952) and Dobrowolski (1966)). A narrow band filter normally has a relative bandwidth of 15% or less and in this case the overall design is considered to be a single entity. The Fabry—Perot filter is probably the simplest example of a narrow band pass filter and can either be metal—dielectric or all-dielectric (Heavens (1955) and Baumeister (1963)). Smith (1958) discussed the use of multiple half-wave filters for band pass applications; Berning and Turner (1957) designed the induced transmission filter by optimising the performance of metal—dielectric band pass filters. Metal—dielectric multilayers for use in Fabry—Perot and induced transmission filters have been discussed in detail by Macdonald (1971) and will not be included in this text.

A beam splitter (figure 2.5) is a device for dividing a beam of light into two parts; this may either be a division of energy throughout the spectrum — such a filter is an achromatic beam splitter — or one may wish to obtain a spectral division whereby the incident light is split into different colour components — this occurs if a dichroic beam splitter is used. Two dichroic beam splitters are used in colour television cameras in order to produce the red, green and blue primary colour beams. In this latter application, the filters used are very similar to the edge filter, but are designed for use at non-normal incidence. The achromatic beam splitter is also often used at a high angle of incidence and as a result the two components tend to be highly polarised. Banning (1947) devised a polarising beam splitter by incorporating a multilayer filter in a glass prism in such a way that light is

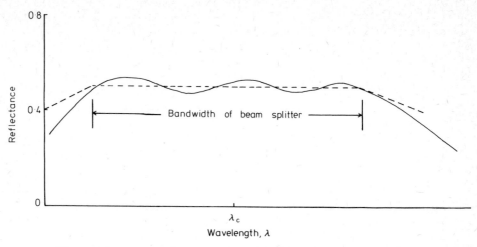

Figure 2.5   Spectral characteristics of an achromatic beam splitter.

incident on the multilayer at an angle greater than the critical angle for the materials. This is necessary because the Brewster angle for a multilayer stack consisting of certain commonly used materials may be greater than 90° referred to air as the medium of incidence, i.e. it is greater than the critical angle for the materials concerned. The Brewster condition for an interface between two materials of different refractive index may always be satisfied for some angle of incidence; in this case the reflectance of the p-component of polarisation will be zero, whereas the s-component will have nonzero reflectivity. The latter may be enhanced by the use of the multilayer stack, while that of the p-component can be kept at, or very close to, zero. Thus, the effect of the filter is such that the reflected beam is mostly composed of the s-component of polarisation and the transmitted beam is basically the p-component of polarisation.

The above discussion provides a very brief introduction to the various types of multilayer filter which occur in practice, so that reference can be made in this and subsequent chapters to particular designs; full and detailed descriptions, illustrated by many practical examples of these and other filters, are to be found in Macleod (1969). One or two designs included in chapters 4 and 5 do not fall into these main classifications, but are special purpose filters, designed (often as a 'one off' exercise) for particular applications.

2.2   Achromatised designs for antireflection coatings (Liddell 1966) — an illustration of the graphical method

The equation for the reflectance of a single film on a substrate was given by (1.19); from this it may be deduced that the conditions for a single layer to have zero reflectance at normal incidence for some wavelength λ_0 are that the optical thickness of the layer must be $\lambda_0/4$ and its index must be given by

$$n_1 = (n_0 n_{sub})^{1/2}, \qquad (2.1)$$

i.e. the index of the film must be equal to the geometric mean of the indices of the surrounding media. When these conditions are satisfied, the film is said to 'match' the surrounding media at the wavelength λ_0. Condition (2.1) is often difficult to satisfy using practical materials, so two- or three-layer coatings are used instead; these have the additional advantage of having a wider low-reflectance band than the single-layer coating. The thicknesses of the layers in the earlier coatings tended to be quarter-wave or half-wave. The spectral reflectivity of some multiple quarter-wave coatings is shown in figure 2.6. In order to produce a coating to antireflect a surface at a particular wavelength, the graphical method, discussed in the previous chapter, may be used. Although multiple reflections are ignored, the results produced are fairly accurate.

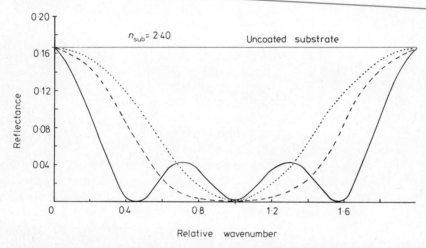

Figure 2.6 Multiple quarter-wave antireflection coatings: dotted curve, single layer, $n_1 = 1\cdot55$; broken curve, double layer, $n_1 = 1\cdot38$, $n_2 = 2\cdot10$; full curve, triple layer, $n_1 = 1\cdot35$, $n_2 = 1\cdot55$, $n_3 = 1\cdot85$.

The resulting reflectance from any coating is approximately equal to the vector sum of the Fresnel coefficients of the interfaces, so it follows that zero reflectance for any wavelength will be obtained if $r_1, r_2, \ldots, r_{N+1}$ form a closed polygon at that wavelength. If fixed index materials are used, this condition may be met by treating the thicknesses as the design variables. The process may be illustrated by the following example:

A two-layer coating of cerium oxide ($n_2 = 2\cdot30$) and magnesium fluoride ($n_1 = 1\cdot38$) on glass ($n_{sub} = 1\cdot52$) (figure 2.7(a) illustrates the configuration)

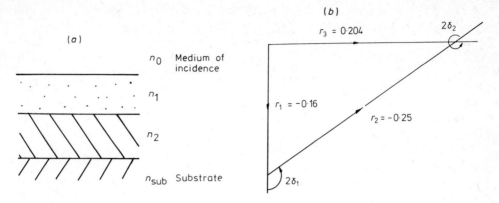

Figure 2.7 (*a*) Configuration for a 2-layer antireflection coating. (*b*) Graphical construction.

is required to give zero reflectance at 632·8 nm for normal incidence. Using equation (1.14)

$$r_1 = \frac{1·00 - 1·38}{1·00 + 1·38} = -0·160,$$

$$r_2 = \frac{1·38 - 2·30}{1·38 + 2·30} = -0·246,$$

$$r_3 = \frac{2·30 - 1·52}{2·30 + 1·52} = 0·204.$$

If we construct a triangle whose sides are proportional to r_1, r_2 and r_3 (figure 2.7 (*b*)), the values for δ_1 and δ_2, the phase thicknesses, may be measured. These are approximately 63° and 160° respectively. Using equation (1.2) i.e.

$$\delta_m = 2\pi n_m d_m/\lambda, \qquad m = 1, 2,$$

we obtain $d_1 = 80$ nm and $d_2 = 122$ nm. The calculation may be checked using the usual matrix formulation (1.27) and (1.28); for the two-layer case we have

$$\begin{pmatrix} E_0 \\ H_0 \end{pmatrix} = \begin{bmatrix} \cos\delta_1 & \dfrac{i}{n_1}\sin\delta_1 \\ in_1\sin\delta_1 & \cos\delta_1 \end{bmatrix} \begin{bmatrix} \cos\delta_2 & \dfrac{i}{n_2}\sin\delta_2 \\ in_2\sin\delta_2 & \cos\delta_2 \end{bmatrix} \begin{pmatrix} 1 \\ \mu_{sub} \end{pmatrix} E_{sub}^+,$$

$$= \begin{bmatrix} 0·454 & 0·646i \\ 1·230i & 0·454 \end{bmatrix} \begin{bmatrix} -0·940 & 0·149i \\ 0·787i & -0·940 \end{bmatrix} \begin{pmatrix} 1 \\ 1·52 \end{pmatrix} E_{sub}^+,$$

$$= \begin{pmatrix} -0·935 - 0·819i \\ -0·927 - 0·799i \end{pmatrix} E_{sub}^+,$$

so

$$\mathcal{R}=\left|\frac{E_0-H_0}{E_0+H_0}\right|^2=\frac{(0\cdot008)^2+(0\cdot02)^2}{(1\cdot862)^2+(1\cdot618)^2},$$

i.e. $\mathcal{R}\simeq 0\cdot00008.$

The resulting value for $\mathcal{R}$ at the design wavelength is less than 0.01%.

For some applications one requires a coating to antireflect at more than one wavelength. Such a coating is said to be achromatised. Vasicek (1952) and Turner (1950) have discussed this problem in some detail; one way of obtaining this result from the simple graphical model necessitates the vector diagram closing in symmetric positions on either side of some reference wavelength for two zeros of reflectance; for achromatisation at three wavelengths, the vector diagram should also close at the reference wavelength (figure 2.8). For a three-layer coating, $r_1+r_3=r_2+r_4$, so this means that the quadrilateral formed by r_1,r_2,r_3 and r_4 circumscribes a circle; thus

$$p=\frac{r_1}{r_2}=\frac{\sin\dfrac{y_2}{2}\sin\dfrac{(y_2+y_3)}{2}}{\sin\dfrac{y_4}{2}\sin\dfrac{y_1+y_2}{2}},$$

$$q=\frac{r_1}{r_3}=\frac{\sin\dfrac{y_2}{2}\sin\dfrac{y_3}{2}}{\sin\dfrac{y_1}{2}\sin\dfrac{y_4}{2}},\tag{2.2}$$

$$r=\frac{r_1}{r_4}=\frac{\sin\dfrac{y_3}{2}\sin\dfrac{y_2+y_3}{2}}{\sin\dfrac{y_1}{2}\sin\dfrac{y_1+y_2}{2}},$$

where

$$y_i=\pi-2\delta_i,\qquad i=1,2,3$$

and

$$y_1+y_2+y_3+y_4=2\pi,$$

so that for given phase thicknesses, the appropriate values of n_1, n_2 and n_3 may be obtained. In order to obtain practical values for these indices, Turner suggests using layers whose optical thicknesses are in the ratio $1:2:3:\ldots:N$ for an N-layer filter, where the first layer has an optical thickness of a

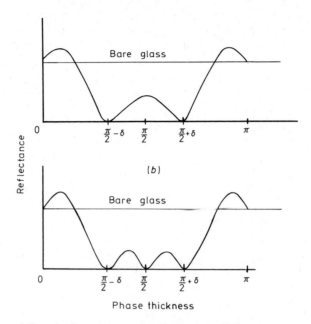

(a)

(b)

Phase thickness

Figure 2.8   A three-layer achromatised antireflection coating, (*a*) achromatised at two points, (*b*) achromatised at three points.

quarter wave at the central reference wavelength. The technique is best illustrated by reference to a practical problem:

The helium–neon laser may be made to operate at 3390 nm and at 632·8 nm; certain elements in the system need to be antireflecting at both these wavelengths. For a suitable three-layer antireflection coating for quartz (n_{sub} for quartz = 1·457 at 632·8 nm and 1·409 at 3390 nm), we proceed as follows, making use of the periodic property of multilayer reflectance; the ratio of the wavelengths to be achromatised is 5·357, so we may consider reflectances at phase thicknesses $\pi/2$, $\pi/2 \pm \delta$, $5\pi/2$, $5\pi/2 \pm \delta$. For real values of refractive index, exact achromatisation may be obtained for $\delta \simeq 5°$, $6°$ and $7·5°$. However, the calculations summarised in table 2.1 indicate that the reflectivity is low for values of δ between $0°$ and $30°$. Let x_1, x_2 ($= 2x_1$) and x_3 ($= 3x_1$) represent the phase thicknesses of the layers at $\pi/2 - \delta$; we may plot the values of n_1, n_2 and n_3 against x_1, (figure 2.9) and use the diagram to obtain a suitable set of indices for any particular value of x_1. If we take $x_1 = 65°$, $\delta = 25°$, then

$$\lambda_0 = \frac{450 \times 632\cdot8}{450 - \delta}\ \text{nm} = 669\cdot4\ \text{nm},$$

Table 2.1 Parameters for an achromatised antireflection coating designed for use with a helium–neon laser.

δ (deg)	5	7·5	15	20	25	27·5
x_1 (deg)	85	82·5	75	70	65	62·5
p	0·5671	0·5823	0·6830	0·8440	1·2993	2·1567
q	−1·0313	−1·0731	−1·3660	−1·8794	−3·5016	−6·7959
r	−4·849	−4·6639	−3·7322	−2·8794	−1·9383	−1·4631
n_1	1·2641	1·2784	1·2903	1·3319	1·4716	1·8052
n_2	1·9634	1·9574	1·8783	1·8722	1·9782	2·3595
n_3	1·5288	1·5354	1·5594	1·6085	1·7752	2·1682
$\mathscr{R}_{632·8\,nm}$ (%)	0·0023	0·002	0·0098	0·0247	0·098	0·015
$\mathscr{R}_{3390\,nm}$ (%)	0·0257	0·0192	0·0573	0·066	0·0347	0·1696

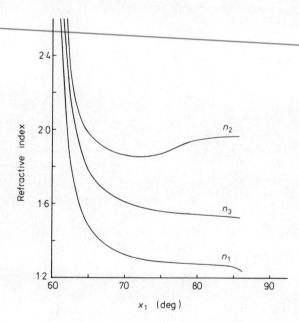

Figure 2.9 Combinations of indices for the achromatised coating for the He–Ne laser.

and a coating achromatised at both wavelengths (neglecting the effects of dispersion and absorption) may be obtained by using

15 $\lambda_0/4$ layers of lead fluoride ($n_3 = 1\cdot76$),

10 $\lambda_0/4$ layers of tin oxide ($n_2 = 1\cdot96$),

5 $\lambda_0/4$ layers of barium fluoride ($n_1 = 1\cdot47$).

A check calculation based on the exact equations gives $\mathscr{R} = 0.083\%$ at 632·8 nm and $\mathscr{R} = 0.097\%$ at 3390 nm. Although both dispersion of index and absorption have been neglected, one might expect such a coating to provide an approximation to the required design.

2.3   The 'two effective interface' method

A Fabry–Perot interferometer consists basically of two reflecting surfaces separated by a spacer. Any non-absorbing multilayer may be considered as such a system by selecting one layer, bounded by interfaces M and N, to act as a spacer and then treating the layers to the left of and including M as one reflecting surface, and the layers to the right of and including N to act as the other (Smith 1958). This is illustrated in figure 2.10; r_1, t_1, r'_1, t'_1, r_2, t_2, r'_2, t'_2 are the Fresnel amplitude reflection and transmission coefficients

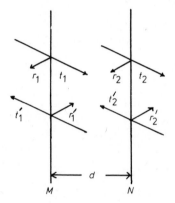

Figure 2.10   Schematic representation of the two effective interfaces (after Smith 1958).

at the interfaces. The transmittance of the system at wavelength λ is given by

$$\mathscr{T}(\lambda) = \frac{|t_1 t_2|^2}{|1 - r'_1 r_2 \exp(-2i\delta)|^2}, \tag{2.3}$$

where

$$\delta = \frac{2\pi n d \cos\theta}{\lambda}, \tag{2.4}$$

n and d are the refractive index and physical thickness of the spacer and θ is the angle of incidence. (This equation may be compared with (1.20) noting that in the case of a single layer, $r_1' = -r_1$. Also we assume that the final medium has the same refractive index as the medium of incidence.)

Let

$$r_1' = |r_1'| \exp(i\psi_1),$$
$$r_2 = |r_2| \exp(i\psi_2),$$
$$(2.5)$$

where ψ_1, ψ_2 are the phase changes on reflection from the two reflecting systems. Then (2.3) becomes

$$\mathscr{T}(\lambda) = \frac{|t_1 t_2|^2}{[1 - |r_1'||r_2|\cos(\psi_1 + \psi_2 - 2\delta)]^2 + [|r_1'||r_2|\sin(\psi_1 + \psi_2 - 2\delta)]^2}$$
$$(2.6)$$

We may replace $\cos(\psi_1 + \psi_2 - 2\delta))$ by $1 - 2\sin^2\frac{1}{2}(\psi_1 + \psi_2 - 2\delta)$ and the amplitude reflection and transmission coefficients may be expressed as energy transmittances and reflectances, giving

$$\mathscr{T}(\lambda) = \frac{\mathscr{T}_1(\lambda)\,\mathscr{T}_2(\lambda)}{[1 - \mathscr{R}(\lambda)]^2} \times \frac{1}{\left(1 + \dfrac{4\mathscr{R}(\lambda)}{(1 - \mathscr{R}(\lambda))^2}\sin^2\frac{1}{2}(\psi_1 + \psi_2 - 2\delta)\right)}, \qquad (2.7)$$

($\mathscr{R}$ is defined by equation (2.11) below)

which may be written

$$\mathscr{T}(\lambda) = \frac{\mathscr{T}_{\max}(\lambda)}{1 + F(\lambda)\sin^2\eta}, \qquad (2.8)$$

where

$$\mathscr{T}_{\max}(\lambda) = \frac{\mathscr{T}_1(\lambda)\,\mathscr{T}_2(\lambda)}{(1 - \mathscr{R}(\lambda))^2}, \qquad (2.9)$$

$$F(\lambda) = \frac{4\mathscr{R}(\lambda)}{(1 - \mathscr{R}(\lambda))^2}, \qquad (2.10)$$

$$\mathscr{R} = (\mathscr{R}_1\mathscr{R}_2)^{1/2}, \qquad (2.11)$$

$\mathscr{R}_1$, $\mathscr{R}_2$ and $\mathscr{T}_1$, $\mathscr{T}_2$ are the reflectances and transmittances of the mirror coatings,

$$\eta = \frac{2\pi nd\cos\theta}{\lambda} - \psi(\lambda) \qquad (2.12)$$

and $\psi(\lambda)$ is the average value of the phase change on reflection in the spacer at the spacer–mirror boundaries for wavelength λ. From equation (2.8) it is seen that transmission bands will occur when $\eta = m\pi$. The integer m is the order number of the filter, and the quantity F is sometimes called the 'finesse' of the filter. If the transmittance and energy absorption of the coatings are $\mathcal{T}$, $\mathcal{A}$ (assumed small), the maximum transmittance is

$$\mathcal{T}_{max} = \frac{1}{(1 + \mathcal{A}/\mathcal{T})^2}, \tag{2.13}$$

since $\mathcal{R} + \mathcal{T} + \mathcal{A} = 1$. Thus it is important that the absorption be as low as possible. Typical values for silver coatings (Heavens 1955) are $\mathcal{R} = 0.95$, $\mathcal{T} = 0.01$, $\mathcal{A} = 0.04$, giving $\mathcal{T}_{max} = 4\%$; a much better performance is achieved by using dielectric multilayers, for which maximum transmittances of more than 90% may be obtained (Baumeister 1963). Another important characteristic of the Fabry—Perot filter is the 'halfwidth' or width at half maximum, $\Delta\lambda$ or $\Delta\sigma$:

$$\frac{\Delta\lambda}{\lambda} = \frac{\Delta\sigma}{\sigma} = \frac{(1 - \mathcal{R}(\lambda))}{\mathcal{R}^{1/2}(2\pi n d - \partial\psi/\partial\sigma)}. \tag{2.14}$$

For metal films the dispersion of phase change is negligible so (2.9) becomes

$$\frac{\Delta\lambda}{\lambda} = \frac{(1 - \mathcal{R})}{m\pi\mathcal{R}^{1/2}}, \tag{2.15}$$

since $\psi \simeq \pi$. For dielectric films, the dispersion of phase change is significant and its sign in the high reflecting region is such as to decrease $\Delta\lambda$. We shall return to this point later in the chapter when the design of broad band high-reflectance coatings for use in interferometry is discussed.

Smith applied his effective interface (or 'split filter') concept to the design of a new type of narrow band transmission filter, known as the double half-wave filter, which has the desirable characteristics of more rapid transition from stop band to pass band and a flatter top to the pass band. The simplest DHW system is HHLHH (H or L is used to denote a single quarter-wave high- or low-index layer), and the system is split by choosing the first half-wave as the spacer. Using Smith's notation as shown in figure 2.11 we see that

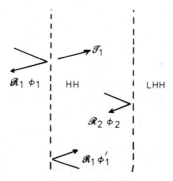

Figure 2.11 Analysis of the HHLHH double half-wave filter (after Smith 1958).

$\mathcal{R}_1$ and $\mathcal{T}_1$ are not dependent on wavelength as they represent the reflectance and transmittance of the single H—air surface $\phi_1, \phi_2, \phi_1', \phi_2'$ are the phase changes associated with the reflection coefficients r_1, r_2, r_1', r_2'. Thus in this case, $\phi_1 = \pi$, $\phi_1' = 0$. The transmittance of the DHW system is then

$$\mathcal{T}(\lambda) = \frac{\mathcal{T}_1(\lambda) \; \mathcal{T}_2(\lambda)}{(1 - \mathcal{R}(\lambda))^2} \frac{1}{1 + F(\lambda) \sin^2(\phi_2(\lambda)/2 - 2\pi n d/\lambda)}. \qquad (2.16)$$

Writing

$$\mathcal{T}_0(\lambda) = \frac{\mathcal{T}_1(\lambda) \; \mathcal{T}_2(\lambda)}{(1 - \mathcal{R}(\lambda))^2}, \qquad (2.17)$$

and

$$\theta = \frac{\phi_2(\lambda)}{2} - \frac{2\pi n d}{\lambda}, \qquad (2.18)$$

we see that at λ_0 (where $2\pi n d/\lambda = \pi$), $\theta = 0$, since $\phi_2 = 0$ at λ_0. $\theta = 0$ also at two points equally spaced in wavenumber on either side of λ_0; at these points the phase change of the spacer equals that of the reflector LHH. The reflectance of the filter and the individual reflecting elements is shown in figure 2.12, from which it may be seen that $\mathcal{R}_1 = \mathcal{R}_2$ at the points where $\theta = 0$. At these points

$$\mathcal{T}_0(\lambda) = \frac{(1 - \mathcal{R}_1(\lambda))(1 - \mathcal{R}_2(\lambda))}{(1 - \mathcal{R}(\lambda))^2} = 1, \qquad (2.19)$$

so the transmission is complete. This property is typical of all double half-wave systems. In order to obtain a narrow band filter, the trough of the reflectance $\mathcal{R}_2$ must be narrowed at the same time as ensuring that $\mathcal{R}_2$ is only slightly less than $\mathcal{R}_1$. These requirements are satisfied by the system HLHHLHLHLHHLH with $n_H = 4.0$ and $n_L = 1.35$ — the computed

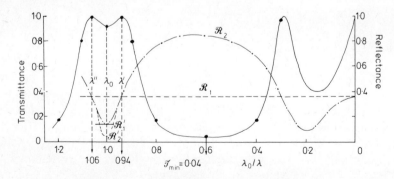

Figure 2.12 Computed transmittance of the HHLHH filter and of its component reflectors (after Smith 1958).

44

transmittance curve of this system is shown in figure 2.13. Smith also gives the conditions necessary to produce a low-pass filter based on the double half-wave design.

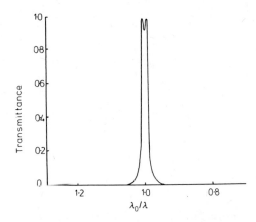

Figure 2.13 A practical double half-wave filter, HLHHLHLHLHHLH (after Smith 1958).

Thetford (1969) used the effective interface idea to design three-layer antireflection coatings. The system is analysed in such a way that the central layer forms the spacer, the outer layers and their boundary media the reflecting surfaces. Conditions for zero reflectance are given by

$$\mathcal{R}_1 = \mathcal{R}_2 \tag{2.20}$$

and

$$\phi_1(\lambda) + \phi_2(\lambda) - 4\pi n d/\lambda = 2\pi N, \tag{2.21}$$

where N is a positive integer. In order to apply his method, the approximation (1.82) is used i.e.

$$\mathcal{R}_1 = r_1^2 + r_2^2 + 2r_1 r_2 \cos 2\delta_1, \tag{2.22}$$

$$\mathcal{R}_2 = r_3^2 + r_4^2 + 2r_3 r_4 \cos 2\delta_3. \tag{2.23}$$

For given refractive indices, it is fairly easy to find appropriate thicknesses to satisfy equations (2.20)–(2.23) for a single wavelength λ_0. However, for broad band antireflection it is necessary to extend the analysis to find the appropriate conditions for zero reflectance at two wavelengths; generally the resulting designs for the achromatisations exhibit low reflectance over a broad band. A pair of values δ_1, δ_3 satisfying (2.20), (2.22) and (2.23) may be selected and the appropriate value of δ_2 calculated from (2.21). The various reflectances expressed in the above equations may be represented on an Argand diagram. In order to obtain the condition for zero reflectance at two wavelengths, $\mathscr{R}_1$ and $\mathscr{R}_2$ should have the characteristics indicated in figure 2.14. To obtain the mathematical conditions for this second

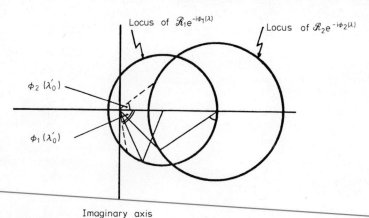

Figure 2.14 Representation of single film reflectances used in the design of a 3-layer antireflection coating (after Thetford 1969).

reflectance zero at λ_0', equations (2.22) and (2.23) are differentiated and the condition

$$\Delta(\mathscr{R}_2) = \Delta(\mathscr{R}_1) \tag{2.24}$$

applied. This gives the result

$$\frac{\lambda_0}{\lambda_0'} - 1 = \frac{(r_3 r_4 \sin 2\delta_3)(\pi - 2\delta_3)}{\delta_3 r_3 r_4 \sin 2\delta_3 + \delta_1 r_2 r_1 \sin 2\delta_1}, \tag{2.25}$$

which corresponds to satisfying the amplitude condition ((2.20) above) at λ_0'. The phase condition

$$\frac{2\lambda_0 \delta_2}{\lambda_0'} = 2\pi - \phi_1(\lambda_0') - \phi_2(\lambda_0') \tag{2.26}$$

must also be satisfied. If this is not the case for the pair of values δ_1, δ_3 chosen, new values must be tried. A few calculations of this nature soon enable the designer to choose suitable values for the δ without too much difficulty in most cases, unless a combination of materials has been chosen which will not produce two zeros of reflectance. Results of four three-layer coatings designed by this method are shown in figure 2.15.

The split filter concept is clearly a very useful one for the multilayer filter designer, as seen by the wide variety of problems to which it may be applied. It is also a useful tool for error analysis – this application will be discussed in detail in chapter 7.

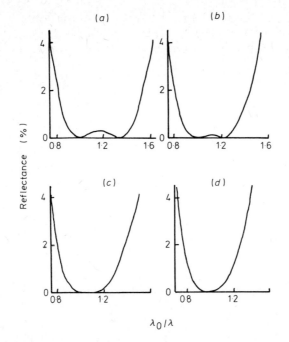

	(a)	(b)
n_0	1·52	1·52
n_1	1·8	1·8
n_2	2·0	2·1
n_3	1·38	1·38
n_4	1·00	1·00
$n_1 h_1$	0·132 λ_0	0·152 λ_0
$n_2 h_2$	0·336 λ_0	0·359 λ_0
$n_3 h_3$	0·205 λ_0	0·220 λ_0

	(c)	(d)
n_0	1·52	1·52
n_1	1·8	1·8
n_2	2·2	2·4
n_3	1·38	1·38
n_4	1·00	1·00
$n_1 h_1$	0·170 λ_0	0·181 λ_0
$n_2 h_2$	0·388 λ_0	0·445 λ_0
$n_3 h_3$	0·227 λ_0	0·247 λ_0

Figure 2.15 The reflectance of four 3-layer antireflection coatings (after Thetford 1969).

2.4 Design of broad band high-reflectance coatings

We have seen that the limiting fractional width of the reflectance band of a classical stack is given by

$$\frac{\Delta\lambda}{\lambda_0} = \frac{4}{\pi} \sin^{-1}\left(\frac{n_H - n_L}{n_H + n_L}\right). \qquad (2.27)$$

Thus the only way of producing a large fractional width for this type of stack is to use a high ratio n_H/n_L; unfortunately, there are severe practical limitations to this procedure. For the visible region, it is difficult to find materials for which n_H/n_L is greater than about 2; however, in the near infrared, where semiconducting materials of high index may be used, n_H/n_L may be as high as 3·65, giving a fractional bandwidth of 0·77. A practical way of producing extended bandwidths in the visible region is to take realisable values for refractive indices of the layers and to attempt to adjust the layer thicknesses to produce the desired response. This application is very suitable for automatic design programs and examples of such designs will be given in chapter 4. However, one or two other special purpose methods have been developed for the problem. Penselin and Steudel (1955) were probably the first workers to try the idea of staggering the layer thicknesses throughout the stack to form a regular progression; in this way, at any wavelength, a fairly wide range of layers have optical thicknesses close enough to a quarter wave to produce the high reflectance. Figure 2.16 shows some results obtained by Penselin and Steudel for 13-layer filters whose

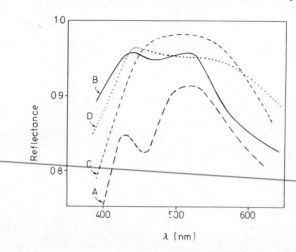

Figure 2.16 Results of Penselin and Steudel.

layer thicknesses varied according to an arithmetic progression. The idea was extended by Heavens and Liddell (1966) who computed reflectances of 15-, 25- and 35-layer filters whose layer thicknesses formed either arithmetic or geometric progressions; for the arithmetic progression filters common differences in the range -0.05 to $+0.05$ were used, whereas for the geometric filters the common ratio ranged from 0.95 to 1.05. For all filters, the high index was assumed to be 2.36 (CeO_2), the low index 1.39 (MgF_2) and the substrate 1.53 (glass). The reflectances of two of the best filters are shown in figure 2.17; table 2.2 gives a comparison of the bandwidths of some of the filters discussed above. The Baumeister and Stone design (1956) was obtained using a 'successive relaxation' technique (see chapter 4).

One important property of these 'staggered filters' is their high phase dispersion which gives rise to two interesting characteristics if the filters are used as the reflecting elements of a Fabry–Perot filter: (1) it may be seen from equation (2.14) that since $\partial\psi/\partial\sigma$ is a negative quantity, the bandwidth of the filter is considerably smaller than if classical stacks are used; (2) according to the theory produced by Giacomo et al (1959), the effect of layer thickness errors in the reflectors on the width of the pass band is minimised if

$$\left|\frac{\partial\psi}{\partial\sigma}\right| = 4\pi n D_m , \qquad (2.28)$$

48

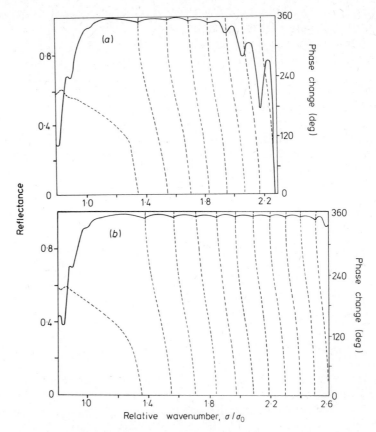

Figure 2.17 The results of Heavens and Liddell: (*a*) 25-layer filter; (*b*) 35-layer filter (after Heavens and Liddell 1966).

Table 2.2 Comparison of bandwidths for various types of broad band reflecting filters.

Type of filter	Bandwidth (Å) $\mathscr{R}\,(>90\%)$	$\lambda_0 = 1/\sigma_0$ (Å)
13-layer classical stack	4300–6100	5000
Limiting value for infinite classical stack	4250–6200	5000
Penselin and Steudel filter (13 layers)	3800–6100	
Baumeister and Stone filters (15 layers)	4100–7400	
Asymmetric arithmetic filters ($k = -0.02$)		
15 layers	4190–6250	6000
25 layers	4180–7250	7000
35 layers	3300–8400	8000
Asymmetric geometric filters ($k = 0.97$)		
15 layers	3940–6250	6000
25 layers	3420–7300	7000
35 layers	3000–8260	8000

where n is the spacer index and D_m the total thickness of one of the reflecting stacks – the staggered filters come close to fulfilling this condition over the entire reflectance band of the system. The phase dispersion properties were discussed further by Baumeister and Jenkins (1957) and Baumeister *et al* (1959).

One of the simplest methods for extending the high-reflectance region was suggested by Turner and Baumeister (1966) and consists of placing a quarter-wave stack centered at one wavelength over another centered at a different wavelength. Such stacks are said to be 'mismatched'. However, in this process care must be taken to avoid a peak of transmission in the centre of the high-reflectance band – this will occur if the outer quarter-wave layers are of the same index. The problem may be overcome by using stacks of the form $(0.5_L H 0.5_L)^m$ or $(0.5_H L 0.5_H)^m$. Figure 2.18 shows the reflectance of such a filter, designed for use in the infrared.

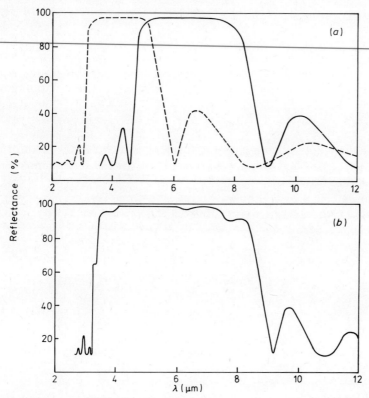

Figure 2.18 (*a*) Measured reflectances of two stacks $BaF_2 \mid 0.5_L$ H $0.5_L \mid$ Air. H and L are films of stibnite and chiolite a quarter-wave thick at reference wavelength $\lambda_0 = 4.06$ (broken curve) or 6.3 nm (full curve). (*b*) Measured reflectance of these two stacks superimposed in a single coating for an extended high-reflectance region (after Turner and Baumeister 1966).

2.5 Use of equivalent index techniques in multilayer design

Herpin (1947) showed that at a single wavelength, any sequence of films in a multilayer may be represented by a fictitious bi-layer with characteristic matrix $\mathbf{M}_a\mathbf{M}_b$. Since both these matrices (and also their product) are unitary, one has three independent elements from which to determine the two equivalent indices and thicknesses of the films forming the bi-layer. Thus, one of the four parameters must be chosen arbitrarily; Epstein (1952) suggested that one of the indices should be chosen equal to that of its neighbouring medium (either the medium of incidence or the substrate). Equating the matrix product of the multilayer with that of the bi-layer, we obtain

$$\mathbf{M} = \begin{bmatrix} A & iB \\ iC & D \end{bmatrix} = \begin{bmatrix} \cos\alpha & \dfrac{i}{N}\sin\alpha \\ iN\sin\alpha & \cos\alpha \end{bmatrix} \begin{bmatrix} \cos\beta & \dfrac{i}{n_{\text{sub}}}\sin\beta \\ in_{\text{sub}}\sin\beta & \cos\beta \end{bmatrix},$$

(2.29)

where N is the equivalent index of the first layer and α, β are the equivalent thicknesses. For a symmetrical system, $A^2 = D^2 = 1 - BC$, and hence for this case

$$\beta = 0, \qquad \cos\alpha = A, \qquad N^2 = C/B, \qquad (2.30)$$

i.e. the system reduces to a single equivalent layer of index N and thickness α. The analysis may be extended to give results for the general unsymmetrical case (Liddell 1966).

We may consider as a simple example the three-layer symmetrical system ABA, whose characteristic matrix is given by:

$$\begin{bmatrix} \cos\delta_A & \dfrac{i}{n_A}\sin\delta_A \\ in_A\sin\delta_A & \cos\delta_A \end{bmatrix} \begin{bmatrix} \cos\delta_B & \dfrac{i}{n_B}\sin\delta_B \\ in_B\sin\delta_B & \cos\delta_B \end{bmatrix} \begin{bmatrix} \cos\delta_A & \dfrac{i}{n_A}\sin\delta_A \\ in_A\sin\delta_A & \cos\delta_A \end{bmatrix},$$

(2.31)

so using (2.30) above

$$\cos\alpha = \cos 2\delta_A \cos\delta_B - \tfrac{1}{2}(n_B/n_A + n_A/n_B)\sin 2\delta_A \cos\delta_B,$$

$$N^2 = \frac{n_A^2\,[\sin 2\delta_A \cos\delta_B + \tfrac{1}{2}(n_B/n_A + n_A/n_B)\cos 2\delta_A \sin\delta_B - \tfrac{1}{2}(n_A/n_B - n_B/n_A)\sin\delta_B]}{\sin 2\delta_A \cos\delta_B + \tfrac{1}{2}(n_B/n_A + n_A/n_B)\cos 2\delta_A \sin\delta_B + \tfrac{1}{2}(n_A/n_B - n_B/n_A)\sin\delta_B},$$

(2.32)

which may be solved to give α and N. This may be extended easily to cover any symmetrical period. A multilayer consisting of S identical periods each with an equivalent phase thickness α and equivalent index N is equivalent to a single layer of thickness $S\alpha$ and index N since

$$\begin{bmatrix} \cos\alpha & \dfrac{i}{N}\sin\alpha \\[2mm] iN\sin\alpha & \cos\alpha \end{bmatrix}^S = \begin{bmatrix} \cos S\alpha & \dfrac{i}{N}\sin S\alpha \\[2mm] iN\sin S\alpha & \cos S\alpha \end{bmatrix}.$$

In a practical computation of equivalent index, the designer will discover there are regions where $\cos\alpha < -1$ and hence (2.32) cannot be solved for real α. Both α and N take imaginary values; this corresponds to the case $|x| > 2$, discussed in the previous chapter (equation (1.57)), and indicates a 'high-reflectance zone' or 'stop band'. Outside such zones where the equivalent index and thickness are real, we have a 'pass band'. The band edge occurs when $\cos\alpha = 1$.

The equivalent index technique for symmetric systems is probably the most useful analytical technique available and is the method of design preferred by many designers: it has been particularly successful when applied to the design of low-reflection coatings and band pass filters. Figure 2.19

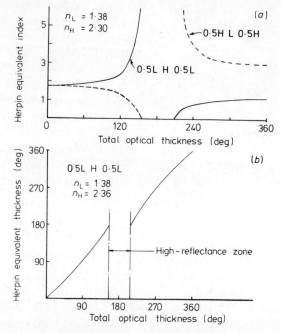

Figure 2.19 Dispersion of (a) equivalent index and (b) equivalent thickness (after Epstein 1952).

illustrates the dispersion of equivalent index and thickness for the symmetrical combinations $0.5_L H 0.5_L$ and $0.5_H L 0.5_H$ with respect to total phase thickness. This shows that for multilayers whose component thicknesses are small compared with the wavelength, the equivalent index assumes a value which is almost constant and which lies between the values of the component film indices, while the equivalent thickness is nearly equal to the sum of the component thicknesses. Costich (1970) showed that the value of N at $0°$ phase thickness is $(n_H n_L)^{1/2}$ for both combinations; at $360°$ phase thickness, the value for $0.5_L H 0.5_L$ is given by $n_L (n_L/n_H)^{1/2}$, whereas for $0.5_H L 0.5_H$ it is $n_H (n_H/n_L)^{1/2}$.

In the application of equivalent index techniques to the design of three-layer antireflection coatings, Berning (1962) showed that if the thicknesses are small

$$N \simeq n_L \frac{q + n_H/n_L}{q + n_L/n_H} \quad , \tag{2.33}$$

$$\gamma \simeq \delta \left(1 + \frac{(n_L - n_H)^2 q}{n_L n_H (1+q)^2} \right), \tag{2.34}$$

where q is the ratio of thicknesses and $\delta = 2\delta_H + \delta_L$, the total thickness of the layers in the combination. Thus N is approximately a constant whose value lies between n_L and n_H; any particular value for N may be obtained by varying q. This result is useful for antireflection purposes when one needs an index to match the surrounding media; the range of application of (2.33) and (2.34) is surprisingly large – equation (2.34) will hold for values of δ up to and exceeding $90°$. Film coatings for which the total thickness is $90°$ or $270°$ are of especial interest in the design of antireflection coatings. Epstein (1952) gives results for equivalent indices of some symmetric thin-film combinations which may be used for this purpose – these are shown in table 2.3. Further results have been given by Young (1961).

Baumeister (1963) and Young and Cristal (1966) applied the equivalent index method to the design of edge filters. If a multilayer stack is used as an edge filter, subsidiary reflectances spoil the passing performance near the edge; however, the stack could be constructed of the thin-film combination $(0.5_L H 0.5_L)$ repeated q times – the multilayer is then symmetrical and equivalent to a single layer whose equivalent index is equal to that of the basic combination and whose equivalent thickness is q times that of the basic combination. One may estimate the Herpin equivalent index for the stack at the subsidiary reflectance maxima and apply coatings to match the stack to the substrate at the stack–substrate interface and to match it to air at the air–stack interface. Unfortunately, the dispersion of equivalent index is usually large at these points, so in practice, any solution which attempts to suppress more than one subsidiary reflectance maximum is necessarily a compromise. Baumeister (1963) gives an example of a low-(frequency) pass

Table 2.3 Results for equivalent indices of some symmetrical thin-film combinations.

$\delta = 2\delta_1 + \delta_2$	$90°$	$90°$	$270°$	$270°$
n_1	1·38	2·30	1·38	2·30
n_2	2·30	1·38	2·30	1·38
δ_2	N	N	N	N
$0°$	1·380	2·300	1·380	2·300
$10°$	1·514	2·096	1·258	2·523
$20°$	1·657	1·916	1·151	2·758
$30°$	1·800	1·763	1·060	2·995
$40°$	1·938	1·638	0·985	3·222
$50°$	2·061	1·540	0·926	3·426
$60°$	2·162	1·468	0·882	3·598
$70°$	2·238	1·418	0·852	3·726
$80°$	2·283	1·390	0·834	3·806
$90°$	2·300	1·380	0·828	3·833

filter of 19 layers

$$\text{Air}\,(0\cdot5\text{L H }0\cdot5\text{L})^9\,\text{Glass,}$$

where $n_L = 1\cdot38$, $n_H = 2\cdot30$, $n_{sub} = 1\cdot52$ and the layers have a quarter-wave optical thickness at $1\cdot0\,\mu$m. This filter would have subsidiary reflectance maxima at $6850\,\text{cm}^{-1}$ and $7750\,\text{cm}^{-1}$. Using figure 2.19, we see that the Herpin indices at these wavenumbers are $2\cdot48$ when $\sigma = 6850\,\text{cm}^{-1}$ ($\delta = 123°$) and at $\sigma = 7750\,\text{cm}^{-1}$, $N = 3\cdot44$. At $7750\,\text{cm}^{-1}$, a single quarter-wave layer of index $2\cdot30$ is needed to match the Herpin layer to glass and a quarter-wave layer of index $1\cdot85$ is needed to match it to air, whereas at $6850\,\text{cm}^{-1}$, the quarter-wave layers should have indices $1\cdot95$ and $1\cdot57$ respectively. Thus, as a compromise, the design

$$\text{Air}\,(\text{film A})\,(0\cdot5\text{L H }0\cdot5\text{L})^9\,(\text{film B})\,\text{Glass}$$

was proposed, where film A has index $1\cdot70$ and film B index $2\cdot10$; both have quarter-wave optical thickness at $\sigma = 7500\,\text{cm}^{-1}$. The resulting design is shown in figure 2.20 and it is seen that the overall transmittance in the region from $8100\,\text{cm}^{-1}$ to $6300\,\text{cm}^{-1}$ is considerably improved. Both Young (1967) and Thelen (1971) have extended the method still further to design optical minus filters — these have regions of high transmittance on both sides of the high-reflectance band.

Some of the methods described in subsequent chapters could be classified as 'analytical techniques'. Certain of these were developed from electrical filter design work and are therefore included in chapter 3; the class of methods known as 'Fourier transform methods' are described in chapter 5, which is devoted to this topic—it is a subject which has become very

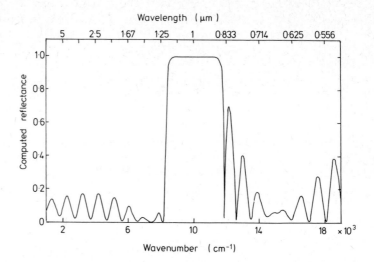

Figure 2.20 Band pass filter, Air $\mid$ L$'$(0·5L H 0·5L)^{9}H$'$ $\mid$ Glass, designed by the equivalent index technique. Index of glass = 1·52, $n_{L'}$ = 1·70, $n_{L'}d_{L'}$ = 0·3333μ, n_L = 1·38, $n_L d_L$ = 0·25μ, n_H = 2·3, $n_H d_H$ = 0·25 μ, $n_{H'}$ = 2·10, $n_{H'}d_{H'}$ = 0·3333 μ (after Baumeister 1963).

important for filter designers in the last few years following the work of Sossi (1974, 1976) and Dobrowolski and Lowe (1978); in the latter case, a combination of earlier analytical techniques with automatic computer design methods has produced an extremely powerful-looking design strategy.

3 Application of Electrical Filter Design Techniques

Over the past few decades, much independent development in the theory of filter design has taken place in the fields of linear circuit theory and microwave quarter-wave transformer theory. The methods developed in these subjects are the outcome of years of research in filter synthesis from which a fairly sophisticated theory has evolved. Many of the techniques are totally unlike those which are generally used for optical filter design, but some of the results may be applied to the latter problem. No attempt will be made to give a complete account of all the electrical filter synthesis methods here; we shall consider only the methods which have been modified so as to be directly applicable to multilayer filter design. For a more detailed treatment of filter synthesis, the reader is referred to the books by Van Valkenburg (1960) and Knittl (1976). Note that the notation used is different from that used by optical filter designers.

3.1 Basic notation and definition of terms used in network synthesis

The electrical engineer tends to work in terms of the impedance and admittance of a medium rather than in terms of its refractive index. These quantities may be defined as follows: the characteristic impedance of a medium is inversely proportional to its refractive index, and the characteristic admittance is the reciprocal of impedance. Thus

$$\frac{Y_1}{Y_2} = \frac{Z_2}{Z_1} = \frac{n_1}{n_2}, \tag{3.1}$$

We may also define the amplitude reflection coeficient, r, at the boundary between two media in terms of these quantities. For normal incidence (the electrical engineer is seldom confronted with an angle of incidence complication!)

$$r = \frac{Z_2 - Z_1}{Z_2 + Z_1} = \frac{Y_1 - Y_2}{Y_1 + Y_2} = \frac{n_1 - n_2}{n_1 + n_2}. \tag{3.2}$$

The response of any 'lumped constant' network (i.e. an electrical network containing resistances, capacitances and inductances rather than a transmission line which is a 'distributed' network) can be considered in two ways, either as a time domain response, $f(t)$, or as a frequency domain response, $F(i\omega)$. These are related by means of a Fourier transformation:

$$F(i\omega) = \int_{-\infty}^{+\infty} f(t)\, e^{-i\omega t}\, dt,$$

$$f(t) = \frac{1}{2\pi} \int_{-\infty}^{+\infty} F(i\omega)\, e^{i\omega t}\, d\omega. \qquad (3.3)$$

Generally in circuit theory synthesis it is more convenient to work in terms of a complex frequency, s, defined by

$$s = \sigma + i\omega. \qquad (3.4)$$

$F(s)$ is related to $f(t)$ by a Laplace transformation

$$F(s) = \int_{-\infty}^{+\infty} f(t)\, e^{-st}\, dt,$$

$$f(t) = \frac{1}{2\pi i} \int_{-\infty}^{+\infty} F(s)\, e^{st}\, ds. \qquad (3.5)$$

Another quantity used to describe the response of the network is the 'insertion loss function', P_{loss}; this is defined as the ratio of the incident power to the transmitted power, i.e.

$$P_{loss} = \frac{1}{\mathscr{T}}, \qquad (3.6)$$

and it is related to the amplitude reflection coefficient by

$$|r|^2 = \frac{P_{loss} - 1}{P_{loss}}. \qquad (3.7)$$

The impedance, $Z(s)$, of the network is given by

$$r(s) = \frac{Z(s) - Z_{load}(s)}{Z(s) + Z_{load}(s)}, \qquad (3.8)$$

where Z_{load} is called the 'load impedance' (the load corresponds to the substrate in the optical case). Thus, if Z_{load} and P_{loss} are known, Z may be calculated.

One important result concerning 'realisability' was obtained by Brune (1931); a necessary and sufficient condition for the impedance of the network to represent a physically realisable LCR circuit is that $Z(s)$ must be a 'positive real' function. This means that

$$\mathrm{Re}(Z(s)) \geqslant 0, \quad \text{for} \quad \mathrm{Re}(s) \geqslant 0$$

and

$$Z(s) \text{ is real whenever } s \text{ is real,}$$

i.e. the zeros of $Z(s)$ must lie in the left hand half of the (complex) s-plane. For fuller details of the mathematical properties of these functions, the reader is again advised to consult the book by Van Valkenburg (1960).

Darlington (1939) used this result to develop a method for constructing lossless transmission circuits (these are analogous to antireflection coatings in the multilayer case) with a resistive termination to obtain optimum realisable performance. The next important development was made by Richards (1948) who extended the theory to include transmission line synthesis by use of the transformation

$$s = i \tan \theta, \qquad (3.9)$$

where θ represents the electrical length of a section of transmission line,

$$\theta = 2\pi l/\lambda_g \text{ radians}, \qquad (3.10)$$

l is the physical length of the waveguide section and λ_g is the guide wavelength. However, he makes the following assumptions: (1) the elements of the transmission line are lossless; and (2) the elements are commensurate. This transformation effectively extends application of network theory to the optical region, since transmission lines are very similar mathematically to multilayers; however, there is one important consideration to bear in mind for multilayer synthesis — often a configuration is fixed in advance and, more important, there are only a few materials available for use. Thus, for some applications it becomes necessary to manipulate the circuit prototype to accept these restrictions on data. Two important applications of filter synthesis techniques to the multilayer design problem have been made by Young (1961) and Seeley (1961), working independently. Their methods will be discussed in detail in subsequent sections. Knittl (1967) has applied a rational function technique to the problem and has also described the use of a pole and zero plot of the reflectance function.

3.2 Young's synthesis of antireflection coatings (1961)

One procedure for circuit filter synthesis may be described as follows: the insertion loss function P_{loss} is specified as a function of frequency; this specification will not in general be exactly realisable for a finite number of circuit elements unless a degree of allowable tolerance is also specified. This tolerance allows the designer to determine the degree of the polynomial to be employed in a curve fitting procedure. Tschebysheff polynomials of the first kind are generally employed for this purpose; they may be defined as follows

$$T_k(\bar{\omega}) = \begin{cases} \cos (k \cos^{-1} \bar{\omega}), & \text{for } |\bar{\omega}| \leqslant 1, \\ \cosh (k \cosh^{-1} \bar{\omega}), & \text{for } |\bar{\omega}| > 1. \end{cases} \qquad (3.11)$$

58

These polynomials have the following properties:

(1) $T_k(\bar{\omega})$ oscillates between ± 1 for $-1 \leqslant \bar{\omega} \leqslant 1$;
(2) the zeros are all located in $-1 \leqslant \bar{\omega} \leqslant 1$, with the intervening extrema having values ± 1;
(3) outside the range $-1 \leqslant \bar{\omega} \leqslant +1$ the polynomial quickly becomes very large compared to unity; for large values of $\bar{\omega}$

$$T_k(\bar{\omega}) \rightarrow 2^{k-1}(\bar{\omega})^k.$$

Simple graphs of Tschebysheff polynomials of order 2, 3, 4, 5 and 6 are shown in figure 3.1.

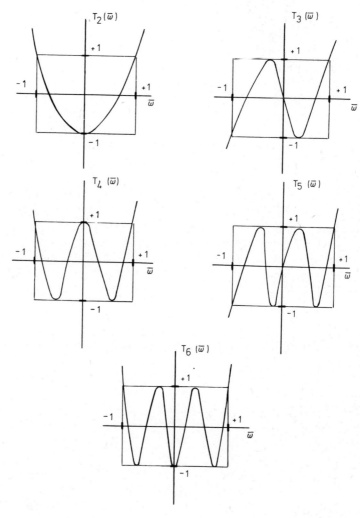

Figure 3.1 Tschebysheff polynomials for small values of $\bar{\omega}$.

Young synthesises antireflection coatings using the technique which Riblet (1957) applied to the design of a lossless waveguide quarter-wave transformer, consisting of a number of cascaded waveguide sections of equal lengths $\lambda_g/4$ at the central frequency (λ_g is the 'guide wavelength'). The assumption is made that there are no absorption losses, so any energy loss is due to reflection at the interfaces. If this reflection loss is minimised, the plot of reflection coefficient against reciprocal wavelength will show an equi-ripple characteristic (figure 3.2(*a*)). In the limiting case of perfect match over vanishingly small bandwidth, the response becomes 'maximally flat' as shown in figure 3.2(*b*).

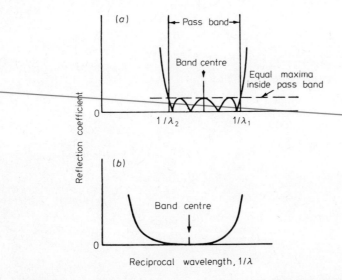

Figure 3.2   Typical performance of transformer or multilayer filter (after Young 1961). (*a*) Equi-ripple response, (*b*) maximally flat reponse.

Riblet's method was based on a theorem of Richards (1948) concerning the reduction of degree of the numerator and denominator of a rational impedance function $Z(s)$. Physically, this process corresponds to the removal of a section of transmission line at the input end of the transformer; the section removed is the first transformer section and its characteristic impedance can now be found. The process is repeated until the final impedance function is a constant, equal to the characteristic impedance of the output waveguide. The method is perhaps best illustrated by the following example (Young (1961), following Riblet): We attempt to apply the method to the design of an antireflection coating for a substrate of index 2·27, the refractive index of the medium of incidence being unity. We also specify that the amplitude reflection coefficient must be less than or equal to 0·025 over the range 408 nm, to 767·2 nm. The specification of this degree of tolerance enables us to calculate that three quarter-wave layers will be required. The insertion loss function for a multilayer film of k layers is given by

$$P_{\text{loss}} = 1 + \frac{(n-1)^2 T_k(\cos\theta/\mu_0)}{4nT_k^2(1/\mu_0)}, \qquad (3.12)$$

where n is the ratio of refractive index of the first medium to that of the last, $T_k(x)$ is a Tschebysheff polynomial of degree k and

$$\mu_0 = \sin\left(\tfrac{1}{2}W\frac{\pi}{2}\right),$$

where

$$W = 2\left(\frac{\lambda_2 - \lambda_1}{\lambda_2 + \lambda_1}\right), \qquad (3.13)$$

and λ_1 and λ_2 are the limiting wavelengths in the pass band. For the data given above, $W = 0.611$, $\mu_0 = 0.464$ and assuming $k = 3$, then

$$\frac{(n-1)^2}{4n}\frac{1}{T_3^2(1/\mu_0)} = 1.578 \times 10^{-4}.$$

Expressing the amplitude reflection coefficient in terms of P_{loss},

$$|r|^2 = \frac{P_{\text{loss}} - 1}{P_{\text{loss}}} = \frac{0.253\cos^6\theta - 0.0817\cos^4\theta + 0.00659\cos^2\theta}{0.253\cos^6\theta - 0.0817\cos^4\theta + 0.00659\cos^2\theta + 1}$$

$$= \frac{0.1779 + 0.0685\,s^2 + 0.00659\,s^4}{1.1779 - 2.9315\,s^2 + 3.00659\,s^4 - s^6}, \qquad (3.14)$$

using Richards' transformation (equation (3.9)). The roots of the determinant of this expression are

$$s_1 = \pm(0.868 + 0.249\mathrm{i}),$$

$$s_2 = \pm 1.294,$$

$$s_3 = \pm(0.868 - 0.294\mathrm{i}).$$

Retaining only the roots whose real parts are negative, and then forming a polynomial from the latter, we obtain

$$D(s) = s^3 + 3.030\,s^2 + 3.085\,s + 1.086 \qquad (3.15)$$

and

$$r = \text{constant} \cdot \frac{T_3\,(\cos\theta/\mu_0)\,(s^2 - 1)}{D(s)} \qquad (3.16)$$

If the constant is chosen so that

$$r = \frac{1-n}{1+n} \quad \text{when} \quad s = 0,$$

since $s = 0$ corresponds to zero optical thickness, then for the example we are considering

$$r = \frac{-0\cdot081\,s^2 + 0\cdot422}{s^3 + 3\cdot030\,s^2 + 3\cdot085\,s + 1\cdot086}. \qquad (3.17)$$

Then, using (3.2), the admittance is found to be

$$Y_1(s) = \frac{s^3 + 3\cdot111\,s^2 + 3\cdot085\,s + 1\cdot508}{s^3 + 2\cdot949\,s^2 + 3\cdot085\,s + 0\cdot664}. \qquad (3.18)$$

We can now obtain the first refractive index by setting $s = \pm1$. This gives $n_1 = Y(1) = 1\cdot13$. We then construct a new admittance function

$$Y_2(s) = n_1 \frac{n_1 s - Y_1(s)}{s\,Y_1(s) - n_1}. \qquad (3.19)$$

$Y_1(s)$ is one degree less than $Y(s)$ in both numerator and denominator since both are divisible by $(s^2 - 1)$. This enables us to obtain the refractive index of the second layer as $n_2 = 1\cdot50$. The admittance of the final layer is

$$Y_3(s) = n_2 \frac{n_2 s - Y_2(s)}{s\,Y_2(s) - n_2}, \qquad (3.20)$$

giving $n_3 = 2\cdot20$. As a check on the working we see the film terminates with

$$Y_4(s) = n_3 \frac{n_3 s - Y_3(s)}{s\,Y_3(s) - n_3}, \qquad (3.21)$$

from which we obtain $n_4 = 2\cdot27$, the refractive index of the substrate. The physical thicknesses of the layers are of equal optical thickness; their physical thicknesses are 117·9 nm, 88·8 nm and 65·9 nm respectively.

Unfortunately, many of the results obtained from this method and from Knittl's technique are not realisable in practice because of the unavailability of materials with the appropriate refractive indices. However, Epstein (1952) has shown how the concept of equivalent index may be used to transform designs such as these into a more practical configuration.

3.3 Seeley's synthesis of interference filters

While Young was developing the technique described above in the USA, in England, Seeley was applying electrical filter methods to the problem of designing interference filters (1961) which contain from one to four half-wave layers. The method is similar to that used for the synthesis of an equivalent low-pass filter consisting of a 'ladder network' which had been extended to distributed circuit filters. This latter application has the disadvantage that the transmission properties of the network elements are frequency dependent and the method is not very successful for filters whose bandwidth is greater than 10%; however, it can be useful for the design of multilayer interference filters.

The type of structure considered is shown in figure 3.3. It consists of k half-wave layers of the same material surrounded by highly reflecting stacks.

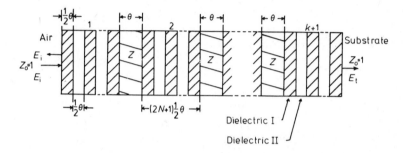

Figure 3.3 Arrangement of dielectric layers in a generalised filter (after Seeley 1961).

For a stack of $2N + 1$ layers, the matrix product of the layers at the central frequency of the pass band is

$$M = \begin{bmatrix} 0 & \dfrac{i}{n_H}\left(\dfrac{n_H}{n_L}\right)N \\ in_H\left(\dfrac{n_L}{n_H}\right)N & 0 \end{bmatrix}. \tag{3.22}$$

Thus as a first approximation, we may represent these stacks by a matrix of form

$$\begin{bmatrix} 0 & i/r \\ ir & 0 \end{bmatrix} \tag{3.23}$$

at all frequencies in the pass band. The characteristic matrix for a half-wave of refractive index n_C is

$$M = \begin{bmatrix} \cos\theta & \dfrac{i}{n_C}\sin\theta \\ in_C\sin\theta & \cos\theta \end{bmatrix}, \tag{3.24}$$

so if we consider only bandwidths of $0.1\omega_C$, we may approximate $\cos\theta$ by -1 and $\sin\theta$ in the M_{21} term by 0 (this will cause an error of less than 1% in the bandwidth of a Fabry–Perot filter, provided r is greater than 2.5), thus obtaining a fairly simple model for the synthesis, namely

$$\mathbf{M} = \begin{bmatrix} M_{11} & iM_{12} \\ iM_{21} & M_{22} \end{bmatrix} = \begin{bmatrix} 0 & \dfrac{i}{r_1} \\ ir_1 & 0 \end{bmatrix} \begin{bmatrix} -1 & \dfrac{i}{n_C}\sin\theta \\ 0 & -1 \end{bmatrix} \begin{bmatrix} 0 & \dfrac{i}{r_2} \\ ir_2 & 0 \end{bmatrix}$$

$$\cdots \begin{bmatrix} -1 & \dfrac{i\sin\theta}{n_C} \\ 0 & -1 \end{bmatrix} \begin{bmatrix} 0 & \dfrac{i}{r_{n+1}} \\ ir_{n+1} & 0 \end{bmatrix}.$$

$$(3.25)$$

For a symmetric filter, $r_{n+1} = r_1$, $r_n = r_2$, etc so this provides further simplification of the functions involved.

Let us now consider the appropriate prototype transmission function. As we have seen, the two most commonly used for electrical filter design are the Tschebysheff function

$$\mathcal{T} = \frac{1}{1 + h^2(\mathrm{T}_k(\bar{\omega}))^2}, \qquad (3.26a)$$

giving

$$\frac{1}{\mathcal{T}} - 1 = h^2(\mathrm{T}_k(\bar{\omega}))^2, \qquad (3.26b)$$

and the maximally flat Butterworth function

$$\mathcal{T} = \frac{1}{1 + [(\bar{\omega}')^k]^2}, \qquad (3.27a)$$

or

$$\frac{1}{\mathcal{T}} - 1 = (\bar{\omega}')^{2k}. \qquad (3.27b)$$

In both cases, $-1 \leqslant \bar{\omega} \leqslant +1$ in the pass band ($\bar{\omega}$ is a normalised frequency variable). If all refractive indices in the multilayer filter are normalised with respect to those of the external media (which are assumed to be equal to preserve symmetry — if this is not the case an antireflection layer may be added to the design) we obtain from (3.25)

$$\frac{1}{\mathcal{T}} - 1 = \frac{1}{4}(M_{12} - M_{21})^2. \qquad (3.28)$$

The right hand side of equation (3.28) is a polynomial in $\sin\theta$ whose coefficients depend on the values of the r_i. Since we are assuming also that the relative bandwidths of the filters are fairly small

$$\sin\theta \simeq \pi\frac{(\omega_C - \omega)}{\omega_C}, \qquad (3.29)$$

where ω_C is the central frequency in the pass band. Before we can equate (3.28) with either (3.26b) or (3.27b), the frequency in the multilayer description must also be normalised:

$$\sin\theta \simeq t\bar\omega \quad \text{or} \quad t'\bar\omega'. \tag{3.30}$$

The scale factor t or t' is chosen so that

$$t = -\pi\frac{(\omega_C - \omega_1)}{\omega}, \qquad \text{for the equi-ripple function,}$$

$$\tag{3.31}$$

$$t' = -\pi\frac{(\omega_C - \omega_1)}{h^{1/n}\,\omega_C}, \qquad \text{for the maximally flat function,}$$

since $\mathcal{T}$ must equal $1/(1 + h^2)$ at the band edge (ω_1).

The synthesis is completed by equating coefficients of appropriate powers of $\bar\omega$ in the multilayer and prototype representations. In general, the Tschebysheff prototype is preferred since its rate of cut-off at the band edge is greater; however, one then has to assume that the transmittance may fall to $1/(1 + h^2)$ in the pass band.

Seeley applied this method to the design of double, triple and quadruple half-wave filters; the results are shown in figure 3.4. The multilayer transmittance characteristics are very close to the prototype functions for the most part; the reduction in specified pass band width is caused by the neglect of the frequency variation in phase shift in the reflecting multilayers. However, the major disadvantage of the method from the point of view of multilayer design is that the values of r obtained must be realisable, and only a limited number of values correspond to practical material combinations.

3.4 The multilayer circuit analogy method

The methods described in the previous sections have been special purpose techniques applied to the design of antireflection coatings and narrow band interference filters respectively. Another type of filter is very important both in multilayer application and in the electrical filter counterpart — this is the edge filter, which may have either a low-(frequency) pass, a high-pass or a band-pass performance. Once again on consideration of the most suitable prototype for this kind of filter, we turn to the Tschebysheff equi-ripple polynomial function; however, we need to find a means of carrying over the analytic form of the function from the circuit to the multilayer. Seeley (1961, 1965) and Smith and Seeley (1968) have provided a method which enables us to do this by establishing a correspondence between the two structures in such a way that each inductance or capacitance in the circuit corresponds to a layer in the multilayer, the circuit termination corresponds

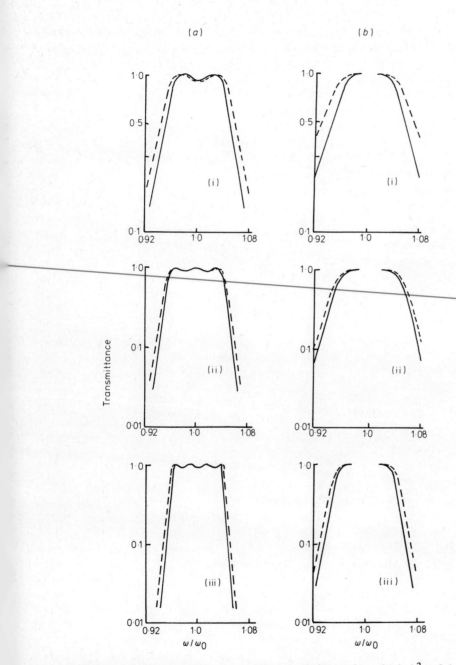

Figure 3.4 Transmission characteristics of filters for which $h^2 = 0 \cdot 1$ and $t = -0 \cdot 04$. (i) 2 cavities, (ii) 3 cavities, (iii) 4 cavities. Broken curve, prototype functions; full curve, exact transmission of filters. (*a*) Equal-ripple transmission, (*b*) maximally flat transmission (after Seeley 1961).

to the substrate and the circuit source corresponds to the medium of incidence of the multilayer. However, because of the frequency dependence of the multilayer, this correspondence is only exact at one frequency; all other frequencies are then normalised with respect to this design frequency. The choice of design frequency is very important; in a low- or high-pass filter it seems most reasonable intuitively to choose the value at the edge of the stop band. It is also convenient to normalise admittances (i.e. refractive indices) with respect to those of the surrounding media (assumed equal, as before). Let us now consider the correspondence between the multilayer and circuit elements: the characteristic matrices of three layers p, q, r within the multilayer sequence are

$$\mathbf{M}_\mathrm{I} = \ldots \begin{bmatrix} \cos\theta_p & \dfrac{in_\mathrm{sub}}{n_p}\sin\theta_p \\ \dfrac{in_p}{n_\mathrm{sub}}\sin\theta_p & \cos\theta_p \end{bmatrix} \begin{bmatrix} \cos\theta_q & \dfrac{in_\mathrm{sub}}{n_q}\sin\theta_q \\ \dfrac{in_q}{n_\mathrm{sub}}\sin\theta_q & \cos\theta_q \end{bmatrix}$$

$$\times \begin{bmatrix} \cos\theta_r & \dfrac{in_\mathrm{sub}}{n_r}\sin\theta_r \\ \dfrac{in_r}{n_\mathrm{sub}}\sin\theta_r & \cos\theta_r \end{bmatrix} \ldots \qquad (3.32)$$

where n_p, θ_p are refractive index and phase thickness of the pth layer at the edge of the pass band, etc; for the circuit, the sequence takes the form

$$\mathbf{M}_\mathrm{II} = \ldots \begin{bmatrix} 1 & 0 \\ ig_p & 1 \end{bmatrix} \begin{bmatrix} 1 & ig_q \\ 0 & 1 \end{bmatrix} \begin{bmatrix} 1 & 0 \\ ig_r & 1 \end{bmatrix} \ldots \qquad (3.33)$$

Thus the matrices in (3.32) have to be manipulated to take the form (3.33). This manipulation is shown physically in figure 3.5. Further details of the process are given by Smith and Seeley (1968) and by Seeley *et al* (1973). In order to achieve the final correspondence, scaling factors N_{qp} and N_{qr} are introduced which are the mathematical counterpart of the scaling property of an electric circuit transformer. They are defined as follows:

$$N_{qp} = N_{qr},$$

$$N_{pq}N_{qp} = 1 - \frac{n_q}{n_p}\tan\frac{\theta_p}{2}\tan\frac{\theta_q}{2}, \qquad (3.34)$$

$$N_{qr}N_{rq} = 1 - \frac{n_q}{n_r}\tan\frac{\theta_q}{2}\tan\frac{\theta_r}{2}.$$

On completion of the process, we are able to express the circuit admittances, g_i, in terms of the multilayer parameters; for example, if the qth layer is of

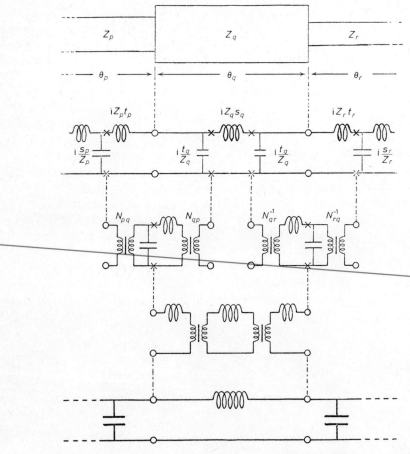

Figure 3.5 Manipulation of electric circuit elements, $s = \sin\theta$, $t = \tan\theta/2$ (after Seeley *et al* 1973).

low index (with respect to that of the surrounding media)

$$g_q = N_{qp}N_{qr}\frac{n_{\text{sub}}}{n_q}\sin\theta_q + \frac{N_{qp}}{N_{rq}}\frac{n_{\text{sub}}}{n_p}\tan\frac{\theta_p}{2} + \frac{N_{qr}}{N_{pq}}\frac{n_{\text{sub}}}{n_r}\tan\frac{\theta_r}{2}. \quad (3.35)$$

A similar result is obtainable for *high*-index layers. For any standard prototype function, expressions for the circuit elements g_q, needed to realise the desired response, are available from a standard reference text (Saad 1968); for example, for the Tschebysheff prototype of order m, with ripple of height h

$$g_k g_{k+1} = \frac{4\sin\dfrac{(2k-1)\pi}{2m}\sin\dfrac{(2k+1)\pi}{2m}}{\gamma^2 + \sin^2\dfrac{k\pi}{m}}, \quad (3.36)$$

and

$$g_1 = \frac{2 \sin \dfrac{\pi}{2m}}{\gamma},$$

where

$$\gamma = \sinh \left(\frac{1}{m} \sinh^{-1} \frac{1}{h} \right).$$

We see from (3.36) that $g_k = g_{m-k+1}$, so the filter is symmetric.

Expression (3.35) is general; no constraints have been placed on the number of different materials used. However, it would be useful to be able to represent the usual situation in multilayer practice of having two fixed indices for the layers and then to solve (3.35) to obtain the multilayer phase thicknesses θ_i. An alternative approach might be to impose an equal thickness constraint and extract values of n_i for each layer; however, we have noted earlier in the chapter that this tends to produce values of index for which no materials are available, so we shall concentrate on the former procedure. Equation (3.35) is rather complicated to solve as it stands, but if we make the approximations

$$N_{pq} = N_{qr} \simeq \left(1 - \frac{n_L}{n_H} \tan^2 \theta_q/2 \right)^{1/2},$$

$$\tan \theta_p/2 + \tan \theta_q/2 \simeq 2 \tan \theta_q/2, \tag{3.37}$$

then (3.35) becomes

$$g_q = (n_{sub}/n_L + n_{sub}/n_H) \sin \theta_q, \tag{3.38a}$$

while for a high-index layer

$$g_p = (n_H/n_{sub} + n_L/n_{sub}) \sin \theta_p. \tag{3.38b}$$

For a first or la layer

$$g_1 = (n_{sub}/n_L + n_{sub}/2n_H) \sin \theta_1, \qquad \text{if low-index,}$$

$$g_1 = (n_H/n_{sub} + n_L/2n_{sub}) \sin \theta_1, \qquad \text{if high-index.} \tag{3.38c}$$

It should be noted that in the derivation of formula (3.35), certain terms in $\tan \theta$ in the expansion of the layer matrices of the first and last layers cannot be incorporated into the LC network analogy and are ignored, resulting in larger errors of approximation in these layer thicknesses than in the internal layers. This error may be corrected by Chen's iteration process which will be described in the next section.

We may illustrate the method by working through the equations for the design of an 11-layer filter using a combination of materials commonly used in the visible region, namely zinc sulphide ($n_H = 2 \cdot 30$) and magnesium fluoride ($n_L = 1 \cdot 38$) on a crown glass substrate ($n_{sub} = 1 \cdot 52$). This will give us rejection $> 2 \times 10^2$ since $(2 \cdot 30/1 \cdot 38)^{11} \simeq 275$, and a pass band ripple of about 2.5% ($\mathcal{T}_{min} = (1 + h^2)^{-1}$) since

$$h = \frac{n_H/n_{sub} - n_{sub}/n_L}{n_H/n_{sub} + n_{sub}/n_L} = \frac{1 \cdot 513 - 1 \cdot 101}{1 \cdot 513 + 1 \cdot 101} = 0 \cdot 158.$$

The rule for choosing the index of the first layer can also be adapted from transmission line filter theory, namely, the substrate having the greatest imittance (relative to the substrate) should be used for odd numbered layers. For the filter we are considering, $n_{sub}/n_L = 1 \cdot 101$ and $n_H/n_{sub} = 1 \cdot 513$, so we commence with a high-index layer. The parameter γ, to be used in obtaining the g_i values is given by

$$\gamma = \sinh\left(\frac{1}{m} \sinh^{-1} \frac{1}{h}\right) = \sinh\left(\frac{1}{11} \sinh^{-1} \frac{1}{0 \cdot 158}\right) = 0 \cdot 2333.$$

The other factors required are summarised in table 3.1. Substituting these values in equation (3.36) we obtain

$$g_1 = \frac{2 \times 0 \cdot 1424}{0 \cdot 2333} = 1 \cdot 221,$$

$$g_1 g_2 = \frac{4 \times 0 \cdot 4154 \times 0 \cdot 1424}{0 \cdot 0544 \times 0 \cdot 0794} = 1 \cdot 768, \qquad g_2 = 1 \cdot 449,$$

etc.

Table 3.1 Values required for calculation of the g_i factors in the design of an 11-layer band pass filter for use in the visible region.

k	1	2	3	4	5
$\sin \dfrac{(2k-1)\pi}{22}$	0·1424	0·4154	0·6549	0·8412	0·9595
$\sin k\pi/11$	0·2817	0·5406	0·7557	0·9096	0·9898
$\sin^2 k\pi/11$	0·0794	0·2923	0·5712	0·8274	0·9797

The remaining calculations, based on equations (3.38) are summarised in table 3.2. The performance of the low-pass filter thus designed is illustrated in figure 3.6; results of the refinement of the design using the least squares method (see next chapter) are also shown. It can be seen that the design is not altered much by the refinement process, indicating that the circuit

Table 3.2 Extraction of parameters for the 11-layer low-pass filter.

Layer	Index	g parameter	$\left(\dfrac{n_{sub}}{n_L}+\dfrac{n_{sub}}{n_H}\right)$	$\left(\dfrac{n_H}{n_{sub}}+\dfrac{n_L}{n_{sub}}\right)$	$\sin\theta$	θ (deg)	Fractional thickness
Substrate	1·52						
1	2·30	1·221		1·967	0·620	38·3	0·55
2	1·38	1·449	1·762		0·822	55·3	0·80
3	2·30	2·165		2·421	0·894	63·4	0·92
4	1·38	1·627	1·762		0·922	67·4	0·97
5	2·30	2·250		2·421	0·930	68·4	0·99
6	1·38	1·649	1·762		0·935	69·3	1·0
7	2·30	2·250		2·421	0·930	68·4	0·99
8	1·38	1·627	1·762		0·922	67·4	0·97
9	2·30	2·165		2·421	0·894	63·4	0·92
10	1·38	1·449	1·762		0·822	55·3	0·80
11	2·30	1·221		1 967	0·620	38·3	0·55
Substrate	1·52						

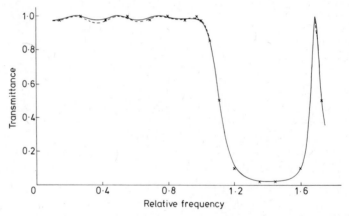

Figure 3.6 Refinement of the circuit analogy design with respect to a Tschebysheff specification for an 11-layer filter for use in the visible region. Full curve, design based on Seeley's method; broken curve, refined design — square wave specification; ×, design points for refinement (after Seeley *et al* 1973).

analogy result is close to being an 'optimal' design for a low-pass filter. Seeley and Smith (1966) give examples of 14-layer low- and high-pass filters using infrared materials — for the case of filters with an even number of layers, one must have

$$n_H > n'_{sub} > n_L,$$

where

$$n'_{sub} = n_{sub}\,\frac{g_{last}}{g_{first}},$$

(3.39)

and in this case the symmetry of the final design thicknesses is lost, although the overall variation is fairly symmetrical. The thicknesses for the high-pass multilayer are obtained by subtracting the θ_i for the low-pass filter from 180°; the design parameters for both filters are given in table 3.3 and the resulting transmittances are shown in figure 3.7.

Table 3.3 Equal-ripple parameters.

Layer	Index	g para-meter	$(n_{sub}/n_L + n_{sub}/n_H)$ etc	$\sin \theta$	Low-pass θ (deg)	Low-pass fraction	High-pass θ (deg)	High-pass fraction
Sub	4·0							
1	Low, 2·2	1·27	2·21	0·575	35·1	0·545	144·9	1·25
2	High, 5·1	1·44	1·82	0·793	52·5	0·815	127·5	1·10
3	Low, 2·2	2·22	2·61	0·851	58·3	0·905	121·7	1·05
4	High, 5·1	1·60	1·82	0·880	61·6	0·955	118·4	1·025
5	Low, 2·2	2·33	2·61	0·894	63·4	0·985	116·6	1·01
6	High, 5·1	1·625	1·82	0·896	63·6	0·985	116·4	1·01
7	Low, 2·2	2·34	2·61	0·897	63·8	0·99	116·2	1·005
8	High, 5·1	1·64	1·82	0·902	64·4	1·0	115·6	1·0
9	Low, 2·2	2·34	2·61	0·897	63·8	0·99	116·2	1·005
10	High, 5·1	1·62	1·82	0·892	63·1	0·98	116·9	1·01
11	Low, 2·2	2·30	2·61	0·882	61·9	0·96	118·1	1·025
12	High, 5·1	1·56	1·82	0·858	59·1	0·92	120·9	1·045
13	Low, 2·2	2·055	2·61	0·788	52·0	0·805	128	1·10
14	High, 5·1	0·892	1·55	0·576	35·0	0·545	145	1·255
Anti-reflect	Low, 2·2					2·0		0·5

3.5 Chen's iteration for the circuit analogy method

Two major approximations occur in the circuit analogy design process described above; first, the correspondence is only exact at the edge frequency, and the transmittance might well be expected to depart from that of the prototype at points away from this frequency. This is seen to be the case, particularly for the high-pass design, although it is still recognisable as 'equi-ripple'. The second point concerns the degree of approximation involved in expressions (3.37) and (3.38c); on substituting the values of θ_i obtained from (3.38) for the 17-layer filter described by Chen (1970) into the more accurate formulae (3.35), an immediate error is seen for all but the central layer. The values of the right hand side of equations (3.35) are shown in table 3.4 under the heading f_n. In nearly all cases f_n is less than g_n. Chen has shown that a solution to (3.35) may be obtained from the circuit analogy values by applying a linear iteration process to the equations ; the final values are shown in the table as θ_i'. The differences between θ_i and θ_i' are small for layers in the centre

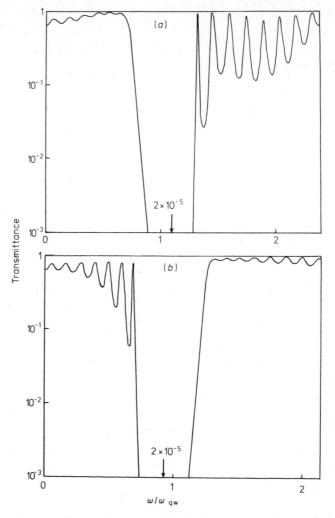

Figure 3.7 Computed 14-layer Tschebysheff filters for use in the infrared. (*a*) Low-pass, (*b*) high-pass (after Seeley *et al* 1973).

but increase towards the outer layers of the filter; thus it appears that the approximation $\theta_p \simeq \theta_q \simeq \theta_r$ is partly to blame for the discrepancy. Also, we have noted above that the equations (3.38*c*) involved a major approximation, and because of this, the numerical values of f_1 are deliberately excluded from the table. We may write

$$g_1 = f_1(\theta_1, \theta_2),$$
$$g_2 = f_2(\theta_1, \theta_2, \theta_3),$$
$$\cdots\cdots\cdots\cdots\cdots$$
$$g_9 = f_9(\theta_8, \theta_9, \theta_{10}),$$

(3.40)

Table 3.4 Results of Chen's iteration for a 17-layer low-pass filter.

n	g_n	f_n'	f_n	θ_n	θ_n'
1	1·223			$38°27'$	$43°52'$
2	1·457	1·403	1·457	$55°46'$	$59°30'$
3	2·184	2·137	2·186	$64°26'$	$66°0'$
4	1·640	1·621	1·641	$68°31'$	$70°0'$
5	2·281	2·273	2·282	$70°25'$	$71°18'$
6	1·674	1·662	1·668	$71°43'$	$72°0'$
7	2:299	2·303	2·300	$71°47'$	$72°12'$
8	1·683	1·677	1·679	$72°11'$	$72°20'$
9	2·305	2·296	2·305	$72°41'$	$72°30'$

remembering that $\theta_8 = \theta_{10}$ etc. The accurate value of θ_1 can be found as the solution of the system formed by omitting the first of these equations and making the more reasonable assumption that $\theta_8 \simeq \theta_9$. This is necessary because we have now only eight equations for the thicknesses, so we cannot have more than eight design variables! This is the basis of Chen's method. The values of the right hand sides of equations (3.35) obtained with these corrected values θ are also shown in table 3.4 under the heading f_n' and comparison of these values with the corresponding g_n values indicates that this simple correction procedure is very successful. These more accurate design parameters give a multilayer performance which is an improvement on the circuit analogy design in all respects. However, the design is unlikely to be optimal even then, because of the lack of correspondence with the prototype at all frequencies but the edge; Chen therefore proposed an alternative method of design for the problem – the turning value method; this is basically a merit function technique so we shall postpone consideration of the method until the next chapter as it would be more appropriate to consider it in comparison with other techniques of that nature.

4 The Use of Merit Function Techniques in Multilayer Design

The problem of designing a multilayer filter with specified reflectance or transmittance properties is very complex and there is no simple method of solution for all problems, although we have seen that for certain standard prototype responses, methods similar to those used in electrical filter synthesis may be employed. The digital computer offers considerable scope for automatic design methods; the response of the filter is specified for the appropriate spectral range and the design parameters are varied in order to achieve an approximation to the specification to within some prescribed tolerance criteria.

We may characterise the fit between the specified response and that corresponding to a particular multilayer configuration by a suitably chosen 'merit function'. The objective is then to minimise the merit function with respect to the design variables. If one were to obtain a perfect fit to the desideratum, this minimum value would be zero; normally this does not happen and one hopes that the minimum obtained for a particular problem is low enough to meet the allowed tolerance requirements of the specification. Since the merit function is generally a non-linear function of the design parameters, one of a number of standard optimisation techniques may be used for the minimisation. Unfortunately, most of the more efficient techniques only produce a global optimum for convex functions, whereas the merit functions associated with this type of work are almost certainly not convex; however, it is not necessary always to find the global (or lowest) minimum in design work – any optimum which satisfies the tolerance requirements is suitable. One also has to consider practical considerations of a design, such as ease of manufacture and susceptibility to error; sometimes a subsidiary minimum gives a design which is better in realisation than a theoretically better optimum. Some examples of beam splitter designs discussed later in the chapter may help to emphasise this point.

Another problem is that the most powerful optimisation techniques were developed on the assumption that the function to be optimised is fairly well approximated by a quadratic function in the region of the minimum; the multilayer response is not quadratic – such information as we have for particular types of structure indicates that an m-layer filter has a behaviour similar to an mth order Tschebysheff function. In the experience of the author, the most useful optimisation methods for optical design applications are those which do not require evaluation of derivatives; it is fortunate that most merit functions may be formulated as a sum of squared terms and there are particularly efficient methods available for dealing with this type of problem. (For a more detailed discussion of the types of optimisation method available, the reader is referred to appendix 1.)

Multilayer filters have two characteristics which can be considered as 'design parameters', namely, refractive indices and thicknesses of the layers. In the previous chapter, a reference to the lack of availability of suitable materials for multilayer use was made; from the practical point of view, it might therefore be better to use fixed values of refractive index and to treat thicknesses only as design variables. However, the development of co-evaporation techniques (Jacobsson and Martensson 1966, Fujiwara 1963a,b) for producing films of any intermediate index between the two index values of the materials used in the sources opens up the possibility of using indices as design variables in addition to the thicknesses. Most of the techniques we shall consider in this chapter do not at present take advantage of this new development, but could easily be adapted to accommodate refractive indices in place of, or in addition to, layer thicknesses.

The merit function techniques fall into two categories—those for refining an existing design, and automatic design methods for which no approximate design need be known. Generally, the second class of method can also be used for refinement, so it is a very valuable tool for the multilayer filter designer.

4.1   Baumeister's successive approximations method

The method of successive approximations, developed by Baumeister (1958), is basically a 'relaxation' design procedure rather than a merit function technique, but is included here because of its similarity with the latter. Small changes are made in the design variables in order to produce a better approximation to the desired result than that given by the initial design. The process is iteratively applied until a result is obtained which gives the required overall improvement in performance. Usually the specification is for reflectance or transmittance of the filter, but other optical properties, such as phase change on reflection or transmission or first derivatives of any of these properties with respect to either wavenumber or angle of incidence, may be used instead.

The change in reflectance $\Delta \mathcal{R}_j$ or transmittance $\Delta \mathcal{T}_j$ of an N-layer filter at some wavenumber σ_j caused by alterations Δd_i in the layer thicknesses is given by

$$\Delta \mathcal{R}_j = -\Delta \mathcal{T}_j = \sum_{i=1}^{N} \frac{\partial \mathcal{R}_j}{\partial d_i} \Delta d_i + \mathrm{O}(\Delta d_i)^2, \tag{4.1}$$

assuming that the values of refractive index remain constant. Thus, if we have a multilayer filter which differs from the required specification at a finite number of points (m), we may estimate the difference in reflectance

76

at these m points and solve the system of equations given by (4.1) for $j = 1, \ldots , m$. If m is less than N the system is underdetermined, so we also specify that $\Sigma_{i=1}^{N}(\Delta d_i)^2$ be a minimum — i.e. the change in thickness of each layer should be minimal. The calculation may be performed either by using a finite difference calculation or by an exact method, since $\partial \mathscr{R}/\partial d_i$ may be calculated relatively easily (see chapter 6). The latter procedure is preferable since numerical differentiation is a technique which is prone to error. Since the second order terms in (4.1) are neglected, the changes $\Delta \mathscr{R}_j$ should be small, so the process is repeated iteratively until the fit to the specification is satisfactory. Figure 4.1 shows the computed reflectance

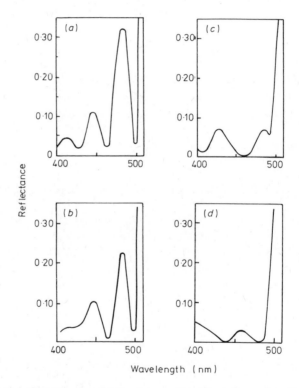

Figure 4.1 Computed reflectance as a function of wavelength of four stages of a high-pass filter design. (a) Stage 1; (b) stage 3; (c) stage 6; and (d) stage 9, the final design (after Baumeister 1958).

of the successive stages in a high-pass filter design — the thicknesses of the designs are given in table 4.1. An example of a broad band reflector design obtained by Baumeister and Stone (1956) using this refinement process is shown in figure 4.2 (bandwidth characteristics were included in table 2.2); this example provides a useful comparison with other methods.

Table 4.1 Optical thickness and index of refraction of each of the films of the multilayers whose reflectance curves are shown in figure 4.1.

Layer	Index of refraction	Wavelength in millimicrons at which the optical thickness of the layer is a quarter wavelength			
		Stage 1	Stage 3	Stage 6	Stage 9
substrate	1·52	massive	massive	massive	massive
1	1·38	599	602	606	616
2	2·30	599	609	628	672
3	1·38	599	610	626	646
4	2·30	599	607	610	601
5	1·38	599	601	594	585
6	2·30	599	595	585	590
7	1·38	599	590	583	596
8	2·30	599	589	588	589
9	1·38	599	595	599	577
10	2·30	599	602	605	573
11	1·38	599	606	602	582
12	2·30	599	603	594	597
13	1·38	599	598	594	606
14	2·30	599	600	610	610
15	1·38	599	603	637	620
16	2·30	599	612	647	639
17	1·38	300	302	303	306
air	1·00	massive	massive	massive	massive

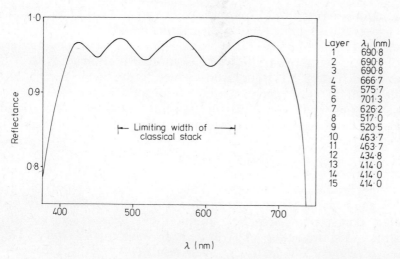

Layer	λ_i (nm)
1	690·8
2	690·8
3	690·8
4	666·7
5	575·7
6	701·3
7	626·2
8	517·0
9	520·5
10	463·7
11	463·7
12	434·8
13	414·0
14	414·0
15	414·0

Figure 4.2 High-reflectance coating of Baumeister and Stone.

4.2 Automatic design methods

Baumeister's method of design has one serious limitation; the designer must start with a multilayer configuration whose response is a reasonable approximation to the specification. However, there are certain design problems where it is difficult to provide this approximate design. A good automatic design technique should be able to reach an appropriate minimum of the merit function from any starting point in the parameter space of the design variables. This condition is hard to fulfill; it can be done by means of an 'exhaustive search' technique – the parameter space may be divided into a mesh of points; each of N design variables is then evaluated at p different values, so p^N evaluations of the merit function are needed to cover each node of the mesh in order that the lowest value be selected as the optimum. Clearly, unless both p and N are small, the computer time required for such a process is formidable. One version of the 'Least Squares' method (Heavens and Liddell 1968), described in detail in the next section, uses a restricted form of this process for an initial search only, but even here it has not been applied for filters with more than six layers.

A variation of the exhaustive search idea was applied by Elsner (1964); in order to limit the number of function evaluations, he reduced the number of design variables by keeping fixed the values of refractive indices and some layer thicknesses. The remaining thicknesses were allowed to take the values $m\lambda_0/4$, where $m = 1, 2, \ldots, 6$. Then every time the transmittance of the multilayer obeyed the relation

$$F_1(\lambda) \leqslant \mathcal{T}(\lambda) \leqslant F_2(\lambda), \qquad \lambda_0 \leqslant \lambda \leqslant \lambda_1, \qquad (4.2)$$

the functions $F_1(\lambda)$ and $F_2(\lambda)$ were adjusted to provide stiffer criteria. Elsner's results for an 11-layer high-reflection coating are shown in figure 4.3. The computation took 3½ hours on the Moscow State University computer.

Shatilov and Tyutikova (1963) developed an evolutionary type of design method; at each stage a further layer is added to the design and its thickness adjusted until the best approximation to the specification is obtained; this is basically a univariate search method with one linear search for each design variable. The merit function they used was

$$\Delta m^2 = \int (\mathcal{R}_0(\lambda) - \mathcal{R}_m(\lambda, d_1, \ldots, d_N))^2 \, d\lambda, \qquad (4.3)$$

where the integral is evaluated using Simpson's rule. They report that systems of up to eight layers were designed this way without the aid of a digital computer! One cannot help but admire their obvious agility with hand calculators – the evaluation of $\mathcal{R}$ at a single wavelength involves the multiplication of eight 2×2 matrices. Their result for an 8-layer low-reflection coating is shown by the full curve in figure 4.4 – the broken curve shows

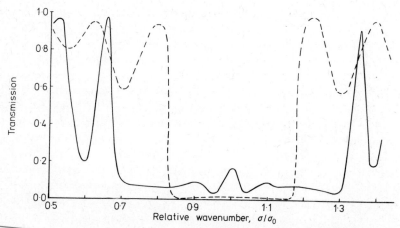

Figure 4.3 Elsner's broad band reflector. Broken curve, classical stack; full curve, Elsner's filter, $n_H = 2.50$, $n_L = 1.38$.

the result obtained by Dobrowolski (1965). There are, however, some problems where the method breaks down, notably in the design of a thin-film system having the reflectance characteristics of a multilayer stack. One obvious source of error is the assumption that the design variables are completely uncorrelated.

Ermolaev *et al* (1962) used both refractive indices and thicknesses as design variables, defining their merit function as

$$F_m(x) = \int_{\lambda_1}^{\lambda_2} \rho(\lambda) \, |\mathscr{R}(x,\lambda) - \mathscr{R}_0(\lambda)|^k \, d\lambda, \qquad k > 0, \qquad (4.4)$$

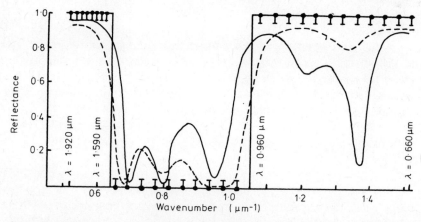

Figure 4.4 Shatilov and Tyutikova's problem: full curve, Shatilov and Tyutikova's design; broken curve, Dobrowolski's 11-layer filter design (after Dobrowolski 1965).

where **X** is the vector of design variables, ρ is a wavelength dependent weighting function and R_0 is the specified curve. To optimise F they used a steepest descent technique which included a parabolic interpolation for the minimum along each direction of search. They also attempted to solve the problem of finding the global optimum by proceeding as follows: after each minimum was found, a series of merit functions were calculated which differed from the original function by one parameter; if any of these calculations produced a value of F which was smaller than the minimum value, the minimisation procedure would be restarted from this new point. Unfortunately, this process will not work indefinitely, and it does tend to produce a large number of merit function evaluations. They applied their method to the design of low- and high-pass filters, similar to the example given by Baumeister (1958) (figure 4.1), with a fair amount of success. However, no allowance for absorption and dispersion was made and some of the index values required were rather unrealistic.

4.3 The least squares method of Heavens and Liddell

One disadvantage of the methods described in the previous section is that the methods used to optimise the merit functions are inefficient. One important criterion for the designer is economy of computer time in producing his results, particularly for specialised 'one-off' designs. There are many very efficient optimisation techniques described in the literature which are already coded in the form of library subroutines (and usually available on request), so it seemed sensible to use such a routine to save both development and production time in the program (production time is saved both by the efficiency of the method, and by the efficient coding provided by expert programmers).

For systems of current practical importance incorporating up to fifteen or more layers, certain restrictions must be imposed on the range of design parameters to be used. The least squares method is generally applied with fixed values of refractive index and a prespecified total number of layers in the design. Quite often, to ease manufacture, two materials only are used.

The method derives its name from the form of merit function used, namely

$$F(\mathbf{x}) = \sum_{k=1}^{m} (\mathscr{R}_0(\lambda_k) - \mathscr{R}(\mathbf{x}, \lambda_k))^2, \tag{4.5}$$

where **x** is the vector of design variables, $\mathscr{R}_0$ is the specified reflectance at λ_k and $\mathscr{R}$ is the computed value of reflectance at λ_k for a particular value of **x**. Since $m \gg N$, this is essentially a curve fitting problem where the well known 'least squares' criterion is applied. The computer program based on the method contains three basic requirements: (1) a routine for computing the reflectance of a multilayer with specified layer thicknesses, entailing the evaluation of expressions of the form (1.16) and (1.17); (2) a means of comparing the resultant reflectance at any wavelength with the specified value – namely, the evaluation of $F(x)$; and (3) a systematic method for adjusting the design variables in order to produce a minimum of $F(x)$. The flow diagram of the method is shown in figure 4.5.

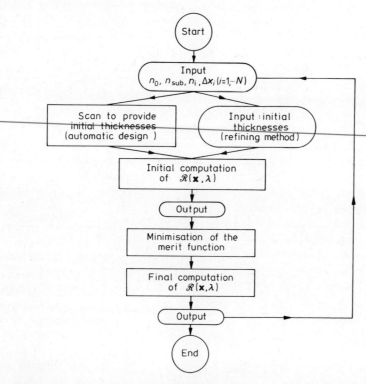

Figure 4.5 Flow diagram for the least squares method (after Heavens and Liddell 1968).

The least squares method may be used either to refine an initial design, or to generate a completely automatic design. In practice, an experienced designer will generally apply the former option since he will have an intuitive idea of the type of configuration required to meet a certain specification, but occasionally one may have to produce a completely new type of design; in this case the automatic design option is invaluable. The difference between the two programs is the initial scan to locate a suitable starting value which is incorporated in the automatic design program. This design or the initially provided design in the other version of the program, may then be refined by applying the method developed by Powell (1965). Powell's method is particularly efficient as it was designed for functions which are sums of squared terms; in each direction of search, a linear search based on Powell's quadratic interpolation method is performed. The method is guaranteed to converge for quadratic functions and most functions can be reasonably well approximated by a quadratic in the region of the minimum, and is easy to use since it does not require the derivatives of the merit function to be supplied. Unfortunately, the merit functions arising in multilayer design are not well approximated by a quadratic generally, so unless a reasonable approximation to the starting design is provided, the program is highly likely to converge to an unsatisfactory subsidiary minimum; thus for automatic design applications, it has been found necessary to incorporate a less efficient preliminary scan procedure to limit the area of search for the library subroutine.

Two forms of scan have been used; the exhaustive search technique described in the previous section may be used for filters with a few layers (this technique is described as 'complete scan' in the examples); for more complicated structures, a type of univariate search called the N^2 scan method was employed. This may be described as follows: we consider a system of N layers and vary the phase thickness of the first layer over some prescribed range, the thicknesses of the remaining layers being held constant, and select the value of x_1 which minimises $F(x)$; the procedure is repeated for the remaining $N-1$ layers yielding a first approximation to the design; the sequence is then repeated, starting the next iteration with the second, third, . . . , Nth layer and ending with the first, and so on; in the final iteration, the Nth layer is varied first, then the first, second, . . . and finally the $(N-1)$th. Thus, if q values of thickness are investigated for each layer (the nodes of the mesh), a total of $q \times N^2$ function evaluations will be needed in place of the q^N required for the complete scan process.

This method has been successfully applied to a large number of design problems during the past eight years. One of the earliest tests was the production of a filter whose reflectance characteristics were identical to those of a five-layer classical stack; this was the example that failed with Shatilov and Tyutikova's method. The least squares method gave the results shown in table 4.2 and figure 4.6. The complete scan thickness results are close to those of the stack, whereas in the shorter N^2 scan, the thicknesses depart significantly from the 'correct' values; however, the reflectance curves of both filters agree closely with the given specification. Another application of interest for purposes of comparison with other methods is the 13-layer broad band high-reflectance coating, based on the configuration suggested by Baumeister and Stone (1956). For 13 layers the complete scan is prohibitive, so the N^2 scan and a refinement of the design given by two mismatched classical stacks were applied, producing the results shown in figure 4.7 and table 4.3.

Two more recent applications of the method are also of interest; when

Table 4.2 5-layer classical stack.

Layer number	Index	Phase thickness			
		Complete scan		N^2 scan	
		Initial thicknesses	Final thicknesses	Initial thicknesses	Final thicknesses
1	2·36	80	89·21	120	101·92
2	1·39	110	90·61	60	81·20
3	2·36	80	91·07	90	89·86
4	1·39	80	87·49	120	100·15
5	2·36	110	92·58	30	66·34
Number of design wavenumbers		9		9	
Initial value F		$1·27 \times 10^{-2}$		$8·38 \times 10^{-2}$	
Final value F		$9·75 \times 10^{-6}$		$2·06 \times 10^{-3}$	

Thetford (1969) produced his method of design for three- and four-layer antireflection coatings, the least squares method was applied, using the multilayer configuration suggested by Thetford. The results produced by the N^2 scan and the complete scan methods were identical to the refinement of Thetford's original designs and are shown in figures 4.8 and 4.9. These figures also show the effects of dispersion of refractive index. The second application was concerned with the design of achromatic beam splitters, reported by Clapham (1971). The specification required approximately equal reflectance and transmittance throughout the visible spectrum, for a surface enclosed in a cemented cube for unpolarised light at 45° angle of

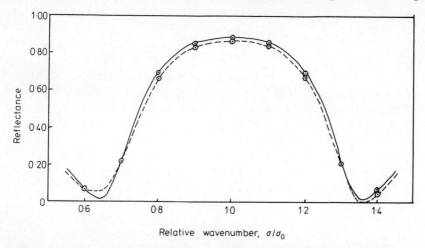

Figure 4.6 The 5-layer classical stack design obtained by the least squares method. Full curve, complete scan; broken curve, N^2 scan (after Heavens and Liddell 1968).

Table 4.3 Broad band reflecting multilayers.

Layer number	Index	Phase thickness			
		N^2 scan design		Refined design	
		Initial thickness	Final thickness	Initial thickness	Final thickness
1	2·36	80	91·50	75	60·29
2	1·39	160	156·81	75	76·70
3	2·36	100	94·74	75	75·39
4	1·39	120	121·60	75	77·82
5	2·36	80	83·86	75	74·59
6	1·39	160	162·62	75	65·34
7	2·36	100	89·21	75	72·95
8	1·39	80	82·45	90	100·15
9	2·36	80	80·38	110	102·38
10	1·39	80	80·50	110	110·62
11	2·36	80	83·62	110	116·46
12	1·39	80	76·77	110	99·96
13	2·36	100	95·91	110	117·85
14	1·39	60	67·47	110	107·32
15	2·36	80	72·60	110	109·28
Number of design wavenumbers		17		17	
Initial F		$8·91 \times 10^{-2}$		$1·68 \times 10^{-1}$	
Final F		$8·18 \times 10^{-2}$		$1·39 \times 10^{-1}$	
Atlas time		7 min		2 min	

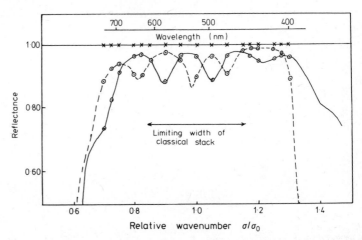

Figure 4.7 High-reflectance coating design obtained using the least squares method (after Heavens and Liddell 1968). Full curve, N^2 scan result; broken curve, refinement of an initial design provided by two mismatched stacks.

85

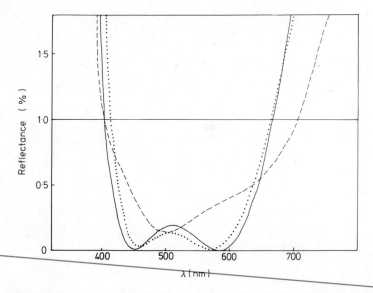

Figure 4.8 3-layer antireflection coating using indices suggested by Thetford (1969), showing effects of dispersion. Full curve, original design; dotted curve, effect of dispersion; broken curve, refined design to allow for dispersion.

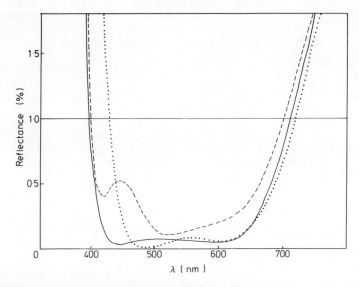

Figure 4.9 4-layer antireflection coating using indices suggested by Thetford (1969), showing effects of dispersion. Full curve, original design; dotted curve, effect of dispersion; broken curve, refined design to allow for dispersion.

incidence. An intuitive design was developed by Clapham and the least squares program used to refine this intuitive design and also to produce an automatic design, using the complete scan process; the latter application produced the result shown in figure 4.10, which also contains Clapham's intuitive design. The latter was not significantly improved by the refinement process, so the refined design is not included in the figure. Table 4.4 shows the characteristics of both designs.

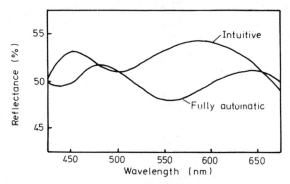

Figure 4.10 Theoretical performance of intuitive and automatic designs for an achromatic beam splitter (after Clapham 1971).

Table 4.4 (*a*) 'Intuitive' design of achromatic beam splitter for use with unpolarised light at 45° in cemented glass prisms of index 1.51.

Layer number	Material	Physical thickness (nm)	Phase thickness (deg), 45° incidence in glass	Phase thickness, (deg), normal incidence
1	MgF$_2$	136	90	142
2	ZnS	57	90	101
3	MgF$_2$	91	60	95
4	ZnS	76	120	135
5	MgF$_2$	136	90	142
6	ZnS	107	169	190

(*b*) Automatic design of achromatic beam splitter for use with unpolarised light at 45° in cemented glass prisms of index 1.51.

Layer number	Material	Physical thickness (nm)	Phase thickness (deg), 45° incidence in glass	Phase thickness, (deg), normal incidence
1	MgF$_2$	178	119	187
2	ZnS	98	160	179
3	MgF$_2$	117	79	124
4	ZnS	58	96	107
5	MgF$_2$	151	101	159
6	ZnS	136	223	250

If one is using a sophisticated automatic design technique, it is important that any data used in the program be as accurate as possible. In particular we know that refractive index is a dispersive quantity and it is essential to have accurate knowledge of its dispersion throughout the spectral range of the design. In the next chapter, various methods for obtaining this information will be discussed. Figures 4.8 and 4.9 illustrate the effects of dispersion in the design of antireflection coatings; it is clear from these that a design program which has 'built in' dispersion should be used in place of a 'fixed index' version, particularly if the design range extends towards the ultraviolet region of the spectrum.

Other options have also been added to the program during the past few years; these include: (1) the ability to 'fix' some design parameters (thicknesses) and thus reduce the number of variables for the optimisation; alternatively, some layers may be constrained to have equal optical thicknesses i.e. one can ensure the configuration is symmetric by keeping the $(N - k)$th and $(k + 1)$th layers equal ($k = 1, 2, \ldots, N/2$); (2) allowing the thicknesses to vary only between certain fixed values, so that the layers are neither too thin nor too thick to be manufactured conveniently. To ensure that the thicknesses x_i obey the relationship $A \leqslant x_i \leqslant B$, one may optimise with respect to y where

$$\left(\frac{x_i - A}{B - A}\right) = \sin^2(y_i); \tag{4.6}$$

(3) a weighting factor w_k may be attached to each term in the sum of squares on the right hand side of equation (4.5); and (4) a restart facility is provided by allowing several calls of the optimisation routine – this facility is very useful in practice for obtaining a suitable minimum with this particular method. A specification of the program is given in appendix 2, which includes estimates of the time required for various types of design.

4.4 Dobrowolski's method for completely automatic synthesis of thin-film systems

In 1966, Dobrowolski presented a method which overcame many of the disadvantages of successive elimination methods and the earlier automatic design methods of Elsner, Shatilov and Tyutikova, and Ermolaev *et al.* The method is automatic, so no starting design is required; it is an evolutionary method, so the multilayer configuration need not be specified in advance as is necessary for the least squares method. The difficulties of both the exhaustive search method on the one hand, and of Shatilov and Tyutikova's method on the other, are overcome by adding two or three layers at a time to the design and then performing an exhaustive search to find the best values of the parameters for these layers only; the refractive index and

88

thickness for each layer may assume *NI* and *NT* different values respectively; the former are equally spaced between the limits n_L and n_H and the latter are equally spaced between 0 and a predetermined value nd_H ($nd_H = \lambda/4$ or $\lambda/2$, for example). Thus if N_L layers are added, $2[NI(NT-1)+1/N_L$ merit function evaluations are required. For most design problems, $N_L = 2$ is sufficient, but Dobrowolski's program allows N_L to be $1, 2, 3$ or 4. After each addition of new layers, the whole multilayer configuration at that stage is adjusted by a refinement process, based on the successive iterations method of Baumeister. The flow diagram for the method is shown in figure 4.11.

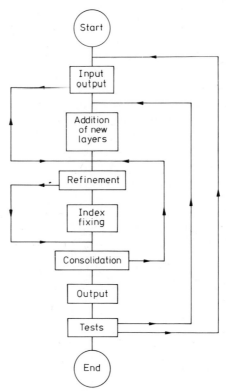

Figure 4.11 Flow diagram for Dobrowolski's method (after Dobrowolski 1965).

Another feature of the automatic synthesis method is the generality of the merit function, which has the form

$$ F = \left(\frac{1}{m} \sum_{j=1}^{m} \frac{|P_j^D - P_j|^K}{\text{Tol}_j} \right)^{1/k}, \tag{4.7} $$

where P_j^D, P_j and Tol_j are the desired value, the actual value and the tolerance of the desired property; the last is generally reflectance or transmittance, but could instead be phase change on reflection or transmission, or the rate of change of any of these quantities with respect to either wavelength or angle of incidence. K is an integer taking one of the values 1, 2, 4 or 16. The higher values of K are useful in particular problems where some properties are much further from the desired values than the others. The normalisation with respect to tolerance is convenient when the merit function is non-homogeneous. When all properties in the merit function are just within tolerance of the desired values, $F = 1$; thus, by setting $F = 0.5$ as the test for end of calculation, one may allow for the fact that some properties usually achieve a higher state of correction at the expense of the others. During refinement, the search for the minimum is based on a univariate search technique, using a quadratic interpolation method in each direction of search. Two other features in the program should also be mentioned: (1) if both thicknesses and refractive indices are taken as design variables, a refractive index list of available materials is read in at the outset; the index fixing routine is bypassed until the desired performance is almost obtained, and at that point the index values obtained in the design process are replaced by the nearest value in the list so that real materials may be used; (2) the consolidation process is activated if during the synthesis the indices of two adjacent layers approach the same value; the two layers are then replaced by a single layer of intermediate index. In addition, the outermost layers will be omitted if their indices approach those of the surrounding media.

Both this method and the least squares method may be applied to the design of filters containing absorbing materials, but in this case, it is easier to fix the (complex) refractive index values and to treat thicknesses only as the design variables. Dobrowolski applied this method initially to several design problems including the synthesis of a 7-layer classical stack, a narrow band transmission filter, an achromatic beam splitter for use at normal incidence, a filter in which the reflectance varies linearly with wavelength, an achromatised antireflection coating for wide angle use and Shatilov and Tyutikova's problem, all with great success. The results for the latter are shown in figure 4.4. Figure 4.12 and table 4.5 show the 50% beam splitter results; curves A and B are 5-layer and 6-layer designs using three fixed indices, curve C is a 5-layer design calculated with variable indices (the index fixing routine ensured that after fixing, the indices had to assume one of the values: 1.30, 1.55, 1.80, 2.05, 2.30). The performance may be compared with the 45° achromatic beam splitter designs obtained using the least squares method (figure 4.10).

Two later applications of the method are of particular interest, since the designs concerned were entirely novel, and therefore presented the designer with a problem for which no intuitive approximation could be made. The first of these was an interference reflector whose reflectance at any desired wavelength may be adjusted continuously over a range of values

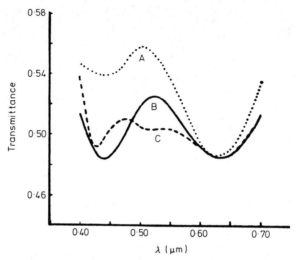

Figure 4.12 Dobrowolski's result for an achromatic beam splitter (after Dobrowolski 1965)

(Dobrowolski *et al* 1968). The wavelength and reflectance are altered by two independent calibrated adjustments. A physical arrangement for this is shown in figure 4.13 — the reflector was mounted on a carriage that was driven by wavelength control which rode on a second carriage driven by reflectance control. Such a continuously adjustable reflector would be of great use in multiple beam interference microscopy where the highest precision of measurement is obtained for maximum contrast of interference fringes; this occurs when the reflectance of the reference flat equals that of the specimen. A continuously adjustable reflector, permanently mounted in the microscope would be most convenient for this application. Dobrowolski produced a

Table 4.5 Achromatic beam splitter with a 50% transmittance for normal incidence of light.

Layer number	Optical thickness (μm)		Refrac- tive Index	Curve C	
	Curve A	Curve B		Optical thickness (μm)	Refrac- tive index
Substrate			1·55		1·50
1		0·5155	1·60		
2	0·0448	0·0732	1·38	0·0567	1·30
3	0·1327	0·1313	1·60	0·1340	1·55
4	0·2298	0·1956	2·30	0·2220	2·30
5	0·1168	0·1093	1·38	0·1158	1·30
6	0·1199	0·1134	2·30	0·1061	2·30
Medium			1·00		1·00

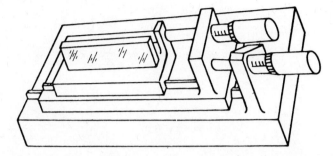

Figure 4.13 A variable interference reflector with independently settable wavelength and reflectance (after Dobrowolski *et al* 1968).

suitable design for this; the reflectance was of the form

$$\mathcal{R} = C \ln (\lambda/d) + D, \qquad (4.8)$$

where $d = d(\nu)$, the thickness of the multilayer, is a function of ν, the linear or angular displacement along the reflector,

$$d = \exp (A\nu) + B. \qquad (4.9)$$

A, B, C and D are constants determined by the range of reflectance and wavelength desired. The resulting theoretical design, the design produced by the synthesis program and two experimental designs are shown in figure 4.14. Table 4.6 gives the multilayer configuration of the reflector — for ease of manufacture, three materials only were used in the design.

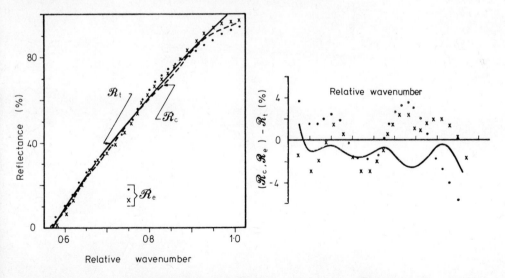

Figure 4.14 Theoretical, $\mathcal{R}_t$, calculated, $\mathcal{R}_c$, and experimental, $\mathcal{R}_e$, results for a 0–90% adjustable reflector (after Dobrowolski *et al* 1968).

92

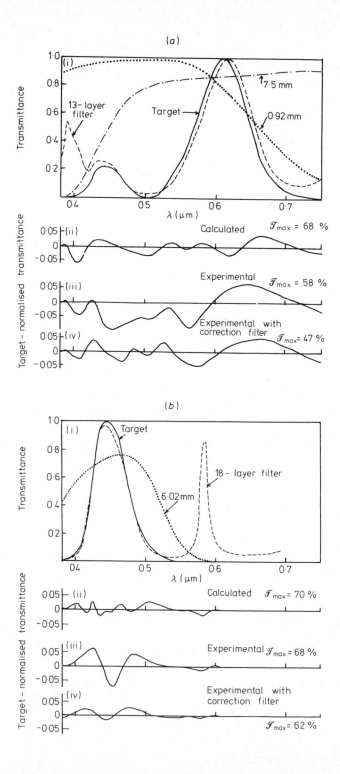

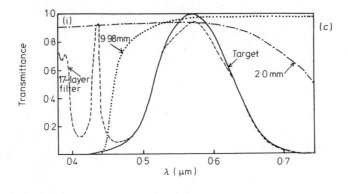

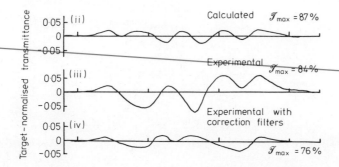

Figure 4.15 Dobrowolski's filter designs for tristimulus colorimetry: (*a*) the $\bar{x}_\lambda$ tristimulus filter; (*b*) the $\bar{y}_\lambda$ tristimulus filter; (*c*) the $\bar{z}_\lambda$ tristimulus filter (after Dobrowolski 1970).

The second new application produced by the method was a set of filters for tristimulus colorimetry, designed to simulate the colour mixture functions of the CIE standard observer when used in conjunction with a Gillod–Boutry photocell (Dobrowolski 1970). Some enhancements had been made to the original program by this stage to allow for (a) dispersion of index of the materials used in the design, (b) a relative spectral transmittance curve in place of the absolute value curve, (c) inclusion of other types of filter, such as glass absorbing systems and (d) a search for a design consisting of several filters in series if a single filter will not produce the solution. The specified $\bar{x}_\lambda$, $\bar{y}_\lambda$ and $\bar{z}_\lambda$ curves are the full curves in figure 4.15; the computed transmittance curves of the resulting designs are shown by broken curves. Glass filters were incorporated to restrict the transmission range; their transmittance is also shown.

Thus it is seen that this method of automatic design is very powerful, but because of its complexity, the computing time involved is inevitably considerable.

Table 4.6 Construction parameters for the 0–90% adjustable reflector nd is the optical thickness in μm.

Layer number	nd	n
Substrate		1·550
1	0·0888	1·380
2	0·0765	1·800
3	0·0568	1·380
4	0·0745	2·300
5	0·1450	1·380
6	0·3705	1·800
7	0·1430	1·380
8	0·1448	1·800
9	0·1468	2·300
10	0·1408	1·380
11	0·2930	2·300
12	0·2278	1·380
13	0·3235	2·300
14	0·2473	1·380
15	0·2473	2·300
Medium		1·000

4.5 Multilayer synthesis method of Pelletier, Klapisch and Giacomo

Pelletier *et al* (1971) published details of a method of automatic filter design which appears to have some advantages over both the least squares method and Dobrowolski's synthesis technique when applied to the problem of designing achromatic reflectance coatings (high reflectors, beam splitters and antireflection coatings) for an extended spectral range.

The merit function is chosen as

$$F = \Omega_1 \left(\frac{1}{L} \sum_{j=1}^{L} | \mathscr{R}(\lambda_j, \mathbf{x}) - \bar{\mathscr{R}} \,|^k \right)^{1/k} + \Omega_2 \,| \, \bar{\mathscr{R}} - \bar{\mathscr{R}}_0 \,|, \qquad (4.10)$$

where $\mathscr{R}(\lambda_j, \mathbf{x})$ is the calculated reflectivity at wavelength λ_j for a multilayer configuration with thicknesses x_i, $i = 1, \ldots, P$; $\bar{\mathscr{R}}$ is the mean of the computed reflectance values over the L design wavelengths,

$$\bar{\mathscr{R}} = \frac{1}{L} \sum_{j=1}^{L} \mathscr{R}(\lambda_j, \mathbf{x}); \qquad (4.11)$$

$\mathscr{R}_0$ is the desired reflectivity at wavelength λ_j, Ω_1, Ω_2 are relative weights for the two parts of the merit function; and k, Ω_1, Ω_2 may be adjusted to suit the needs of a particular design specification. The main advantage of this formulation is that the first term ensures that the amplitude of fluctuation of the design from its mean value is minimised, as well as the difference between this mean value and the desired value; the latter is accomplished by the minimisation of the second term in (4.10). The spectral range of the design may be split into several sections, each having different values of Ω_1 and Ω_2; if a large contrast C_0 is required between a region of high reflectivity (λ_1, λ_2) and an adjacent region of low reflectivity (λ_2, λ_3), a term of the form

$$\left| \frac{\bar{\mathscr{R}}\lambda_1\lambda_2}{\bar{\mathscr{R}}\lambda_2\lambda_3} - C_0 \right| \tag{4.12}$$

may be included in the merit function. In addition, transmittance, phase change on reflection or transmission, or the rate of change of any of these quantities may be used in place of $\mathscr{R}$. However, care was taken to ensure that of layers, such as broad band high-reflection coatings, it is worthwhile to in execution.

The non-linear simplex method, developed by Nelder and Mead (1965) was used for the minimisation. This particular method was chosen because it requires no evaluation of derivatives of the merit function, nor does it assume that the function is differentiable and continuous over the domain of interest. It has the additional advantage that the user can easily ensure that the design variables take only positive values. However, it should be noted that numerical comparisons (for example, Fletcher (1965)) indicate that it is far less efficient than some other methods which require no evaluation of derivatives, notably, the sum of squares method of Powell (1965), which is used in the least squares method of design. Pelletier and his co-workers provide four stopping criteria: (1) little change in the merit function value for several iterations, indicating that the function is close to the minimum value obtainable for that starting point; (2) a sufficiently small value of the merit function (i.e. less than some prespecified value), indicating that a solution has been obtained to within the desired level of tolerance; (3) little change in the design variables; and (4) a maximum number of permissable iterations, in case the method is slow to converge or does not converge at all for a particular problem.

The length of time taken for the calculation increases almost exponentially with the number of design variables. For designs requiring a large number of layers, such as broad band high-reflection coatings. it is worthwhile to limit the number of design variables, either by fixing some thicknesses or by constraining several layers to have equal thicknesses or even to have thicknesses in some predefined arithmetic progression. In general, Pelletier *et al* (1971) suggest using a set of design variables

$$\{\alpha_k\}, \qquad K = 1, \ldots, \pi < P, \quad \text{the number of layers,}$$

and commence their calculations by setting up the relations between the α_k and the thicknesses $x_i, i = 1, \ldots, P$. The flow diagram for their method

96

is shown in figure 4.16. During the later iterations of the program, the constraints may be relaxed; if the initial results do not meet the design requirements, π is increased with the best results being used as the starting point for the next iteration. This process can continue until $\pi = P$. Table 4.7 shows their results for high-reflection coatings with 9–21 layers; the performance of the 21-layer design is also shown in figure 4.17. Figure 4.18

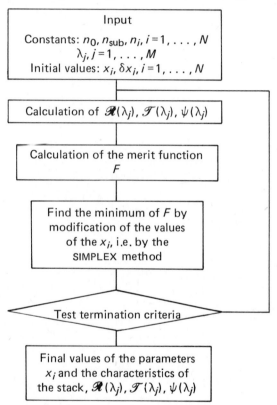

Figure 4.16 The design method of Pelletier *et al* (1971): flow diagram for the first iterations with a reduced number of design variables.

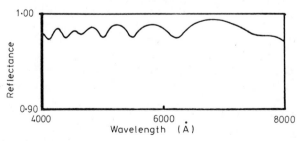

Figure 4.17 Computed reflectance of the 21-layer high-reflectance coating (after Pelletier *et al* 1971).

Table 4.7 High-reflection coatings. Thicknesses of the layers in angstrom, counted from the substrate. C, cryolite; S, zinc sulphide.

No of layers	9	9	11	13	15	15	15	17	17	19	21
Spectral domain (Å)	4000–8000	4500–7000	4500–7000	4500–7000	4000–8000	4000–7000	4500–7000	4000–8000	4000–7000	4000–8000	4000–8000
Maximum reflectance	0·865	0·917	0·972	0·989	0·978	0·982	0·991	0·984	0·993	0·992	0·994
Minimum reflectance	0·773	0·864	0·919	0·946	0·917 (804)	0·958	0·962	0·929	0·968	0·964	0·973
Physical thickness	861 S	1100 S	1052 S	627 S	804 S	838 S	969 S	422 S	429 S	912 S	1053 S
	1363 C	1350 C	1467 C	2014 C	1649 C	1207 C	1630 C	763 C	891 C	1504 C	1791 C
	737 S	1087 S	584 S	572 S	807 S	746 S	653 S	489 S	496 S	786 S	696 S
	1285 C	1096 C	2002 C	1169 C	1408 C	1260 C	1853 C	972 C	846 C	1351 C	1557 C
	600 S	590 S	590 S	1089 S	708 S	675 S	600 S	526 S	425 S	808 S	654 S
	1033 C	938 C	1157 C	1098 C	1507 C	1117 C	1238 C	874 C	838 C	1245 C	1530 C
	499 S	563 S	545 S	548 S	642 S	730 S	1048 S	461 S	500 S	771 S	691 S
	603 C	950 C	1078 C	1106 C	1474 C	997 C	1045 C	929 C	985 C	1325 C	1299 C
	380 S	746 S	555 S	566 S	618 S	579 S	560 S	609 S	533 S	642 S	766 S
			1047 C	1065 C	886 C	937 C	1063 C	1465 C	1076 C	1284 C	1204 C
			549 S	575 S	496 S	475 S	554 S	675 S	775 S	744 S	622 S
				1059 C	941 C	812 C	1099 C	1305 C	1095 C	913 C	1473 C
				570 S	492 S	448 S	555 S	801 S	632 S	475 S	586 S
					879 C	694 C	1042 C	1257 C	1257 C	833 C	952 C
					394 S	425 S	554 S	773 S	765 S	494 S	479 S
								1376 C	1073 C	1009 C	940 C
								927 S	892 S	499 S	490 S
										768 C	943 C
										409 S	514 S
											768 C
											416 S

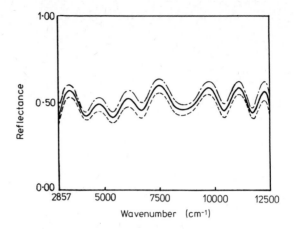

Figure 4.18 The 12-layer achromatic beam splitter design produced by Pelletier *et al* (1971). Broken curve, *p* polarisation; chain curve, *s* polarisation. Angle of incidence, 22°.

is an example of an achromatic beam splitter extending from 800 nm to 3500 nm. All the designs are based on the use of two materials, zinc sulphide and cryolite.

4.6   Chen's turning value method

Chen (1970) and Seeley *et al* (1973) were primarily concerned with a specific class of multilayer design problems, namely, the design of low- and high-pass filters which have a Tschebysheff equi-ripple characteristic in the pass band. This so called optimum response is often used for electrical filter design work, as has been illustrated in chapter 3; there was reason to believe that it is a response which could be realised by a suitable multilayer configuration. The circuit analogy method of Seeley *et al* (1973) was an attempt to do this, but the fit between the specified response and the filter design produced was not exact due to error in the approximations used; an exact design can be produced if the refractive index values are not specified in advance, but this is not a practical procedure. Chen therefore considered a fixed index configuration and developed a method of design which gave a much closer response to the Tschebysheff specification. Figure 4.19 shows the response of a 17-layer filter designed by the circuit analogy method, compared with the Tschebysheff response — comparison with figure 4.20, which illustrates Chen's turning value design, shows that the latter is a significant improvement for this type of design.

When the errors in the circuit analogy method were discussed in chapter 3, two main causes were suggested: (1) the approximations involved in the

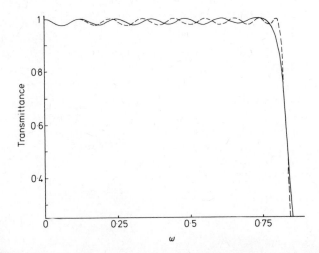

Figure 4.19 The 17-layer filter designed by the circuit analogy method (full curve) for use in the visible region, compared with the Tschebysheff function (broken curve).

design equations (these were corrected by Chen's iteration process); and (2) the electric circuit analogue uses a single frequency variable, whereas inhomogeneous variables, θ_i, the phase thicknesses, are used in the multilayer system; this discrepancy means that the two systems are identical at one point only, namely, the cut-off frequency. At all other frequencies, the difference in frequency variation between the multilayer immittances and those of the electric circuit results in an alteration of the position of the

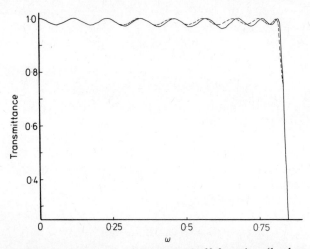

Figure 4.20 Comparison of the Tschebysheff function (broken curve) with 17-layer filters designed by the turning value method (after Seeley *et al* 1973).

pass band ripples. A different approach may be used; an attempt may be made to fit the multilayer response to the Tschebysheff characteristic numerically, as has been done for other specifications using the merit function techniques outlined in the previous sections. Most of these techniques are applied by fitting the multilayer transmittance to the specified response at fixed frequencies; in the case of the Tschebysheff response, these could include the transmittance minima in the pass band. An inherent difficulty arises, however, in that the positions of these minima shift as the multilayer thicknesses are altered. The turning value method (Chen 1970) overcomes this by altering the design frequencies as the design itself is altered, in order to keep them at the transmittance minima.

In chapter 3 we saw that h, the width of the ripple in the pass band, is given by

$$h = \frac{|n_H/n_{sub} - n_{sub}/n_L|}{|n_H/n_{sub} + n_{sub}/n_L|}, \qquad (4.13)$$

and suppose that, for a N-layer symmetric filter, the transmittance minima occur at $\omega_1^*, \omega_2^*, \ldots \omega^*_{(N-1)/2}$ (ω^* is a normalised frequency variable). Then for the filter to have the Tschebysheff response, the following equations must be satisfied:

$$\mathcal{T}(\omega,d_1,d_2,\ldots,d_{(N+1)/2}) = \frac{1}{1+h^2}, \qquad \text{at } \omega = \omega_i \qquad (4.14)$$

$$\frac{\partial \mathcal{T}}{\partial \omega} = 0; \qquad \text{at } \omega = \omega_i \qquad \text{for } i = 1, 2, \ldots, (N-1)/2. \qquad (4.15)$$

We also have to specify the rate of cut-off at the band edge. We do this by specifying two frequencies: ω_p, in the pass band, which characterises the frequency of the transmittance maxima nearest to the band edge, i.e.

$$\mathcal{T}(\omega_p) = 1, \qquad (4.16)$$

and ω_r in the rejection band. To specify the latter, we need to know the optimum rate of cut-off for the filter; the circuit analogy method produces a rate of cut-off that is less than the Tschebysheff response; the multilayer stack has a higher rate of cut-off but its pass band performance is poor; thus, although we take the Tschebysheff response as the basis for ω_r, it is useful in practice to be able to choose ω_r to be lower than that corresponding to the Tschebysheff function, i.e.

$$\mathcal{T}(\omega_r) = \epsilon, \qquad (4.17)$$

where ϵ is an arbitrarily chosen value of transmittance at ω_r. (4.14)–(4.17) are the design equations; we may simplify them by ignoring the transmittance of the minimum at the low-frequency end of the spectrum, since this is close to the design value (even for a classical stack) and is not very sensitive to changes in the d_i. To obtain the solution we define a merit function, F, which will have a minimum of zero if all the equations are satisfied, or whose minimum will give the 'best' solution (in the least squares sense) if the equations cannot be satisfied simultaneously. Thus

$$F = \sum_{i=2}^{(N-1)/2} (a_i \Delta \mathcal{T}_i)^2 + \sum_{i=2}^{(N-1)/2} \left[b_i \left(\frac{\partial \mathcal{T}}{\partial \omega} \right)_i \right]^2 + (c\Delta \mathcal{T}_p)^2 + (d\Delta \mathcal{T}_r)^2,$$

(4.18)

where $\Delta \mathcal{T}_i$, $\Delta \mathcal{T}_p$, and $\Delta \mathcal{T}_r$ are the differences between the desired value of transmittance and the calculated value for a particular configuration; a_i, b_i, c and d are weighting factors.

From consideration of the circuit analogy method on the one hand, and the classical stack on the other, we know that limits can be set on the multilayer thicknesses; also, we see from the discussion above that the variables ω_i^* are functions of the d_i. One standard method of optimisation for this type of problem is that developed by Rosenbrock (1960); although there may be more efficient methods for so-called 'well behaved' functions, Rosenbrock's method is both reliable and robust and seemed to work well for this problem. The construction parameters for the 17-layer filter shown in figure 4.20 are given in table 4.8, together with those given by the circuit

Table 4.8 Construction parameters for 17-layer low-pass filters designed (a) by the turning value method, and (b) by the circuit analogy method.

Layer number	Index	Phase thicknesses (deg) Design (a)	Design (b)
massive	1·52	—	—
1	2·30	51·4	38·4
2	1·38	63·5	55·8
3	2·30	67·6	64·4
4	1·38	70·4	68·5
5	2·30	70·5	70·4
6	1·38	72·6	71·7
7	2·30	72·0	71·8
8	1·38	72·5	72·2
9	2·30	71·6	72·7
10	1·38	72·5	72·2
11	2·30	72·0	71·8
12	1·38	72·6	71·7
13	2·30	70·5	70·4
14	1·38	70·4	68·5
15	2·30	67·6	64·4
16	1·38	63·5	55·8
17	2·30	51·4	38·4
massive	1·52	—	—

102

analogy design. Note that the increase in layer thicknesses of the turning value design shows the same trend as the iterative correction of the circuit analogy method (cf table 3.3).

The turning value method has been successfully applied to the design of several low- and high-pass filters for use in the visible and infrared regions of the spectrum. Chen (1970) also suggests that the method could be used for the design of quarter-wave coupled band pass filters; if multilayer stacks are used in place of quarter-wave reflectors, the Tschebysheff or Butterworth transmittance characteristic is distorted; the response could be expected to be considerably improved by application of the turning value method to the problem.

4.7 Reduction of polarisation effects in design

When multilayer interference coatings are used at high angles of incidence, the problems arising from polarisation of the reflected or transmitted light can be quite severe; in particular, the splitting between the s- and p-components of polarisation at the edge of a band pass filter can prove troublesome to the designer as it tends to result in an overall decrease in edge steepness, and on occasion, can cause a 'hump' to appear on the edge. This effect is shown in figure 4.21(a) which illustrates the resultant reflectance for a 13-layer classical stack when light is incident at 45°, the medium of incidence being air. The full line gives the average of the s- and p-components of polarisation; the other low-pass filter designs shown in figure 4.21 are based on the methods described by Baumeister (1958) and Seeley et al (1973). Although the degradation of edge is not so marked as in the former, the steepness is certainly less than that at normal incidence for both these designs; one may obtain an 'order of magnitude' estimate of the splitting between the components of polarisation by using the approximation formulae (1.65) and (1.66). The numerical values given by these formulae, compared with the actual splitting in the three designs are given in table 4.9.

Costich (1970) used a Herpin equivalent index technique to attempt to eliminate the effect by finding combinations of materials which would be 'polarisation insensitive' when used at high angles of incidence; he recommended that this technique be used in conjunction with a second method for reducing polarisation by transforming the boundary massive media to effective massive media having little polarisation splitting of their effective indices. His results for infrared beam splitters are shown in figure 4.22. Mahlein (1974) has developed a technique for producing non-polarising beam splitters for use at a single frequency in conjunction with a laser source.

A different approach was made by Liddell and Fawcett (1969) who modified the least squares method to produce a 'polarisation insensitive'

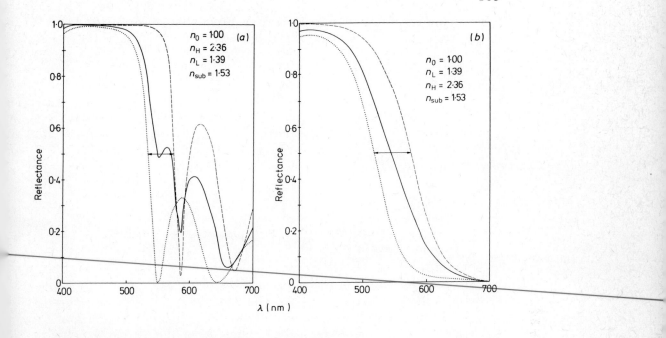

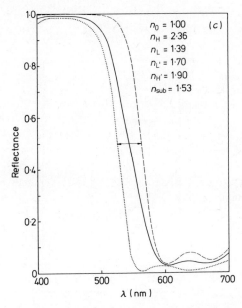

Figure 4.21 Spectral performance of (*a*) a 13-layer classical stack, (*b*) a 13-layer low-pass filter designed using the circuit analogy method and (*c*) a 13-layer low-pass filter designed by Baumeister's method. Dotted lines, *p*-component; broken lines, *s*-component; full lines, average. Angle of incidence = 45°, ↔ shows splitting between components at 50% $\mathscr{R}$.

Table 4.9 Values of the splitting in nm between the s- and p-components of polarisation at 50% point on the edge, $n_0 = 1\cdot00$, $n_H = 2\cdot36$, $n_L = 1\cdot39$, $n_{sub} = 1\cdot53$. The edge frequency is assumed to be 500 nm in all cases.

Type of filter	45° Angle of incidence	20° Angle of incidence
Classical stack	42	6·2
Refinement	32	6·0
Baumeister design	40	7·5
Refinement	28	7·0
Circuit analogy design	58	11·5
Refinement	48	11·0
Value given by formulae (1·50) and (1·51)	42·1	6·1

design. Normally when applying the method at an angle of incidence, the reflectance (or transmittance) used in the merit function is taken to be the average of the s- and p-components; however, if the merit function contains the values of both components and attempts to fit the desired response to both, a design giving reduced polarisation splitting may be obtained. The results of this technique applied to the band pass filter designs illustrated

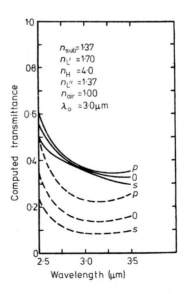

Figure 4.22 Costich's infrared beam splitter design with reduced polarisation dependence. Full curve, Sub/0·75H 1·50L 0·75H/Air; broken curve, Substrate /L' 0·75H 1·50L 0·75H L''/Air (after Costich 1970).

in figure 4.21 are shown in figure 4.23, and it is seen that it is possible to reduce the polarisation splitting effect, but only at the cost of passing performance and stopping performance, although the latter can always be improved by increasing the number of layers in the multilayer configuration.

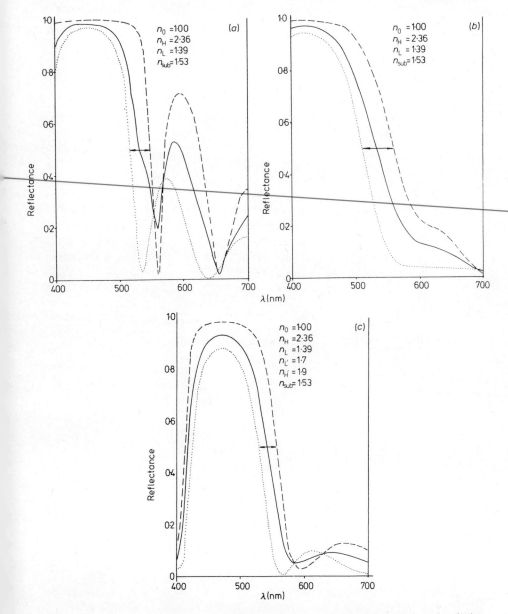

Figure 4.23 Refinement of the designs shown in figure 4.21 to produce reduced polarisation effects.

106

Table 4.9 shows quantitatively the reduction in splitting between the components. The method was also applied to Costich's designs for 50% 'non-polarising' beam splitters for the infrared; the results obtained by refinement of Costich's design and from the automatic design version of the program are illustrated in figure 4.24. These are all fairly acceptable, but when an attempt

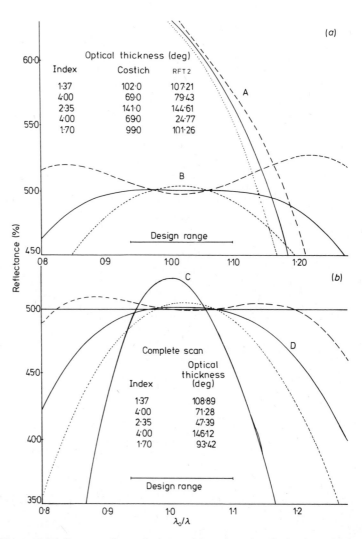

Figure 4.24 Beam splitter designs with reduced polarisation obtained using the least squares method: (*a*) Costich's design, A, and Liddell and Fawcett's refinement design, B; and (*b*) N^2 scan, C, and complete scan, D. Dotted lines, *p*-component; broken lines, *s*-component; full lines, average. Angle of incidence, 45°, $n_{sub} = 1.37$, $n_0 = 1.00$.

was made to produce designs for the visible region, the overall performance was not so impressive, although the percentage improvement was comparable.

One fact that emerges from this application is the comparative versatility of the automatic design programs; they may easily be modified to deal with a variety of design problems.

5 Fourier Transform Methods of Synthesis

The process of synthesis of a dielectric multilayer involves specifying the desired energy reflectance as a function of frequency by means of a series expansion which is then used to deduce the parameters of the system. To make the solution possible, certain simplifying assumptions must be made; in the 'true synthesis' methods, all layers are assumed to be of equal thickness, or of equal effective phase thickness for non-normal incidence, so the problem reduces to one of obtaining the refractive indices for the system. Unfortunately, many indices resulting from such a solution cannot be realised in practice. A comprehensive survey of these methods has been given by Delano and Pegis (1969).

In their review paper Delano and Pegis suggest that synthesis methods may be subdivided into four classes:

(1) special methods, which include some techniques which are not true synthesis methods, and others not generally applicable to all types of filter. This class includes graphical methods, equivalent index techniques and the 'two effective interface' method, all of which were described in chapter 2;
(2) approximate methods, which may be applied to the design of any type of filter, provided one may assume that the Fresnel reflectances are small;
(3) exact methods, which employ rigorous synthesis techniques;
(4) methods of differential correction, which include the successive iteration method of Baumeister and Dobrowolski's automatic design method, both of which were described in chapter 4.

In this chapter, we shall consider examples of methods falling into categories (2) and (3) above; in both cases it is assumed that the desired spectral response $1/\mathcal{T}$ or $\mathcal{R}/\mathcal{T}$ may be expressed as a Fourier cosine series function of frequency or as a function of $\delta = 2\pi n d \cos \theta / \lambda$, the effective phase thickness of the layers. The methods described by Delano and Pegis are restricted to designs with layers of equal effective phase thickness. Sossi (1974, 1976) has extended the Fourier transform method to the design of a refractive index profile for an inhomogeneous layer of infinite extent, which may then be approximated by a finite system of discrete homogeneous layers. The method and its application by Dobrowolski and Lowe (1978) will be discussed in a subsequent section.

108

5.1 The approximate vector method

Extending (1.83) to the case of an N-layer filter, and noting all δ_k are equal, we obtain

$$\rho = \sum_{k=0}^{N} r_k \exp(-2ik\delta), \qquad (5.1)$$

i.e. ρ may be expressed as a finite complex Fourier series in δ, with period π. Then using (1.46)

$$|\rho|^2 = \frac{\mathcal{R}}{\mathcal{T}} = (r_0^2 + r_1^2 + \ldots + r_N^2) + 2(r_0 r_1 + r_1 r_2 + \ldots + r_{N-1} r_N) \cos 2\delta$$

$$+ 2(r_0 r_2 + \ldots + r_{N-2} r_N) \cos 4\delta + \ldots + 2r_0 r_N \cos 2N\delta,$$

$$(5.2)$$

so that $|\rho|^2$ is a finite cosine series. To obtain the required design, one performs a Fourier analysis of the required $\mathcal{R}/\mathcal{T}$ response, giving

$$\frac{\mathcal{R}}{\mathcal{T}} = \sum_{k=0}^{N} c_k \cos 2k\delta. \qquad (5.3)$$

(Methods used to generate this type of series include Tschebysheff polynomial approximations, damped least squares and general optimisation techniques.) We therefore have to solve the following set of $(N + 1)$ simultaneous equations:

$$r_0^2 + r_1^2 + \ldots + r_N^2 \qquad\qquad = c_0,$$

$$r_0 r_1 + r_1 r_2 + \ldots + r_{N-1} r_N = \tfrac{1}{2} c_1,$$

$$r_0 r_2 + r_1 r_3 + \ldots + r_{N-2} r_N = \tfrac{1}{2} c_2, \qquad (5.4)$$

$$\vdots \qquad\quad \vdots$$

$$r_0 r_N \qquad\quad = \tfrac{1}{2} c_N.$$

Pegis (1961) suggested a method of solution (the vector method algorithm) for this system, based on the fact that the c_i may be expressed in terms of the complex variable $Z = e^{2i\delta}$. Then

$$\mathcal{R}/\mathcal{T} = c_0 + \tfrac{1}{2} \sum_{k=1}^{N} c_k (Z^k + Z^{-k}). \qquad (5.5)$$

This may be expressed as a polynomial in $Y = Z + Z^{-1}$

$$\mathcal{R}/\mathcal{T} = \sum_{k=0}^{N} c_k' Y^k. \qquad (5.6)$$

The complex roots Y_i of the resulting polynomial equation may be found, and the quadratics

$$Z + Z^{-1} = Y_i, \qquad i = 1, 2, \ldots, N \qquad (5.7)$$

solved; one member of each reciprocal pair is used to construct the polynomial

$$(Z - Z_1)(Z - Z_2) \ldots (Z - Z_N), \qquad (5.8)$$

whose coefficients are proportional to the r_k. The constant of proportionality is determined from

$$r_0^2 + r_1^2 + \ldots + r_N^2 = c_0. \qquad (5.9)$$

In all, one obtains 2^N physically distinct solutions for the set of values r_k. The refractive indices $n_j, j = 1, 2, \ldots, N$, are then calculated using

$$n_{j+1}/n_j = (1 - r_j)/(1 + r_j). \qquad (5.10)$$

Alternatively, one may use the approximate relation

$$\log\left(\frac{1 + x}{1 - x}\right) \simeq 2x,$$

so that

$$n_{j+1} \simeq n_j \exp(-2r_j). \qquad (5.11)$$

This approximation has the advantage that it does not break down if $|r_j| \geqslant 1$.

Delano and Pegis include a numerical example for the approximate design of an eight-layer neutral density filter with a Tschebysheff-type response, $\mathcal{T} = 50\% \pm 1\%$ over a wide bandwidth. Figure 5.1(a) shows the result obtained with this method and can be compared with the corresponding result using the exact synthesis method described below (figure 5.1(b)).

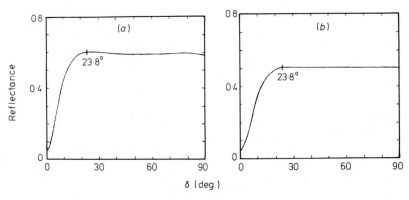

Figure 5.1 Evaluation of an 8-layer neutral density filter (a) using the approximate vector method of Pegis; (b) using the exact synthesis method of Pegis (after Delano and Pegis 1969).

Another approximate method published by Delano (1967) is based on the sampling theorem for periodic functions, which is important in communication theory applications.

5.2   The exact synthesis method

Pegis (1961, 1963) developed a method of synthesis by continued fractions which is an exact synthesis method, using the recurrence relations for amplitude transmission and reflection coefficients (1.41), namely

$$T_{j-1} = \frac{t_{j-1}\, T_j \, \exp(-i\delta_j)}{1 + r_{j-1}\, R_j \, \exp(-2i\delta_j)} \tag{5.12}$$

$$j = 1, 2, \ldots, N+1,$$

$$R_{j-1} = \frac{r_{j-1} + R_j \, \exp(-2i\delta_j)}{1 + r_{j-1} R_j \, \exp(-2i\delta_j)} \tag{5.13}$$

with $T_{N+1} = 1$ and $R_0 = 0$.

Then using the notation described for the approximate method above,

$$R_{j-1} = r_{j-1} + \frac{(1 - r_{j-1})^2}{(r_{j-1} + Z/R_j)} \tag{5.14}$$

and we may express the amplitude reflection coefficient for the entire filter as

$$R = r_0 + \cfrac{(1 - r_0^2)}{r_0 + \cfrac{Z}{r_1 + \cfrac{(1 - r_1^2)}{r_1 + \cfrac{Z}{\ddots}}}}$$

$$\cfrac{(1 - r_{N-1}^2)}{r_{N-1} + \cfrac{Z}{r_{N-1} + \cfrac{Z}{r_N}}}.$$

$$\tag{5.15}$$

Thus if the specified response may be expressed in a similar form, the R_j could be evaluated by comparing coefficients. For a multilayer with N layers of equal optical thickness, $1/\mathcal{T}$ may be expressed as a truncated cosine series

$$1/\mathcal{T} = (1 + c_0) + c_1 \cos 2\delta + \ldots + c_N \cos 2N\delta = 1/(1 - \mathcal{R}). \tag{5.16}$$

To obtain the value of R from $\mathscr{R}$, the vector method algorithm mentioned above may be employed and one obtains an expression for R as the complex quotient

$$R = \frac{E_0^-}{E_0^+} = \frac{d_0 Z^N + d_1 Z^{N-1} + \ldots + d_N}{k_0 Z^N + k_1 Z^{N-1} + \ldots + k_N}. \tag{5.17}$$

The coefficients k_i are real functions of the Fresnel reflectances r_k, and only one set of k_i are physically realisable. The vector method algorithm will generate a large number of possible solutions for the d_i and the k_i. In order to compare this with (5.15), the above equation may be written

$$R = A_0 + \cfrac{1}{B_0 + \cfrac{Z}{A_1 + \cfrac{1}{B_1 + \cfrac{Z}{\ddots \cfrac{}{A_{N-1} + \cfrac{1}{B_{N-1} + \cfrac{Z}{A_N}}}}}}}, \tag{5.18}$$

where A_m, B_m are calculated from the recurrence relations

$$A_m = d_0^{(m)}/k_0^{(m)}, \qquad d_{j-1}^{(m)} = d_j^{(m)} - A_m k_j^{(m)}.$$
$$B_m = k_{n-m}^{(m)}/d_{n-m-1}^{(m+1)}, \qquad k_0^{(m+1)} = k_0^{(m)},$$

$$k_j^{(m+1)} = k_j^{(m)} - B_m d_{j-1}^{(m+1)}$$
$$\text{for } j = 1, 2, \ldots, n - m.$$

The numerator and denominator at each stage must be multiplied by an undetermined constant before equating coefficients, since the form of the continued fraction is arbitrary to within these constants. Then by equating coefficients with (5.15), all the r_k, and hence the n_k may be evaluated.

Other methods of exact synthesis have been presented by Young (1961), Seidel and Rosen (1967) and by Knittl (1967). These are largely based on methods developed for electrical engineering design purposes; Young's method was described in detail in chapter 3. Full details and numerical examples for all these methods are included in the paper by Delano and Pegis (1969).

5.3 The thin-film synthesis program of Dobrowolski and Lowe

Sossi (1974, 1976) turned his attention to the Fourier transform method and extended its application in such a way that no assumptions are made about the number of layers in the filter, nor about the thicknesses and refractive indices of the layers. A refractive index profile is obtained for an inhomogeneous layer of infinite extent which may then be approximated by a finite system of discrete homogenous layers. This method was developed further by Dobrowolski and Lowe (1978) in such a way that it may be combined with other design procedures which place a control on the thickness and refractive index values so that they conform to current practical limitations.

Sossi proved that the spectral transmittance of an inhomogeneous layer is related to its refractive index profile by the following approximate expression

$$\int_{-\infty}^{+\infty} \frac{dn}{dx} \frac{1}{2n} \exp(ikx) \, dx = Q(k) \exp(i\phi(k)) = f(k), \qquad (5.20)$$

where the wave vector $k = 2\pi/\lambda$, $Q(k)$ is an even function of the desired transmittance (the actual form it should take is discussed more fully later),

$$x = 2 \int_0^z n(u) \, du$$

is twice the optical path, z is the geometrical coordinate within the layer and $\phi(k)$ is a phase factor which must be odd for $n(x)$ to be real. From (5.20) we obtain a direct expression for $n(x)$

$$n(x) = \exp\left(\frac{2}{\pi}\int_0^\infty \frac{Q(k)}{k} \sin\left(\phi(k) - kx\right) dk\right), \qquad (5.21)$$

the refractive index profile for an inhomogeneous layer. The success of the method depends on obtaining a good approximation for $Q(k)$, an even function of the desired transmittance. We have seen that in the methods described by Delano and Pegis, $\mathcal{R}(k)/\mathcal{T}(k))^{1/2}$ is used as the desired function, but Dobrowolski and Lowe, following Sossi, suggest that better results are obtained using

$$Q(k) = \left[\frac{1}{2}\left(\frac{1}{\mathcal{T}(k)} - \mathcal{T}(k)\right)\right]^{1/2}. \qquad (5.22)$$

With this formulation the integration in (5.21) need only be performed over the range $k_L \leqslant k \leqslant k_H$ where the transmittance differs from unity.

Figure 5.2 shows a block diagram of the method. The various stages of the calculation are:

(1) The desired transmittance $\mathcal{T}(k)$ and phase factors are provided; since the

114

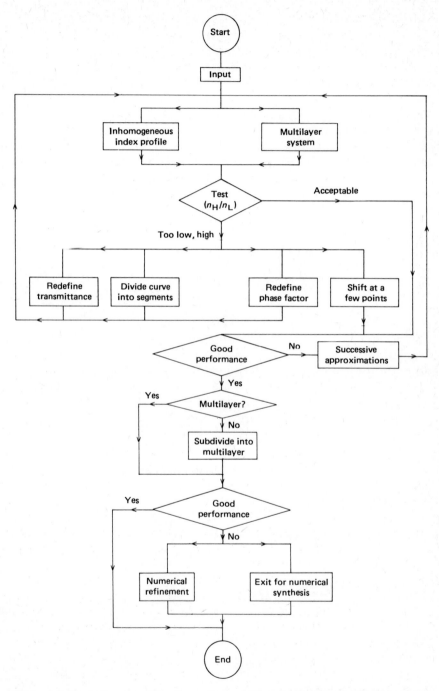

Figure 5.2 Block diagram of the flow of calculations in Dobrowolski and Lowe's calculations (after Dobrowolski and Lowe 1978).

transmittance is normally specified as unity outside the region of interest in order to reduce the range of integration, this means $\mathcal{T}(k)$ is specified at a number of wavelengths within the spectral region concerned. The phase factor is assumed zero unless defined otherwise. The choice of $Q(k)$ given by (5.22) implies that one cannot specify zero transmittance, but one may approach zero as closely as one desires; this will result in an increase in the refractive index ratio n_H/n_L for highest and lowest indices calculated from (5.21).

(2) The refractive index profile for the inhomogeneous layer of infinite extent is computed from (5.21) using a standard numerical integration technique (Dobrowolski and Lowe suggest the trapezoidal rule).

(3) Sometimes the transmittance may be allowed to depart from unity at higher frequencies than those in the region of interest, and in this case one may find a homogeneous multilayer system giving the desired spectral response, with a refractive index profile defined by

$$n(x) = \exp\left(\frac{4}{p}\sum_{m=-\infty}^{+\infty} F\left(\frac{m}{p}\right)\right),\qquad(5.23)$$

where $F(x)$ is the Fourier transform of $f(k)$, defined by equation (5.20), and it is assumed that the desired transmittance is initially defined completely in the wave vector interval $0 \leqslant k \leqslant p$, elsewhere it is unity; then if p is the wave vector displacement between adjacent harmonics, m harmonics are added to the original curve. Equation (5.23) is evaluated only for integral values of $x = (m/p)$; for intermediate values n is constant. Note that in this case all layer optical thicknesses must be an integral multiple of some basic thickness.

(4) Refractive index control; if the ratio of the highest to the lowest index in the profile obtained at step (2) exceeds the values obtainable in practice, this must be rectified. There are several possible courses of action – the transmittance may be redefined outside the spectral region of interest, the curve may be divided into segments or the phase factor may be redefined. If the practical limits are exceeded at only a few points, discontinuous steps may be introduced into the profile to bring them within limits without affecting the overall performance.

(5) The spectral response of the inhomogeneous layer is next evaluated by subdividing it into a large number of thin homogeneous films, as suggested by Jacobsson (1963). The performance of this multilayer is evaluated using the normal matrix methods, but due to the approximations used to define $Q(k)$ (equation (5.22)), the response may be significantly different from that desired. This may be improved using a successive approximation method. For the case of a system which had been reduced to a homogeneous multilayer system at step (3), the synthesis should now be complete. However, for the general case, two further steps are required:

116

(6) The inhomogeneous layer must now be divided into a finite number of discrete layers, characterised by a minimum index difference between layers and a maximum layer thickness. In order to reduce the total number of layers in the system, the overall performance at this stage may deteriorate; however, the spectral response should be brought back to the desired value during the final stage.

(7) At this stage, either a numerical refinement technique, based on the use of a 'merit function' may be applied or a more powerful automatic design method used (Dobrowolski 1965). Some examples of these methods were described in chapter 4. Dobrowolski and Lowe have found that the combination of the filter synthesis technique and the automatic design methods is a very powerful tool for the designer.

Two particular examples of results obtained from this method are illustrated in figures 5.3 and 5.4. The former is a design of a $\bar{y}_\lambda$ tristimulus filter (Dobrowolski 1970, 1973), which is also used as an example in chapter 4; the second is a somewhat more spectacular example and illustrates the ability to design a filter with almost any specified transmittance curve — the one chosen approximates the silhouette of the Parliament buildings in Ottawa.

This Fourier transform method of design is obviously one of the most powerful techniques yet devised, although it remains to be fully tested in terms of realising the designs produced. Used in conjunction with other refinement and synthesis techniques, it provides a quick and cheap method for designing filters with unusual spectral characteristics. However, it is not the answer for all design problems; it cannot be used for filters with strongly

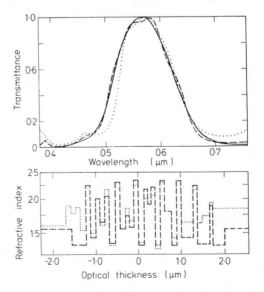

Figure 5.3 The $\bar{y}_\lambda$ tristimulus filter (after Dobrowolski and Lowe 1978).

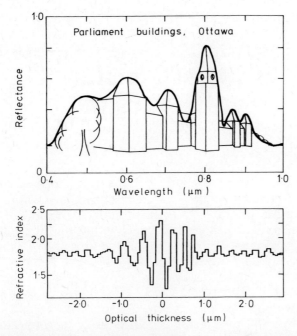

Figure 5.4 Filter with a spectral transmittance curve that approximates the silhouette of the Parliament Buildings, Ottawa (after Dobrowolski and Lowe 1978).

absorbing layers, nor for problems which require a particular response at several angles of incidence or involve polarisation properties. For these problems, the automatic design methods discussed in chapter 4 are the obvious techniques to apply.

6 Theoretical Determination of Optical Constants of Thin Films

In order to be able to apply some of the more sophisticated multilayer design techniques, such as have been described in previous chapters, the designer must have accurate data for refractive index and absorption coefficient of the materials forming the layers within the filter, and also for the dispersion of these quantities over the spectral range for which the filter is to be used. Most results generally available are given for bulk forms of the substances, and there can be sizeable differences between the latter and the thin-film values. Bennett and Booty (1966) give an example of a 346 Å film of silicon whose index ranged from 2·8 to 3·2 in the visible region of the spectrum whereas the bulk value obtained from the literature was quoted as 5·5!

Most of the methods to date for determining optical constants of thin films are applied to a single film on a substrate, one exception being a method due to Hansen (1973), which will be described later; there is of course no guarantee that the optical performance of a similar film *in situ* in the multilayer will be identical to that of the single film, as the substance could be influenced by its neighbouring media during the evaporation process, but one might expect fairly good agreement with the single-film data; the experience of multilayer designers shows that this is indeed the case.

Many of the earlier methods for determining optical constants of thin films have been reviewed by Heavens (1960, 1964); two of the most popular are the 'turning point' method and the Abelès method (1958). The former has the disadvantage that a relatively thick film is needed to obtain adequate dispersion information, the latter is only really applicable to transparent films — in fact, Heavens and Liddell (1965) and also Clapham (1969) have demonstrated that the presence of even a smaller amount of absorption can affect the results appreciably. We shall concern ourselves for the most part with details of more recent computational methods only, which are based on photometric measurements of reflectance and transmittance of the film, rather than on polarimetric measurements; however, one earlier method developed by Hadley and Dennison (1947) will be included as it is useful both as a test for computer programs and as an illustration of the reason for error in some methods.

6.1 Formulae for reflectance and transmittance of a single absorbing film on a transparent substrate

Since the reflectance, $\mathcal{R}$, and the transmittance, $\mathcal{T}$, of a single film on a substrate are functions of n, the refractive index, k, the absorption coefficient and d, the physical thickness of the film, it should be possible, in theory, to find n and k from measured values of $\mathcal{R}$ and $\mathcal{T}$ if all other parameters such as refractive indices of the surrounding media and the film thickness are known. For normal incidence measurements, the following expressions may be used (Heavens 1964):

$$\mathcal{R} = \frac{A \cosh\alpha + B \sinh\alpha - C \cos\beta + D \sin\beta}{E \cosh\alpha + F \sinh\alpha - G \cos\beta + H \sin\beta}, \tag{6.1}$$

$$\mathcal{T} = \frac{8n_2 n_0}{E \cosh\alpha + F \sinh\alpha - G \cos\beta + H \sin\beta}, \tag{6.2}$$

where n_0 is the index of the medium of incidence, n_2 is the index of the substrate, $\alpha = 4\pi kd/\lambda$, $\beta = 4\pi nd/\lambda$ and

$$A = (n^2 + k^2 + n_0^2)(n^2 + k^2 + n_2^2) - 4n^2 n_0 n_2,$$

$$B = 2n[n_2(n^2 + k^2 + n_0^2) - n_0(n^2 + k^2 + n_2^2)],$$

$$C = (n^2 + k^2 - n_0^2)(n^2 + k^2 - n_2^2) + 4k^2 n_0 n_2,$$

$$D = 2k[n_2(n^2 + k^2 - n_0^2) - n_0(n^2 + k^2 - n_2^2)],$$

$$E = (n^2 + k^2 + n_0^2)(n^2 + k^2 + n_2^2) + 4n^2 n_0 n_2,$$

$$F = 2n[n_2(n^2 + k^2 + n_0^2) + n_0(n^2 + k^2 + n_2^2)],$$

$$G = (n^2 + k^2 - n_0^2)(n^2 + k^2 - n_2^2) - 4k^2 n_0 n_2,$$

$$H = 2k[n_2(n^2 + k^2 - n_0^2) + n_0(n^2 + k^2 - n_2^2)].$$

Many methods rely on non-normal incidence measurements, in which case the expressions are much more cumbersome since there are two components of polarisation to consider. Born and Wolf (1959) express the results as follows:

$$\mathcal{R} = \frac{l^2 e^{2v\eta} + m^2 e^{-2v\eta} + 2lm \cos(\phi_{12} - \phi_{01} + 2u\eta)}{e^{2v\eta} + l^2 m^2 e^{-2v\eta} + 2lm \cos(\phi_{12} + \phi_{01} + 2\mu\eta)}, \tag{6.3}$$

for both components, and

$$\mathcal{T}_p = \frac{n_2 \cos\theta_2}{n_0 \cos\theta_0} \frac{f^2 g^2 e^{-2v\eta}}{e^{2v\eta} + l^2 m^2 e^{-2v\eta} + 2lm \cos(\phi_{12} + \phi_{01} + 2u\eta)}, \tag{6.4}$$

$$\mathcal{T}_s = \frac{n_2 \cos\theta_0}{n_0 \cos\theta_2} \frac{f^2 g^2 e^{-2v\eta}}{e^{2v\eta} + l^2 m^2 e^{-2v\eta} + 2lm \cos(\phi_{12} + \phi_{01} + 2u\eta)}, \tag{6.5}$$

where θ_0, θ_2 are the angles of incidence in the medium of incidence and the substrate respectively (the two are related by Snell's law) and

$$l^2 = \frac{[(n^2 - k^2)\cos\theta_0 - n_0 u]^2 + (2nk\cos\theta_0 - n_0 v)^2}{[(n^2 - k^2)\cos\theta_0 + n_0 u]^2 + (2nk\cos\theta_0 + n_0 v)^2},$$

$$m^2 = \frac{[(n^2 - k^2)\cos\theta_2 - n_2 u]^2 + (2nk\cos\theta_2 - n_2 v)^2}{[(n^2 - k^2)\cos\theta_2 + n_2 u]^2 + (2nk\cos\theta_2 + n_2 v)^2},$$

$$\tan\phi_{01} = \frac{2n_0\cos\theta_0[2nku - (n^2 - k^2)v]}{(n^2 + k^2)^2\cos^2\theta_0 - n_0^2(u^2 + v^2)},$$

$$\tan\phi_{12} = \frac{2n_2\cos\theta_2[2nku - (n^2 - k^2)v]}{(n^2 + k^2)^2\cos^2\theta_2 - n_2^2(u^2 + v^2)},$$

$$f^2 = \frac{4n_2^2(u^2 + v^2)}{[(n^2 - k^2)\cos\theta_0 + n_0 u]^2 + [2nk\cos\theta_0 + n_0 v]^2},$$

$$g^2 = \frac{4n_2^2(u^2 + v^2)}{[(n^2 - k^2)\cos\theta_2 + n_2 u]^2 + [2nk\cos\theta_2 + n_2 v]^2},$$

for the p-component of polarisation. For the s-component, $n_i/\cos\theta_i$ ($i = 0, 2$) is replaced everywhere by $n_i\cos\theta_i$.

Also,

$$u^2 - v^2 = n^2 - k^2 - n_0^2\sin^2\theta_0,$$

$$uv = nk,$$

$$\eta = 2\pi d/\lambda.$$

Then

$$\mathscr{R} = (\mathscr{R}_p + \mathscr{R}_s)/2,$$

$$\mathscr{T} = (\mathscr{T}_p + \mathscr{T}_s)/2. \tag{6.6}$$

For both normal and oblique incidence cases, the expressions quoted above are only valid if one makes the assumption that the substrate is of infinite thickness; in practice a correction term must be applied to allow for the effect of reflectance from the back surface of the substrate. This was discussed in chapter 1; if an incoherent source is used, equations (1.68) and (1.69) are applied; for a well-collimated coherent source (1.71) and (1.73) should be used, provided also that the aperture of the detector is small.

We can see from the above formulae that $\mathscr{R}$ and $\mathscr{T}$ are very complicated functions of n and k, and it would be generally impossible to express n and k as explicit functions of $\mathscr{R}$ and $\mathscr{T}$. More important from the practical point of view is the fact that the functions involved can be many valued; this has led to the failure of some of the more straightforward methods of optical constant determination.

6.2   Use of the Hadley–Dennison curves for determining n and k

Hadley and Dennison (1947) produced a set of graphs of $\mathscr{R}$ and $\mathscr{T}$ against d/λ for a range of values of n and k. Figure 6.1 shows the curves for $k = 0.01$ and $n = 2.0$–3.0. In order to find the optical constants of a film whose thickness is known, at a particular wavelength λ, one chooses a number of possible k values and reads off two values of n, corresponding to the $\mathscr{R}$ against d/λ and the $\mathscr{T}$ against d/λ curves for each value of k. The $n(\mathscr{R})$ and

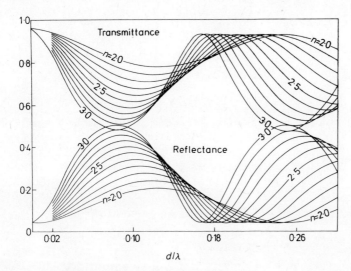

Figure 6.1   The Hadley–Dennison curves for $k = 0.01$, $n = 2.0, 2.1, 2.2, \ldots 3.0$.

$n(\mathscr{T})$ values are then plotted against the k values and graphical interpolation will give the point of intersection of the two curves, thus providing the appropriate value of n and k. The procedure may be illustrated by the following example, first provided by Heavens (1964); for a particular film the following values of $n(\mathscr{R})$ and $n(\mathscr{T})$ were obtained:

k	$n(\mathscr{R})$	$n(\mathscr{T})$
0	2·35	2·50
0·1	2·40	2·30
0·2	2·41	2·06

Figure 6.2 shows the graphical representation of this data; the intersection of the two curves occurs where $n = 2.38$ and $k = 0.054$. In order to obtain maximum accuracy with the method, d should be an odd multiple of $\lambda/4$.

The process can become rather tedious if a large number of values of n and k are required for dispersion behaviour of a particular film; also, in this

122

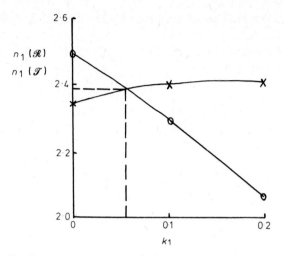

Figure 6.2 Graphical interpolation of data from Hadley's curves (after Heavens 1964).

case, there will inevitably be values of d/λ for which the method becomes insensitive. However, it is a useful technique for problems where only a limited number of values is needed and also it provides a check for results produced by computer programs based on some of the later methods.

6.3   Bennett and Booty's method

We have seen that as n and k cannot be given as explicit functions of $\mathscr{R}$ and $\mathscr{T}$, the mathematical solution of equations (6.3)–(6.5) to produce n and k will be somewhat complicated. The expressions are nonlinear, so the problem may be considered as an optimisation exercise whereby we seek values of n and k to minimise the squares of residuals between the left and right hand sides of the equations; if the equations are to be satisfied exactly, this minimum value will be zero. Fortunately, the availability of large computers makes this kind of problem relatively straightforward to solve, particularly in this case, where at a single wavelength, only two unknowns will be involved.

Bennett and Booty (1966) published a method for determining optical constants which is based on this idea, and applied it to thin metal films. They measured $\mathscr{R}$ and $\mathscr{T}$ for the film at normal incidence and also measured the physical thickness of the film interferometrically, from fringes of equal chromatic order. They then used a thin-film computer program which calculated $\mathscr{R}$ and $\mathscr{T}$ for input values of n, k and d to obtain values of n and k which minimised $|\mathscr{R}_{calc} - \mathscr{R}_{exp}|$ and $|\mathscr{T}_{calc} - \mathscr{T}_{exp}|$ (the subscripts calc and exp refer to the calculated and experimental values respectively). Their method is basically a univariate search technique; first $|\mathscr{R}_{calc} - \mathscr{R}_{exp}|$

is minimised with respect to n, then $|\mathcal{T}_{\text{calc}} - \mathcal{T}_{\text{exp}}|$ is minimised with respect to k; this strategy is not a good one for general optimisation problems, but in this case, n and k are apparently not highly correlated quantities and the technique worked fairly well. Their results for the 346 Å silicon film on fused quartz are shown in figure 6.3. Bennett and Booty have since extended their method to cover the case of a metal film on an absorbing substrate (1969).

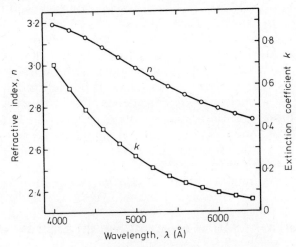

Figure 6.3 Bennett and Booty's results for the 346 Å silicon film (after Bennett and Booty 1966).

6.4 Abelès and Thèye's method

The method of Abelès and Thèye (1966) is also based on the solution of the equations

$$\mathcal{R}_{\text{exp}} - \mathcal{R}(n, k) = 0.$$

$$\mathcal{T}_{\text{exp}} - \mathcal{T}(n, k) = 0, \tag{6.7}$$

but the Newton–Raphson method is used to obtain the solution in place of the univariate search technique. Initial values of n and k are chosen (we may call these n_0 and k_0) either using knowledge of bulk refractive index values, or from other physical considerations, then $\mathcal{R}_0 = \mathcal{R}(n_0, k_0)$ and $\mathcal{T}_0 = \mathcal{T}(n_0, k_0)$ are calculated, together with the partial derivatives $(\partial\mathcal{R}/\partial n)_0$, $(\partial\mathcal{R}/\partial k)_0$, $(\partial\mathcal{T}/\partial n)_0$, $(\partial\mathcal{T}/\partial k)_0$. If second and higher order partial derivatives are ignored

$$\Delta\mathcal{R} = \mathcal{R}_{\text{exp}} - \mathcal{R}_0 = \left(\frac{\partial\mathcal{R}}{\partial n}\right)_0 \Delta n_0 + \left(\frac{\partial\mathcal{R}}{\partial k}\right)_0 \Delta k_0,$$

$$\Delta\mathcal{T} = \mathcal{T}_{\text{exp}} - \mathcal{T}_0 = \left(\frac{\partial\mathcal{T}}{\partial n}\right)_0 \Delta n_0 + \left(\frac{\partial\mathcal{T}}{\partial k}\right)_0 \Delta k_0, \tag{6.8}$$

and the solution to this linear system of two equations in two unknowns provides the values of Δn_0 and Δk_0. The calculation may then be repeated with the better approximations $n_0 + \Delta n_0$ and $k_0 + \Delta k_0$ replacing n_0 and k_0. The iteration is continued until $\mathcal{R}_0$ and $\mathcal{T}_0$ agree with $\mathcal{R}_{exp}$ and $\mathcal{T}_{exp}$ to within desired tolerance values (usually fixed by the experimental accuracy of the measurements).

The main advantage of this method over the previous one is that n and k are varied simultaneously in the search for the solution, and this improves the convergence. In general there may be several possible solutions; the choice of the true one is aided by physical knowledge of the material – if one is obtaining dispersion results at a large number of wavelengths, the results at the previous wavelength may be used as the starting point for the current search. Both the Abelès and Thèye, and the Bennett and Booty methods may be applied at normal or oblique incidence. The former has been used at the Institut d'Optique, Paris for many years, during which time values of optical constants of thin films of metal and alloys have been obtained over a wavelength range 200–2500 nm; however, for fairly thin films (whose thicknesses are of the order of 200–300 nm) of certain materials, there are regions where one cannot obtain the solution of equations (6.8).

6.5 Calculation of optical constants and thickness by Ward *et al*

In the two methods just described, values of physical thickness are measured experimentally for use in the computer program; Ward *et al* (1969) tried to develop a method which would yield the thickness, d, in addition to the values of n and k in the course of the computation. In order to obtain enough 'independent' parameters to determine n, k and d one needs to use measurements of $\mathcal{R}$ and $\mathcal{T}$ at non-normal incidence, with the s- and p-components of polarisation measured separately. In fact, four measurements, $\mathcal{R}_s$, $\mathcal{R}_p$, $\mathcal{T}_s$ and $\mathcal{T}_p$ were made and the function

$$y = (\mathcal{R}_{p\mathrm{exp}} - \mathcal{R}_p(n, k, d))^2 + (\mathcal{T}_{p\mathrm{exp}} - \mathcal{T}_p(n, k, d))^2$$
$$+ (\mathcal{R}_{s\mathrm{exp}} - \mathcal{R}_s(n, k, d))^2 + (\mathcal{T}_{s\mathrm{exp}} - \mathcal{T}_s(n, k, d))^2 \tag{6.9}$$

minimised, using a modified form of the Nelder and Mead simplex technique (1965). However, it was found that unless a very stringent 'stopping' criteria was employed, no unique solution was obtainable for all three parameters and it was necessary to modify the objective function (6.9) by adding the term

$$-c \exp(-(d - D)^2/2\sigma^2),$$

where D is the mean measured thickness, and σ the standard deviation in the measurements. Further investigation of sensitivity of methods for measuring optical constants by Ward and Nag (1970) showed that it is difficult to find regions in the parameter space where *n, k* and *d* could be calculated simultaneously. Unfortunately, this later work involved the solution of ill-conditioned equations, so the results have to be treated with caution. The overall results seem to indicate that $\mathcal{R}_s$, $\mathcal{R}_p$, $\mathcal{T}_s$ and $\mathcal{T}_p$ may not be truly independent parameters for use in this type of work and in general better results are obtained if experimental measurements of film thickness are used.

6.6 Other single wavelength methods

Ruiz-Urbeita *et al* (1971a, b) have developed a variation of the turning value method for determining optical constant data, but unfortunately a very thick film is needed in order to obtain enough turning values for dispersion information over a spectral range. Baldini and Rigaldi (1970) proposed a method for determining optical constants and film thickness based on measurements of reflectance and transmittance from both sides of the substrate; however, this appears to be liable to produce errors arising from non-uniqueness of solution which we have noted in other methods.

One promising method reported in the literature is due to Miller and Taylor (1971), who use an optimised reflection ratio method, based on measurements of the ratio of the reflection coefficient for incident light polarised parallel and perpendicular to the plane of incidence. Unfortunately, their results and sensitivity analysis apply only to values of *n* and *k* lying in the ranges $1 \cdot 0 \leqslant n \leqslant 4 \cdot 0$, $1 \cdot 0 \leqslant k \leqslant 4 \cdot 0$, and the accuracy of the method is limited to ± 5% of the *n* and *k* values, which is far too large to be tolerable for use in multilayer filter design applications. However, it may prove possible to extend the method to cover dielectric thin-film materials, and to improve the tolerance accordingly.

6.7 Hansen's theory for optical characterisation

In the course of research studies on electrochemical and solid state phenomena, Hansen developed a method which may be used to determine the optical properties of many different films over a wide wavelength range. Unlike the methods previously described in this chapter, he considered a thin-film system consisting of several layers deposited on a substrate; in general the optical parameters of the substrate and some of the layers are known, and the remaining unknown optical constants are determined by inverting the set of nonlinear transcendental equations (1.27)–(1.31) which characterise the system. For systems which are well conditioned, the process of numerical inversion can be accomplished with almost negligible error, but care has to be taken that the equations do not become ill conditioned (this would occur in the case of multiple roots, for example). If N optical parameters are to be determined, it is necessary to have N independent optical measurements. Practical limitations in the measurement procedures make it difficult to determine more than three or four optical parameters at one time.

The method used to invert the equations is based on the generalised secant method, described by Barnes (1965), and has certain similarities with methods described by Powell (1965) and Peckham (1970) which have been used by other workers in this field. In order to generate a good starting point for the method, the computer is used to generate a 'proper guess' based on norm and dispersion values supplied to a modified random guess routine. Once values are known at one wavelength, they can be used as initial guesses for neighbouring wavelengths. Hansen found it most convenient to make photometric measurements of $\mathscr{R}$ and $\mathscr{T}$ using a Cary 14 spectrophotometer and to represent these in terms of absorbancies.

The inversion program was also used to determine the error in each of the calculated parameters, caused by the error in measurements. In addition, there are often errors involved in the model used, for example, in assuming that the films are homogeneous and isotropic. In practice the measurement sensitivities may be very low, resulting in a large error in one of the parameters sought. The sensitivity can be expressed in terms of an error matrix: if three energy absorption measurements $\mathscr{A}_1$, $\mathscr{A}_2$ and $\mathscr{A}_3$ are used to calculate n, k and d/λ for a particular film in the configuration, the error matrix is given by

$$
\mathbf{E} = \begin{bmatrix}
\dfrac{\mathscr{A}_1}{n}\left(\dfrac{\partial n}{\partial \mathscr{A}_1}\right)_{\mathscr{A}_2,\mathscr{A}_3} & \dfrac{\mathscr{A}_1}{k}\left(\dfrac{\partial k}{\partial \mathscr{A}_1}\right)_{\mathscr{A}_2,\mathscr{A}_3} & \dfrac{\mathscr{A}_1}{(d/\lambda)}\left(\dfrac{\partial(d/\lambda)}{\partial \mathscr{A}_1}\right)_{\mathscr{A}_2,\mathscr{A}_3} \\[2em]
\dfrac{\mathscr{A}_2}{n}\left(\dfrac{\partial n}{\partial \mathscr{A}_2}\right)_{\mathscr{A}_3,\mathscr{A}_1} & \dfrac{\mathscr{A}_2}{k}\left(\dfrac{\partial k}{\partial \mathscr{A}_2}\right)_{\mathscr{A}_3,\mathscr{A}_1} & \dfrac{\mathscr{A}_2}{(d/\lambda)}\left(\dfrac{\partial(d/\lambda)}{\partial \mathscr{A}_2}\right)_{\mathscr{A}_3,\mathscr{A}_1} \\[2em]
\dfrac{\mathscr{A}_3}{n}\left(\dfrac{\partial n}{\partial \mathscr{A}_3}\right)_{\mathscr{A}_1,\mathscr{A}_2} & \dfrac{\mathscr{A}_3}{k}\left(\dfrac{\partial k}{\partial \mathscr{A}_3}\right)_{\mathscr{A}_1,\mathscr{A}_2} & \dfrac{\mathscr{A}_3}{(d/\lambda)}\left(\dfrac{\partial(d/\lambda)}{\partial \mathscr{A}_3}\right)_{\mathscr{A}_1,\mathscr{A}_2}
\end{bmatrix}
$$

$$(6.10)$$

A value of unity for any element of $\mathbf{E}$ means that the optical parameter has been determined to the same accuracy as the energy absorption, whereas a value of 10 would mean that the relative error of the parameter involved is ten times that of the corresponding energy absorption. Thus one would aim to obtain an error matrix with all elements less than or equal to one. Hansen gives examples of error matrices obtained for a number of metal films. For normal incidence measurements of $\mathscr{T}$, $\mathscr{R}$ and $\mathscr{R}'$ (reflectance from the back surface of the substrate) on a doped tin oxide film at 500 nm, $n = 2 \cdot 0$,

$k = 0.004, d = 1000\,\text{nm}$

$$\mathbf{E}_{\mathscr{TRR}'} = \begin{bmatrix} 0.3 & 1.4 & 0.1 \\ 3 & 0.9 & 3 \\ 5 & 2.5 & 5 \end{bmatrix},$$

whereas the $\mathscr{T}$, $\mathscr{R}$ method (used by Bennett and Booty, and Abelès and Thèye) gives for a copper film with $n = 1.52, k = 2.48, d = 18.5\,\text{nm}$

$$\mathbf{E}_{\mathscr{TR}} = \begin{bmatrix} 2 & 2 \\ 2.2 & 2.9 \end{bmatrix}.$$

It is difficult to obtain optical constants of films with a high k value, and Hansen gives a table of values showing the experimental parameters and resulting error analyses for several methods. This is reproduced in table 6.1. Only the maximum error in each matrix column is given. Unfortunately from the multilayer designer's point of view, he does not give any results for films with very low k values. It is clear, however, that his method is a very powerful one.

6.8   Kramers Kronig analysis method

Nilsson (1968) suggested a method for calculating optical constants using only transmission data for a limited wavelength region. In order to do this, a dispersion relation is used; it is important to remember that no extrapolation outside the measured region should be made when applying this method.

The relation used is that between the amplitude inside the substrate, $(T_{\mathrm{f}})^{1/2}$ and the phase change on transmission τ_{f}. The former is related to the measured transmittance $\mathscr{T}$ by

$$\mathscr{T} = \frac{T_f n_{\mathrm{sub}} \mathscr{T}_{\mathrm{sub}}}{[1 - \mathscr{R}_{\mathrm{back}}(1 - \mathscr{T}_{\mathrm{sub}})]}, \tag{6.11}$$

where $\mathscr{T}_{\mathrm{sub}}$ is the transmittance of the substrate and $\mathscr{R}_{\mathrm{back}}$ the reflectance from the back surface of the film inside the substrate. The function

$$\mathrm{Re}\,\{\ln\,[(T_{\mathrm{f}})^{1/2}\exp{(\mathrm{i}\tau)}]/(v - v_0)\}$$

is integrated along a closed contour in the complex frequency plane and produces an expression for the phase shift

$$\tau(v_0) = \frac{2v_0}{\pi} \int_0^\infty \frac{\ln{(T_{\mathrm{f}})^{1/2}}}{v^2 - v_0^2}\,\mathrm{d}v - 2\pi v_0 d. \tag{6.12}$$

This integral is divided into three parts, separated by the limits of the

Table 6.1 Error analysis, high-k films; $n_1 = 1·52$, $n_3 = 1$, $k_3 = O$. Parallel polarisation, ∥; perpendicular polarisation, ⊥; internal reflection, i; external reflection, e.

Method	n	k	h/λ	θ_1	θ_2	θ_3	$\mathscr{A}_1$	$\mathscr{A}_2$	$\mathscr{A}_3$	Error matrix			Comments
$\mathscr{TR}'\mathscr{R}$	0·062	43	0·05	0	0	0	0·4	0·235	0·223	>64	>12	~100	Useless
$\mathscr{TR}$	0·062	43	0·05	0	0	...	0·4	0·223	...	10·6	10·2	...	Poor
$\mathscr{TR}'$	0·062	43	0·05	0	0	...	0·4	0·235	...	7·4	7·0	...	Poor
$\mathscr{TR}_{\perp i}$	0·062	43	0·05	0	45	...	0·4	0·019	...	0·97	0·99	...	Excellent
$\mathscr{TR}_{\perp i}$	0·062	43	0·05	0	60	...	0·4	0·011	...	0·97	0·99	...	Excellent
$\mathscr{TR}_{\parallel i}$	0·062	43	0·05	0	45	...	0·4	0·11	...	1·66	2·1	...	Excellent
$\mathscr{TR}_{\parallel i}$	0·062	43	0·05	0	60	...	0·4	0·51	...	0·98	0·99	...	Excellent
$\mathscr{TR}_{\parallel i}\mathscr{R}_{\parallel i}$	0·062	43	0·05	0	37	60	0·4	0·30	0·051	1·3	0·99	1·8	Excellent
$\mathscr{TR}_{\perp i}$	0·062	43	0·05	0	37	...	0·4	0·1	...	4	3·7	...	Fair
$\mathscr{TR}_{\perp e}\mathscr{R}_{\perp e}$	0·062	43	0·05	0	37	60	0·4	0·17	0·10	28	19	58	Useless
$\mathscr{TR}_{\perp e}\mathscr{R}_{\parallel i}$	0·062	43	0·05	0	45	...	0·4	0·1	...	10	9·6	...	Poor
$\mathscr{TR}_{\parallel i}\mathscr{R}_{\parallel i}$	0·062	43	0·025	0	37	65	0·13	0·5	0·03	1·5	1	2·6	Excellent
$\mathscr{TR}'$	0·068	73	0·025	0	0	0	0·63	0·118	0·123	18	17	>100	Useless
$\mathscr{TR}$	0·068	73	0·025	0	0	...	0·63	0·118	...	12	11	...	Poor
$\mathscr{TR}'$	0·068	73	0·025	0	0	...	0·63	0·123	...	...	...	...	Poor
$\mathscr{TR}_{\perp i}$	0·068	73	0·025	0	45	...	0·63	0·01	...	1·0	0·99	...	Good
$\mathscr{TR}_{\perp i}$	0·068	73	0·025	0	60	...	0·63	0·006	...	0·98	0·99	...	Good
$\mathscr{TR}_{\parallel i}$	0·068	73	0·025	0	45	...	0·63	0·073	...	1·3	0·98	...	Excellent
$\mathscr{TR}_{\parallel i}$	0·068	73	0·025	0	60	...	0·63	0·03	...	0·98	0·99	...	Excellent
$\mathscr{TR}_{\parallel i}\mathscr{R}_{\parallel i}$	0·068	73	0·025	0	37	60	0·63	0·24	0·03	4	1·0	...	Good
$\mathscr{TR}_{\perp i}\mathscr{R}_{\parallel i}$	0·068	73	0·025	0	37	60	0·63	0·05	0·005	18	0·9	29	Good for κ only

measured region; the outer integrals are written

$$\frac{2v_0}{\pi} \int_0^{v_1} \frac{\ln{(T_f)^{1/2}}\, dv}{v^2 - v_0^2} = A(v_0) \ln \left| \frac{v_1 + v_0}{v_1 - v_0} \right| , \qquad (6.13)$$

$$\frac{2v_0}{\pi} \int_{v_2}^{\infty} \frac{\ln{(T_f)^{1/2}}\, dv}{v^2 - v_0^2} = B(v_0) \ln \left| \frac{v_2 + v_0}{v_2 - v_0} \right| , \qquad (6.14)$$

where A and B are slowly varying functions of v_0,

$$A(v_0) = \frac{1}{\pi} \left(\ln{(T_f(v_1))^{1/2}} - 2v_0 \ln \left| \frac{v_1 - v_0}{v_1 + v_0} \right| \int_0^{v_1} \frac{\ln{(T_f(v))^{1/2}}\, dv}{v^2 - v_0^2} \right) ,$$

$$\qquad (6.15)$$

$$B(v_0) = -\frac{1}{\pi} \left(\ln{(T_f(v_2))^{1/2}} + 2v_0 \ln \left| \frac{v_2 - v_0}{v_2 + v_0} \right| \int_{v_2}^{\infty} \frac{\ln{(T_f(v))^{1/2}}\, dv}{v^2 - v_0^2} \right) .$$

$$\qquad (6.16)$$

The integration over the measured region $v_1 - v_2$ may be performed using Simpson's rule. The approximation is then made that A and B are independent functions of v_0; this turns out to be valid unless v_0, is chosen close to one of the limits of the measured range, v_1 or v_2, in which case both A and B approach zero. To determine A and B, n and k must be calculated by a different method for two frequency values, so that the phase shifts may be calculated and substituted into equation (6.12). It should also be noted that the formula (6.11), relating T_f and $\mathscr{T}$ also contains $\mathscr{R}_{\text{back}}$, which is dependent on n and k; as a first approximation this is taken to be zero and when prelimininary values of n and k have been determined, better values of $\mathscr{T}_{\text{back}}$, T_f, A and B are obtained and the process repeated.

To perform the calculations over the spectral range (v_1, v_2) one uses as input data the transmittances at the measured frequencies, the two sets of n and k values at the reference frequencies, the film thickness and the refractive index of the substrate. Nilsson illustrates the method by giving results of a CdI film, for which 45 points were used. His results are shown in figure 6.4 and we see from this illustration that there is good agreement with the $\mathscr{R}$, $\mathscr{T}$ method. The full arrows show the frequencies used for the A, B determination; if the frequencies at the broken arrows are used instead, the values of n and k change by about $+0\cdot05$ and $-0\cdot03$ respectively above 3 eV. This method has been used successfully on several hundred samples of different materials, but once again few results are available for weakly absorbing films.

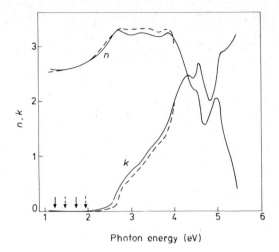

Figure 6.4 The optical constants of a 100 Å CdI$_2$ film obtained from Kramers Kronig analysis of transmission data (full curve) and from the R−T measurements method (broken curve) (after Nilsson 1968).

6.9 Determination of optical constants of weakly absorbing thin films

In 1969 Liddell and Fawcett (1969) developed a program based on Bennett and Booty's method and applied it to dielectric films in which a small amount of absorption was present. Figure 6.5 shows the refractive index results obtained for films of titanium dioxide and magnesium fluoride; it is seen that although the results are acceptable for the most part, allowing for a possible error in thickness measurement, they are not as good as those obtainable for some metal films (the program was tested using the Bennett–Booty data illustrated in figure 6.3, and produced identical results). A slight improvement was obtained when Powell's sum of squares technique (1965) was used in place of the univariate search method.

On extending the investigation to the determination of optical constants in the near ultraviolet, in collaboration with Dr P Clapham of the National Physical Laboratory, the results were far from satisfactory. Very little reliable data is available at present for thin-film materials in the ultraviolet, particularly for relatively high-index materials; the materials studied were the oxides of thorium, aluminium, zirconium and neodymium, together with neodymium fluoride, and this study was an attempt to provide dispersive information over the wavelength range 215–633 nm for these materials.

The films were deposited by electron bombardment onto Spectrosil B substrates; two, denoted by an asterisk, at a temperature of 250°C, the rest

131

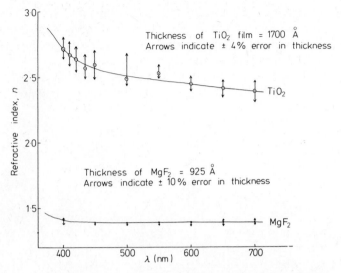

Figure 6.5 Results of Liddell and Fawcett for dielectric films of titanium dioxide and magnesium fluoride.

at the ambient temperature. The measurements of $\mathscr{R}$ and $\mathscr{T}$ were obtained using an instrument based on the design of Shaw and Blevin (1964) and checked on a single beam spectrophotometer and a purpose built single beam reflectometer; the thickness measurements were made using the Talystep mechanical stylus instrument. Particular attention was paid to the polishing of the substrate and to cleaning and deposition procedures in order to keep the scattering losses as low as possible. The overall uncertainty associated with the photometric measurements was estimated as ±0·5 and that of the thickness measurements as ±1 nm (or 1%, whichever is the larger).

Table 6.2 shows the result of applying the program to one of the Al_2O_3 films; although the numerical values are good, the physical behaviour of n

Table 6.2 Results for the 153·7 nm Al_2O_3* film using the Bennett–Booty type program.

λ (nm)	d/λ	n	k	$\Delta\mathscr{R}(\%)$	$\Delta\mathscr{T}(\%)$
215	0·715	1·926	0·0026	0·00	−0·01
225	0·683	1·789	0·0011	0·00	−0·01
250	0·615	1·790	0·0006	0·00	0·00
300	0·512	1·800	0·0005	0·08	0·00
350	0·439	1·680	0·0005	−0·05	−0·21
400	0·384	1·685	0·0010	−0·08	−0·29
450	0·342	1·702	0·0000	0·00	0·00
502	0·306	1·735	0·0000	0·01	0·09
546	0·282	1·659	0·0003	0·00	0·00
633	0·243	1·589	0·0003	0·02	−0·02

132

is unrealistic. In order to investigate this behaviour, and to obtain a clearer picture of the properties of the $\mathscr{R}$ and $\mathscr{T}$ functions than that given by the Hadley–Dennison curves, a library subroutine was used to produce graphs of contours of $\mathscr{R}$, $\mathscr{T}$ and $\mathscr{A}$ as functions of n and k. Figure 6.6 illustrates the results for ranges of values of n and k of interest to the multilayer designer, and it is clear that for both 'sensitive' and 'insensitive' regions, $\mathscr{R}$

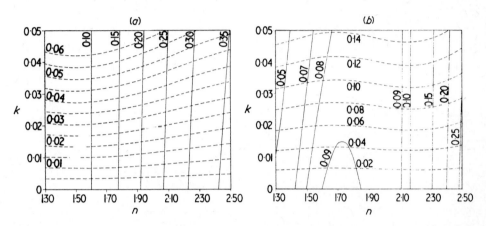

Figure 6.6   Contours of constant $\mathscr{R}$ (full curves) and constant $\mathscr{A}$ (broken curves): (a) for $d/\lambda = 0\cdot12$; (b) for $d/\lambda = 0\cdot25$ (after Liddell 1974).

may be treated as a function of n only and $\mathscr{A}$ $(= 1 - (\mathscr{R} + \mathscr{T}))$ as a function of k only, so in this case the univariate search used by Bennett and Booty is as good as any, whereas for a wider range of values of n and k (figure 6.7), a more efficient optimisation technique, such as that suggested by Abelès and

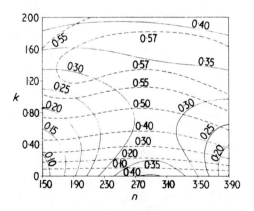

Figure 6.7   Contours of constant $\mathscr{R}$ (full curves) and constant $\mathscr{A}$ (broken curves) for use in metal-film calculations ($d/\lambda = 0\cdot12$) (after Liddell 1974).

Thèye, should be used. Figure 6.6 also shows that for certain values of d/λ, $\mathcal{R}$, $\mathcal{T}$ and $\mathcal{A}$ are slowly varying functions of n, and this can cause problems of ill conditioning of the equations. Nilsson (1968) and Nestell and Christy (1972) used similar curves in their optical constant calculations; the latter analysed a number of methods for obtaining optical constant data from normal and oblique incidence measurements of a selection of two or three of the quantities $\mathcal{R}$, $\mathcal{T}$, $\mathcal{R}_s$, $\mathcal{R}_p$, $\mathcal{T}_s$ and $\mathcal{T}_p$, and also obtained the approximate sensitivity of the n and k values by giving a width to the contours appropriate to the experimental error of measurement. Figure 6.8 illustrates their result for values obtained from measurements of $\mathcal{R}_s$ and $\mathcal{R}_p$ at $60°$ angle of incidence.

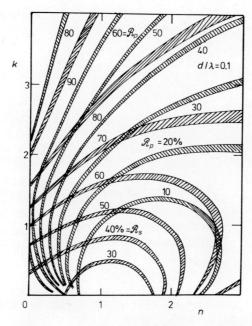

Figure 6.8 Contours of constant $\mathcal{R}_s$ and $\mathcal{R}_p$ at $60°$ angle of incidence and $d/\lambda = 0\cdot1$ (after Nestell and Christy 1972).

6.10   Use of dispersion formulae

The obvious solution to the problem was to attempt to include the appropriate dispersion behaviour of refractive index in the formulation. The absorption values were reasonable both from the numerical and physical point of view, so a dispersion formula for this seemed unnecessary. Two methods were tried by Liddell and Staerck (1972):

(1) The refractive indices of the materials were forced to obey the inequalities

$$n_i > n_{i+1} > 1, \qquad \text{for } i = 1, 2, \ldots$$

and

$$\left| \frac{n_i - n_{i-1}}{\lambda_i - \lambda_{i-1}} \right| < \left| \frac{n_{i-1} - n_{i-2}}{\lambda_{i-1} - \lambda_{i-2}} \right|, \qquad i = 3, 4, \ldots, \qquad (6.17)$$

where n_1, n_2, . . . are measurements of refractive index over a range of increasing values of λ. This is achieved by a standard technique for dealing with simple constraints in optimisation, namely that of transforming the variables n_i into new variables x_i where

$$x_1 = (n_1 - 1)^{1/2},$$

$$x_2 = a \sin \left[\left(\frac{n_2 - 1}{n_1 - 1} \right)^{1/2} \right], \qquad (6.18)$$

$$x_i = a \sin \left[\left(\frac{A - B}{A} \right)^{1/2} \right], \qquad i = 3, 4, \ldots,$$

and

$$A = \frac{n_i - n_{i-1}}{\lambda_i - \lambda_{i-1}}, \qquad B = \frac{n_{i-1} - n_{i-2}}{\lambda_{i-1} - \lambda_{i-2}}.$$

To obtain the appropriate values of x_i, the merit function

$$F(\mathbf{x}) = \sum_{\lambda} (\mathscr{R}_{\exp} - \mathscr{R}_{\text{calc}})^2 \qquad (6.19)$$

was minimised. The values of the absorption coefficient, k_i, at the wavelengths λ_i were then obtained by minimising

$$F(\mathbf{x}) = \sum_{\lambda} [(\mathscr{R}_{\exp} + \mathscr{T}_{\exp}) - (\mathscr{R}_{\text{calc}} + \mathscr{T}_{\text{calc}})]^2, \qquad (6.20)$$

where $x_i = k_i^{1/2}$, which ensures only positive values for k are used in the calculation. The second minimisation could be performed at each wavelength in turn using a single variable technique. Powell's method (1965) was again used for the minimisations.

(2) The second method was based on the assumption that n obeys a dispersion formula of the (modified) Sellmeier form:

$$n^2 - 1 = \frac{\lambda^2}{A + B\lambda^2}. \qquad (6.21)$$

This particular formula gives a good fit for known data on refractive index of dielectric materials in the visible region of the spectrum; its use was suggested by Dobrowolski (private communication, 1968). Powell (1969) also suggested the use of the Drude–Sellmeier formula for determining optical constants of metal films. Again, a range of wavelengths is chosen, n is calculated at each wavelength using formula (6.21), then the function

$$F(A, B) = \sum_{\lambda} (\mathscr{R}_{\text{exp}} - \mathscr{R}_{\text{calc}})^2 \qquad (6.22)$$

is minimised to give the best values of A and B for the spectral range. Once A and B have been found, the functions

$$f(k_i) = (\mathscr{R}_{\text{exp}} + \mathscr{T}_{\text{exp}} - \mathscr{R}_{\text{calc}} - \mathscr{T}_{\text{calc}})^2 \qquad (6.23)$$

can be minimised to give the k values (or equation (6.20) may be used instead). Both Powell's method (1965) and Peckham's method (1970) have been applied to this formulation and give similar results. The flow diagram for the program (RESPECT) is shown in figure 6.9. If the values of n and k are known to be correlated, the minimisation may be performed with respect to the n and k values simultaneously; in this case the merit function may be defined as

$$F(\mathbf{x}) = \sum_{\lambda} [(\mathscr{R}_{\text{exp}} - \mathscr{R}_{\text{calc}})^2 + (\mathscr{R}_{\text{exp}} + \mathscr{T}_{\text{exp}} - \mathscr{R}_{\text{calc}} - \mathscr{T}_{\text{calc}})^2], \quad (6.24)$$

where

$$x_i = k_i^{1/2}, \qquad i = 1, 2, \ldots, m,$$
$$x_{m+1} = A,$$
$$x_{m+2} = B.$$

Note that there are $2m$ independent terms in the sum of squares in (6.24).

Liddell and Staerck (1972) reported the results of preliminary investigations for two Al_2O_3 films. Of the two methods described above, the second was the more successful, so the investigation of other materials was based on this technique (Liddell 1974). Table 6.3(a) shows the results obtained for one of the films and figure 6.10 illustrates the experimental and calculated values of $\mathscr{R}$ and $\mathscr{T}$. These results proved about average for the set; table 6.4(a) shows the best results, obtained for the neodymium fluoride film, and table 6.5(a) the results obtained for the thorium oxide* film, which had the worst value of merit function. These results were obtained using the functions (6.22) and (6.20); however, they were recalculated, using (6.24), to check, and virtually identical results were produced — the final merit function values differed by less than 1% in all cases.

Examination of these results shows discrepancies at certain wavelengths which are larger than one would expect. The pattern of error seemed to suggest a possible error in the thickness measurement, so the thickness was included in the set of design variables and the equations re-optimised. This procedure is quite valid as long as $m > 3$, since equation (6.24) is then overdetermined even with the inclusion of d as x_{m+3}. The results are shown

136

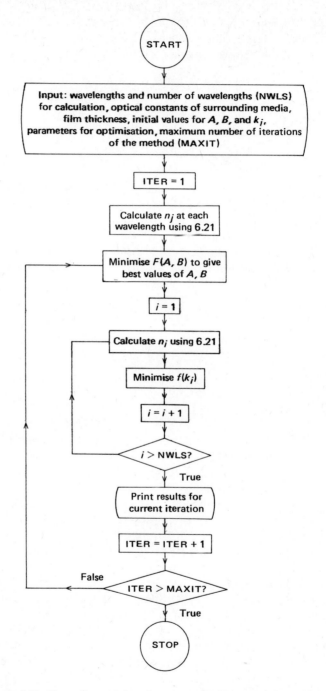

Figure 6.9 Flow diagram for the program RESPECT (after Liddell and Staerck 1972).;

Table 6.3 Dispersion formula results for the Al_2O_3* film (after Liddell 1974).

λ (nm)	(a) Homogeneous film, thickness d_a = 153·7 nm				(b) Homogeneous film with optimised thickness d_b = 158·6 nm				(c) Graded film with optimised thickness d_c = 158·6 nm			
	n	k	$\Delta \mathcal{R}$ (%)	$\Delta \mathcal{T}$ (%)	n	k	$\Delta \mathcal{R}$ (%)	$\Delta \mathcal{T}$ (%)	n	k	$\Delta \mathcal{R}$ (%)	$\Delta \mathcal{T}$ (%)
215	1·808	0·003	−1·2	+1·2	1·805	0·003	+0·1	−0·1	1·805	0·003	+0·1	−0·1
225	1·792	0·001	−0·1	+0·1	1·785	0·001	−0·1	+0·1	1·786	0·001	0·0	0·0
250	1·760	0·001	+1·2	−1·2	1·749	0·001	+0·2	−0·2	1·750	0·001	+0·1	−0·1
300	1·723	0·001	−0·8	+0·8	1·707	0·001	+0·2	−0·2	1·709	0·001	+0·2	−0·2
350	1·703	0·000	−0·7	+0·7	1·684	0·000	−0·1	+0·1	1·686	0·000	−0·1	+0·1
400	1·690	0·000	−0·1	+0·1	1·669	0·000	−0·1	+0·1	1·673	0·000	−0·1	+0·1
450	1·682	0·000	+0·4	−0·4	1·660	0·000	+0·2	−0·2	1·663	0·000	+0·2	−0·2
502	1·675	0·000	+0·2	−0·2	1·653	0·000	+0·2	−0·2	1·657	0·000	+0·1	−0·1
546	1·672	0·000	0·0	0·0	1·649	0·000	+0·2	−0·2	1·653	0·000	+0·1	−0·1
633	1·666	0·000	−0·4	+0·4	1·643	0·000	−0·2	+0·3	1·647	0·000	−0·3	+0·4
A	$-0·639 \times 10^4$ nm²				$-0·760 \times 10^4$ nm²				$-0·736 \times 10^4$ nm²			
B	0·579				0·6072				0·6023			
α	—				—				−0·0040			
Final merit function	$0·486 \times 10^{-3}$				$0·247 \times 10^{-4}$				$0·224 \times 10^{-4}$			

Table 6.4 Dispersion formula results for the NdF film (after Liddell 1974).

λ (nm)	(a) Homogeneous film, thickness d_a = 80·5 nm				(b) Homogeneous film with optimised thickness d_b = 85·9 nm				(c) Graded film with optimised thickness d_c = 88·4 nm			
	n	k	$\Delta\mathcal{R}$ (%)	$\Delta\mathcal{T}$ (%)	n	k	$\Delta\mathcal{R}$ (%)	$\Delta\mathcal{T}$ (%)	n	k	$\Delta\mathcal{R}$ (%)	$\Delta\mathcal{T}$ (%)
215	1·698	0·011	−0·2	+0·2	1·660	0·010	−0·1	+0·1	1·661	0·010	+0·1	−0·1
225	1·684	0·009	+0·1	−0·1	1·651	0·008	−0·1	+0·1	1·652	0·008	−0·2	+0·2
250	1·656	0·004	+0·8	−0·8	1·634	0·004	+0·5	−0·5	1·636	0·004	+0·2	−0·2
300	1·623	0·003	−0·3	+0·4	1·613	0·003	0·0	0·0	1·616	0·003	−0·2	+0·2
350	1·605	0·002	−0·4	+0·4	1·601	0·002	+0·2	−0·2	1·605	0·002	+0·1	−0·1
400	1·594	0·000	−0·3	+0·3	1·594	0·000	+0·1	−0·1	1·598	0·000	+0·1	−0·1
450	1·587	0·000	−0·1	+0·1	1·589	0·000	0·0	0·0	1·593	0·000	0·0	0·0
502	1·582	0·000	0·0	0·0	1·585	0·000	−0·1	+0·1	1·589	0·001	−0·1	+0·1
546	1·578	0·000	+0·1	−0·1	1·583	0·000	−0·1	+0·1	1·587	0·000	−0·1	+0·1
633	1·574	0·001	+0·3	−0·3	1·580	0·001	0·0	0·0	1·584	0·001	0·0	0·0
A	$-0·766 \times 10^4$ nm^2				$-0·516 \times 10^4$ nm^2				$-0·492 \times 10^4$ nm^2			
B	0·696				0·6813				0·6751			
α	—				—				−0·019			
Final merit function	$0·113 \times 10^{-3}$				$0·328 \times 10^{-4}$				$0·137 \times 10^{-4}$			

Table 6.5 Dispersion formula results for the ThO$_2$* film (after Liddell 1974).

λ (nm)	(a) Homogeneous film, thickness d_a = 72·0 nm				(b) Homogeneous film with optimised thickness d_b = 74·3 nm				(c) Graded film with optimised thickness d_c = 71·3 nm			
	n	k	$\Delta \mathscr{R}$ (%)	$\Delta \mathscr{T}$ (%)	n	k	$\Delta \mathscr{R}$ (%)	$\Delta \mathscr{T}$ (%)	n	k	$\Delta \mathscr{R}$ (%)	$\Delta \mathscr{T}$ (%)
215	2·068	0·030	+0·2	−0·2	2·032	0·029	+0·7	−0·8	1·969	0·030	−0·2	+0·2
225	2·038	0·020	+0·1	−0·1	2·008	0·019	0·0	0·0	1·947	0·019	+0·2	−0·2
250	1·984	0·008	−1·0	+1·1	1·963	0·007	−1·8	+1·9	1·906	0·007	+0·1	−0·1
300	1·922	0·007	−2·7	+2·8	1·910	0·006	−2·3	+2·4	1·857	0·006	−0·3	+0·3
350	1·888	0·005	−1·7	+1·9	1·881	0·004	−0·8	+0·8	1·831	0·004	+0·2	−0·2
400	1·868	0·005	−1·0	+1·1	1·864	0·004	−0·2	+0·3	1·814	0·004	+0·1	−0·1
450	1·854	0·003	−0·4	+0·5	1·852	0·003	0·0	0·0	1·804	0·003	0·0	0·0
502	1·845	0·003	0·0	0·0	1·844	0·002	+0·2	−0·2	1·796	0·003	+0·1	−0·1
546	1·837	0·003	+0·1	−0·2	1·838	0·003	+0·1	−0·1	1·791	0·003	−0·1	+0·1
633	1·830	0·003	+0·5	−0·6	1·831	0·004	+0·2	−0·2	1·784	0·004	−0·1	+0·1
A	$-0{\cdot}628 \times 10^4$ nm^2				$-0{\cdot}551 \times 10^4$ nm^2				$-0{\cdot}578 \times 10^4$ nm^2			
B	0·441				0·4387				0·4725			
α	—				—				0·173			
Final merit function	$0{\cdot}129 \times 10^{-2}$				$0{\cdot}966 \times 10^{-3}$				$0{\cdot}237 \times 10^{-4}$			

140

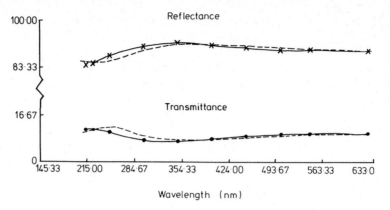

Figure 6.10 Experimental and calculated results for $\mathcal{R}$ and $\mathcal{T}$ for Al_2O_3. Crosses, calculated values of transmittance; full circles, calculated values of reflectance; broken curves, experimental values (after Liddell and Staerck 1972).

in column (*b*) of the tables; there is a marked improvement in all cases with the exception of the thorium oxide* film. In the light of these results, independent measurements of thickness were made on the zirconium oxide and aluminium oxide* samples, using Talystep, multiple beam Fizeau interferometry and the Dyson shearing interferometer; these later measurements agreed reasonably well with the original results, so it appears that the latter were not in error to the extent suggested by the numerical results. One other cause of discrepancy could be that the theoretical model does not take into account the spectral bandwidth of the photometric measurements.

Another possible cause of error is that the refractive index of the film may be inhomogeneous; in order to investigate this, the above method was altered by including a grading of index parameter in the set of design variables after the initial iteration. Two models were used; in the first, the film was split into sub-layers of thickness $d/5$, having indices $n-2\alpha, n-\alpha, n, n+\alpha$, $n+2\alpha$, where n is the index obtained during the first iteration of the program. To avoid unnecessary complication, the dispersion of this grading effect is ignored; this model is based on an idea suggested by Jacobsson (1963). The second model was suggested by Bousquet (1956) and has also been used successfully by Clapham (1972) – the film is split into two sub-layers, the outer having a thickness $2d/3$ and the remaining 'couche de passage' of thickness $d/3$ with a slightly different value of n; this model has been found to give a satisfactory prediction of many effects of inhomogeneity observed in practice. The improvement of results in the current study was similar for both models, although the two-layer structure was marginally better overall and much better for the thorium oxide* film. Tables 6.3–6.5 include the graded index results in column (*c*) – the effect of inhomogeneity is clearly very small for the first two films, but the ThO_2* results give a significant indication of inhomogeneity in structure, which is perhaps not surprising as this was the thinnest film of the set, and could therefore be expected to be influenced more by surface effects than the others.

Neodymium oxide and aluminium oxide have been known to exhibit colour centre absorption, brought about by electron bombardment of the film during its growth (Clapham 1972); this could give rise to discontinuities in the n and k values, so the dispersion formula used for the calculation of n may be oversimplified.

Pelletier (private communication, 1974) has used a number of dispersion formulae in optical constant determination, and obtains good results by using a large number of wavelengths for the calculation. His work seems to indicate that formula (6.21) is oversimplified — a more accurate model for dispersion behaviour is given by

$$n = A + B/\lambda^2 + C/\lambda^4, \tag{6.25}$$

or

$$n = A + B/\lambda^2 + C/\lambda^4 + D/\lambda^6, \tag{6.26}$$

although neither is perfect for all weakly absorbing films. More recently, Pelletier *et al* (1976) have produced results which indicate that for certain films the curve $n(\lambda)$ shows discontinuities due to defects of structure. In order to measure optical constants they use a completely automatic spectrophotometer which measures values of $\mathcal{R}$, $\mathcal{R}'$ and $\mathcal{T}$ at normal incidence over the range 200–700 nm. These measurements provide the data for a computer program in which the values of d, n, and k are successively determined over a large spectral range. This method seems to produce very good results.

7 Thickness Monitoring Techniques and Methods for Analysing Errors in Monitoring

Several classes of design method used for multilayer filters have been discussed in detail and, in the previous chapter, the problem of obtaining optical constant data to a required degree of accuracy was also considered. This leads on to a final type of problem which is encountered by the filter designer; how sensitive is any particular design to errors which may arise during manufacture of the filter? As well as errors in optical constant data, there may be errors in the value of the thickness of any layer and in the uniformity of thickness over the surface of the filter. Macleod (1969) has discussed this latter problem in detail; in this text it is more appropriate to concentrate on the methods used to analyse errors in layer thickness. These methods may also be used to analyse the effect of different refractive index values from those assumed by the designer. The problem of analysing the tolerance of a particular design to errors arising in the manufacturing process has been of interest to filter designers for many years; recently, significant advances in the subject have been made by Macleod and his colleagues, and by Giacomo, Bousquet, Pelletier and their co-workers at Marseilles, France.

Various characteristics such as mass, resistance, optical density, reflectance, transmittance or the rates of change of these quantities with respect to either optical thickness or wavelength may be employed to monitor the film thickness. The two most widely used devices are optical monitoring and the quartz crystal oscillator which measures the mass as the film is deposited. Both are discussed in detail by Macleod in chapter 9 of his book. The main disadvantage of the latter is that its sensitivity decreases as the mass of the film increases: also, it must operate at temperatures below 120°C, so it cannot be used in conjunction with a heated substrate. It is a useful device for controlling the rate of evaporation during deposition, and may therefore often be used to complement an optical thickness monitor. An optical monitoring system consists of a light source illuminating the test substrate, together with a detector for analysing the reflected or transmitted light – originally, the eye was used for this purpose, but normally a photo-electric device is used now. The process is, however, still subject to both operator and instrumental error. The technique most commonly used is the 'turning value' method: the transmittance or reflectance of a single layer (or a stack of equally thick layers) with respect to optical thickness passes through an extremum when the optical thickness is an integral number of quarter waves. If the monitoring wavelength, λ_0, is chosen so that the desired optical thickness of the layer is $\lambda_0/4$, the turning value serves as a convenient point to stop the deposition. Monitoring curves for a 10-layer Fabry–Perot filter are shown in figure 7.7.

Some early work on errors was done by Heavens (1954) who devised a simple method for calculating errors in quarter-wave systems, based on Abelès' representation of the multilayer in which each matrix is characteristic of an interface between the layers in the filter (1948a) (equation 1.25). His results indicated that errors in individual layers in the stack had very little effect on the value of the final reflectance, although they can cause a shift of the wavelength at which the maximum reflectance occurs. Lissberger (1959) described a method for analysing errors which also involved reflectances at the interfaces; when he applied his method to the Fabry–Perot interference filter he showed that the most critical layer with respect to sensitivity to error is the spacer, followed by its neighbouring layers, and as one moves further away from the spacer, the layers become less sensitive.

Giacomo *et al* (1959) investigated the influence of random variations in layer thickness on the width of the pass band of an interference filter, when various types of broad band reflecting multilayers were used as the reflecting elements. As has already been stated in chapter 2, they showed that a necessary condition for such variations to have minimum effect on the position of the pass band is

$$\left|\frac{\partial \psi}{\partial \lambda}\right| = 4\pi n D_m, \qquad (7.1)$$

where $\psi(\lambda)$ is the average value of the phase change on reflection in the spacer at the spacer–mirror boundaries at wavelength λ, n is the refractive index of the spacer and D_m is the geometrical thickness of one of the mirrors. It is interesting to note that a broad band filter such as that reported by Baumeister and Stone (1956) or Heavens and Liddell (1966) comes nearer to fulfilling this condition than a classical stack. Giacomo *et al* also showed that layers at the centre of the filter forming the mirror had the greatest sensitivity to error, and on investigating the effects of 'roughness', they proved that the design least affected by roughness is one in which the sensitivities of all layers are proportional to their thickness.

7.1 Computer simulation of errors in monitoring

Smiley and Stuart (1963) used an analog computer for error analysis; their results for the three-layer configuration

$$\text{Air}/4_H L 4_H/\text{Air}$$

indicated that a 1% error in the thickness of the spacer layer caused an appreciable dip in the centre of the pass band, a 5% error reduced the peak transmittance to 75% and enhanced the dip, whereas a 10% error essentially ruined the pass band. At the present time it would seem to be more sensible to use a digital computer with automatic graph plotting facilities, rather than go to the trouble of setting up an analog computer to simulate the performance of the multilayer. It is a fairly simple matter to write a computer program to simulate the reflectance as measured during filter deposition, which may be treated as a function of optical thickness at any chosen wavelength. The simulation may be extended through any number of layers. This type of program was used in an investigation by Smith and Seeley (1968) to predict the influence of monitoring errors and to facilitate the choice of a suitable monitoring wavelength. Table 7.1 shows the results

Table 7.1 Percentage error in thickness for an assumed 4% observational error in reflectivity for a 10-layer Fabry–Perot filter designed to operate at $15\,\mu$m. L represents a quarter wave of ZnS, H a quarter wave of PbTe.

Layer	Monitoring wavelength			
	$3\lambda_0/4$	$7\lambda_0/8$	λ_0	$9\lambda_0/8$
Substrate (Ge)				
L	4 (min)	2	7 (min)	2
H	11 (max)	1	7 (min)	1
L	3 (min)	4	7 (min)	3
H	18 (max)	3	7 (min)	3
L	6 (min)	5	7 (min)	5
HH	2 (min)	4	7 (min)	5
L	21 (max)	2	7 (min)	2
H	2 (min)	1	7 (min)	0·5
L	12 (max)	9	7 (min)	6
H	1 (min)	2	7 (min)	2

they obtained for a 10-layer Fabry–Perot filter, designed to operate at $15\,\mu$m, when the observational error in reflectivity at termination was assumed to be 4%. The monitoring wavelength, λ_0, was 3·75 μm (i.e. fourth-order monitoring was employed) and other monitoring wavelengths around this value were employed to investigate the comparative effect of errors from a 'turning value' monitoring system (λ_0 or $3\lambda_0/4$) and from monitoring at a wavelength away from the turning value ($7\lambda_0/8$ or $9\lambda_0/8$). It is seen from the table that the former system generally gave rise to larger errors in individual layers than the latter. In addition, the overall effect of errors on the filter pass band was investigated; results for a 6-layer Fabry–Perot filter are shown in table 7.2; In columns (*a*) and (*c*), the filters deposited have errors in the first high-index layer, which gives rise to a change in the turning value of the following (low-index) layer if the monitoring proceeds without correction, but there is no thickness error compensation in the

Table 7.2 Effect of errors on the position of the pass band of a 6-layer Fabry–Perot filter, with and without error compensation. (Monitoring wavelength $3\lambda_0/4$). L represents a quarter wave of ZnS, H a quarter-wave of PbTe.

Layer	Phase thicknesses (deg)			
	(a)	(b)	(c)	(d)
L	270	270	270	270
H	240	240	300	300
L	280	280	260	260
H H	540	540	540	540
L	270	260	270	280
H	270	300	270	240
Reflectance at end of deposition	0·96	0·99	0·96	0·99
Shift of minimum of reflectance (cumulative scale of phase thickness)	$+10°$	$0°$	$-10°$	$0°$

remaining layers; columns (b) and (d) represent filters in which similar errors have been made, but where compensating errors have been made in the corresponding layers on the opposite side of the spacer. Thus, the investigation showed that if all layers are monitored on a single substrate (direct monitoring), there can be an advantage in monitoring at a wavelength away from the turning value, and if no correction is made to allow for previous errors, there is a tendency for errors to accumulate.

Pelletier and Giacomo (1972a) also reported results of computer simulation studies of evaporation monitoring. In particular they studied the situation where an inaccurate knowledge of the refractive indices used lead to a systematically incorrect monitoring of the layer thicknesses (figure 7.1).

7.2 Baumeister's sensitivity analysis method (1962)

It can be seen from equations (1.26)–(1.29) that the transmittance or reflectance of a multilayer is a function of the thickness, d_i, of each layer. Thus, for some wavelength λ_j, the change in transmittance, $\Delta\mathcal{T}_j$, or reflectance, $\Delta\mathcal{R}_j$, produced by errors Δd_i in the layer thicknesses is given by

$$\Delta\mathcal{R}_j = -\Delta\mathcal{T}_j = \sum_{i=1}^{N} \frac{\partial\mathcal{R}}{\partial d_i} \Delta d_i + O(\Delta d_i)^2, \qquad (7.2)$$

if the refractive indices of the layers remain constant. The $\partial\mathcal{R}/\partial d_i$ may be computed either by using a finite difference approximation or by an exact method. Following Baumeister's analysis, the characteristic matrix product

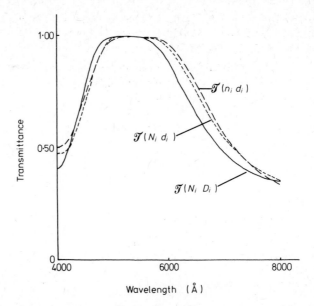

Figure 7.1 Results of a computer simulation for a three-layer coating: n_i, d_i are exact values of index and thickness; N_i represents an index value containing an error, and D_i is the resulting thickness error caused by N_i if the turning value method is used (after Pelletier and Giacomo 1972).

is represented by

$$\mathbf{M} = \begin{bmatrix} C_1 & iC_2 \\ iC_3 & C_4 \end{bmatrix}, \qquad (7.3)$$

then

$$\frac{\partial \mathscr{R}}{\partial \beta_i} = n_0 \frac{\partial \mathscr{R}}{\partial B_1} \frac{\partial C_1}{\partial \beta_i} + n_0 n_{\text{sub}} \frac{\partial \mathscr{R}}{\partial B_2} \frac{\partial C_2}{\partial \beta_i} + n_{\text{sub}} \frac{\partial \mathscr{R}}{\partial B_3} \frac{\partial C_4}{\partial \beta_i} + \frac{\partial \mathscr{R}}{\partial B_4} \frac{\partial C_3}{\partial \beta_i}, \quad (7.4)$$

where $\beta_i = 2\pi n_i d_i / \lambda_j$ and $B_1 = n_0 C_1$, $B_2 = n_0 n_{\text{sub}} C_2$, $B_3 = n_{\text{sub}} C_4$, $B_4 = C_3$. Note that the argument β_i only appears in the ith characteristic matrix product, so

$$\begin{bmatrix} (\partial C_1/\partial \beta_i) & i(\partial C_2/\partial \beta_i) \\ i(\partial C_3/\partial \beta_i) & (\partial C_4/\partial \beta_i) \end{bmatrix} = M_1 M_2 \ldots M_{i-1} M_i' M_{i+1} \ldots M_N, \quad (7.5)$$

and the differentiated matrix $\mathbf{M}_i$ is given by

$$\mathbf{M}_i = \begin{bmatrix} -\sin\beta_i & \dfrac{i}{n_i}\cos\beta_i \\ in_i\cos\beta_i & -\sin\beta_i \end{bmatrix}. \qquad (7.6)$$

This method requires only $4N - 3$ matrix multiplications to evaluate $\partial \mathscr{R}/\partial d_i$

for each layer in the filter, whereas the method based on a finite difference approximation requires N^2 multiplications. The derivatives $\partial \mathcal{R}/\partial d_i$ give a direct indication of the sensitivity of various layers in the filter, and can be computed over any desired spectral range. Often it is convenient to compute the change in reflectance for percentage change in thickness — $(\partial \mathcal{R}/\partial d_i)/d_i$ — in order to compare designs for various spectral regions; $(\partial \mathcal{R}/\partial d_i)/d_i$ is a dimensionless quantity and, in this case, d_i may refer to either optical or to physical thickness. Figure 7.2 illustrates Baumeister's results for a 5-layer

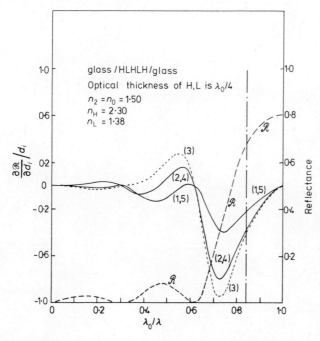

Figure 7.2 The change in computed reflectance per fractional change in thickness of the layers of a five-layer stack (after Baumeister 1962).

quarter-wave stack, and figure 7.3 (*a*) and (*b*) the results obtained by Seeley *et al* (1973) which were used to compare the performance of two low-pass filter designs. These diagrams show the usefulness of the method in indicating at one and the same time which layer is most sensitive to errors and which part of the spectral range is most critical from the error point of view. Another point to note in these designs is that the symmetry of the design produces a corresponding symmetry of error pattern in the layers, so that we have the possibility of thickness-error compensation in layers which are symmetric with respect to the central layer of the filter. However, it would not be easy to extend the technique to analyse cumulative errors in all layers of the filter, so another method of analysis is needed to complement this one.

148

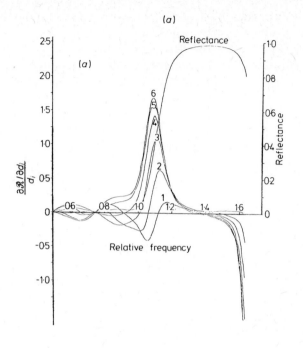

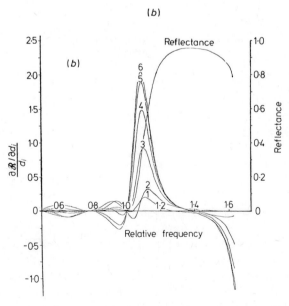

Figure 7.3 Spectral sensitivity of low-pass filter designs: (*a*) circuit analogy design; (*b*) equivalent index design (after Seeley *et al* 1973).

7.3 Ritchie's analysis of random errors in narrow band filters

Baumeister's method has the disadvantage that only the errors in one layer of the filter are considered – the other layers are assumed to be unchanged. Ritchie (1970) adopted an alternative approach of introducing random errors into each layer of the filter, in order to study the effect of simultaneous changes in all layer thicknesses.

The thickness d of each layer in the filter is assumed to be a random variable determined by the Gaussian distribution function

$$P(d) = \frac{1}{\sigma(2\pi)^{1/2}} \exp\left[-(d - \bar{d})/2\sigma^2\right], \tag{7.7}$$

where $\bar{d}$ is the mean thickness of the layer, σ the standard deviation of the distribution and $P(d)$ is the probability that an error $(d - \bar{d})$ will occur. To obtain an approximation to $P(d)$, one may use a computer library subroutine to generate a sequence of K random numbers X_j lying in the range $(0, 1)$ and then apply the formula

$$P_1 = \frac{\sum\limits_{j=1}^{K} X_j - \frac{K}{2}}{(K/12)^{1/2}}. \tag{7.8}$$

P_1 approaches the true normal distribution as $K \to \infty$. Then

$$d = P_1 \sigma + \bar{d}. \tag{7.9}$$

Figure 7.4 shows Ritchie's results for a long-wave pass filter and a double half-wave filter, both designed for use in the infrared. The analysis applies to the case where different monitoring substrates are used for each layer (indirect monitoring), so that if reflectance errors are kept to within 5%, the system should be able to produce both types of filter, but the yield may be low. Another method which uses indirect monitoring is a variant of the turning value method in which the wavelength is chosen so that the final thickness is in excess of a quarter wavelength, i.e. about $0.3\lambda_0$. However, a complication can arise in that a layer deposited on a fresh monitoring surface may exhibit different characteristics from one deposited onto the existing multilayer.

7.4 Investigation of errors in the turning value monitoring method

For the case where turning value monitoring is employed, with all layers deposited on the same substrate, Ritchie's analysis would imply an almost zero yield; however, both Macleod (1972) and Bousquet et al (1972) have shown that an error compensation process occurs which ensures that the

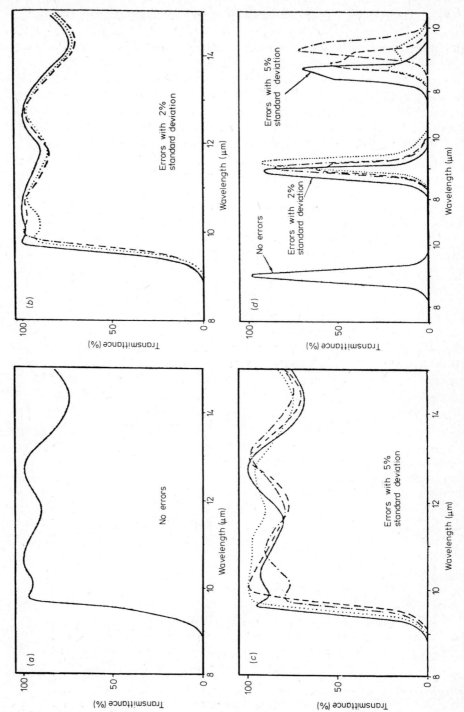

Figure 7.4 Ritchie's design for a long-wave pass filter and a double half-wave filter both designed for use in the infrared (after Macleod 1969).

potential accuracy in monitoring complete narrow band filters is very high. Moreover, Fornier and Pelletier (1971) showed that no other criterion for terminating deposition will allow as good an automatic compensation as the turning value condition.

Macleod (1972) devised a method of error analysis to explain theoretically how this situation occurs. As in Ritchie's method, errors are simulated by a set of random errors, drawn from a normal distribution, but errors in turning value of reflectance rather than in thickness are chosen, and the cumulative effect if all layers are deposited on one substrate is studied. At any stage in the deposition process, the multilayer already deposited may be represented on an Argand diagram by a circle whose centre is $((n^2 + \alpha^2 + \beta^2)/2\alpha, 0)$ ($\alpha + i\beta$ is the equivalent admittance of the previous layers, and n is the refractive index of the layer currently being deposited) and the phase thickness, δ, of the latter may be represented on the same diagram by considering the circle whose centre is $(0, n(\tan \delta - 1/\tan \delta)/2)$ which passes through the point $(n, 0)$. For $\delta = 0, (2k + 1)\pi/2$ (k integral), this locus is the real axis, whereas $\delta = (2k + 1)\pi/4$ produces a circle whose centre is the origin. Both isoreflectance contours and the admittance loci are circles with centres on the real axis, so turning values of reflectance correspond to intersections of the admittance loci with the real axis, whatever the starting point of the layer. Figures 7.5 (a) and (b) illustrate the admittance loci for a 4-layer Fabry–Perot filter for an ideal case and for the case where there are thickness errors in the first two layers. If isoreflectance contours and a δ scale are added to the Argand diagram, then reflectance errors may be converted to layer thickness errors. MacLeod's results for a 10-layer Fabry–Perot filter

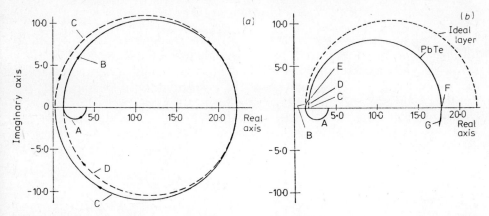

Figure 7.5 (a) Admittance locus of the filter Ge/LHLLH/Air where L represents ZnS ($n_L = 2\cdot3$) and H a 1/4 wave PbTe ($n_H = 5\cdot4$). Curves A, C and E, ZnS; curves B and D, PbTe. (b) Admittance locus of the first two layers of the same filter when there is an overshoot of about 1/8 wave optical thickness in the first layer. Full curve: A, ZnS; B, overshoot − extra ZnS; C, effective starting point of PbTe; D, this part of PbTe missing; E, end of ZnS − start of PbTe; F, turning value, G, overshoot − extra PbTe.

152

are shown in figure 7.6 and table 7.3. In his paper, Macleod also gives results for a double half-wave filter. Although there were large thickness errors in the layers, the overall performance of the filters appears fairly satisfactory; the reason for this is seen by consideration of figure 7.5 again — the layer thickness errors are not as important as the difference between the ideal and actual intersections of the high-index layer with the real axis. However, it should be noted that this error compensation process does not operate if higher-order monitoring is used.

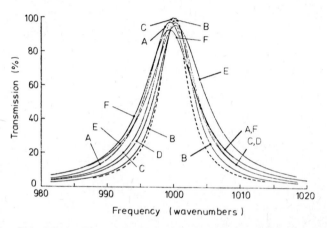

Figure 7.6 Macleod's results for 1% standard deviation reflectance errors in a 10-layer Fabry–Perot filter designed for use in the infrared. The broken curve is the performance without error (first-order monitoring). Table 7.3 gives reflectance and thickness errors for each layer (after Macleod 1972).

Macleod also developed a method for predicting permissible errors in turning value monitoring, which would serve as an indicator for the layers needing higher accuracy in monitoring. The error in any particular layer has two components, corresponding to the overshoot or undershoot in the previous layer and that in the layer itself. Consider two layers K and $K + 1$, whose characteristic admittances are n_K, n_{K+1}, where the thickness of the Kth is in error and the $(K + 1)$th layer has been deposited on the Kth so that it intersects the real axis in the Argand diagram at $n + \Delta n$ instead of n. Macleod proved that

$$\frac{\Delta n}{n} = \frac{(1 + n)^4 (n_{K+1}^2 - n_K^2)}{4n^2(n_K^2 - 1)(n_{K+1}^2 - n^2)} \Delta \mathscr{R} = P(n_K, n_{K+1}, n) \Delta \mathscr{R}, \qquad (7.10)$$

i.e. $\Delta n/n$ is of the same order as $\Delta \mathscr{R}$, even though the thickness errors may be an order of magnitude larger. Also it can be shown that $\Delta n/n$ is propagated through the remaining layers with no change in magnitude. $P(n_K, n_{K+1}, n)$ is therefore a good indicator of the relative tolerance of a particular layer. The

Table 7.3 Reflectance errors at turning values with corresponding layer thickness errors for the infrared filter design illustrated in figure 7.6.

Curve	A		B		C		D		E		F	
Layer	$\mathscr{R}$ error (%)	δ error (%)	$\mathscr{R}$ error (%)	δ error (%)	$\mathscr{R}$ error (%)	δ error (%)	$\mathscr{R}$ error (%)	δ error (%)	$\mathscr{R}$ error (%)	δ error (%)	$\mathscr{R}$ error (%)	δ error (%)
1 (L)	−0·436	−5·842	0·647	7·123	0·879	8·321	0·893	8·390	1·325	10·254	−0·947	−8·642
2 (H)	0·667	15·585	0·145	4·326	0·595	10·518	0·400	8·186	0·090	1·998	0·825	17·916
3 (L)	−0·125	−7·355	−0·848	−7·122	0·860	−0·815	−0·331	−7·158	−2·093	−9·204	−0·028	−7·071
4 (H)	1·419	38·478	0·128	14·605	−0·940	−33·681	0·182	16·151	−1·726	−37·936	−0·919	−31·014
5 (L)	−0·079	−19·717	−1·180	−14·334	1·860	24·900	−0·814	−13·649	−0·072	17·796	0·754	20·670
6 (HH)	1·249	1·942	1·781	4·029	−0·826	−3·495	−1·146	−0·121	0·342	1·063	−1·222	−2·946
7 (L)	−0·788	−35·792	0·045	−1·725	0·557	30·981	0·464	32·819	0·697	23·360	1·401	45·518
8 (H)	−0·628	52·494	−2·093	−21·637	1·352	−46·947	1·057	−47·144	0·668	−49·682	0·358	−63·388
9 (L)	0·819	21·996	0·417	18·420	0·178	3·071	0·252	5·975	−1·910	−29·934	0·397	12·291
10 (H)	−0·779	−37·392	−1·349	−30·504	−0·037	−20·400	−1·956	−28·072	−0·376	50·152	0·410	−31·576
Δ(half-width)	1·07		0·17		0·69		0·51		1·23		1·47	
Calculated half-width (cm⁻¹)	10·4		5·9		8·5		7·5		11·2		12·3	
Measured † half-width (cm⁻¹)	8·8		6·1		7·6		7·3		10·2		9·6	

†i.e. measured from accurately computed curves.

values of P for the Fabry–Perot filter illustrated in figure 7.6 are shown in table 7.4. From these data it may be noted that the most critical layers are the two low-index layers following the spacer. If a low-index spacer is used the spacer itself would be the most critical layer, so it is generally preferable

Table 7.4 Values of the layer sensitivity factor, P, for the filter design illustrated in figure 7.6.

Layer	Index	P
Substrate	4·0	
1 (L)	2·3	1·1
2 (H)	5·4	5·6
3 (L)	2·3	0·5
4 (H)	5·4	25·8
5 (L)	2·3	1·4
6 (HH)	5·4	−1·1
7 (L)	2·3	−175·0
8 (H)	5·4	−0·4
9 (L)	2·3	−39·0
10 (H)	5·4	

to use a high-index spacer. An approximate expression for the increase in bandwidth of the Fabry–Perot was derived:

$$\Delta(\text{half-width}) = \tfrac{1}{2} \left(\left| \sum_a P \cdot \Delta \mathcal{R} \right| + \left| \sum_b P \cdot \Delta \mathcal{R} \right| \right), \tag{7.11}$$

where the summations apply to the reflecting layers on either side of the spacer. Table 7.3 includes values of Δ (half-width), using the P values given in table 7.4. The approximation appears justified for cases where the increase in bandwidth is 20% or less. From further studies Macleod found that the sensitivity to error increases with the number of layers in the filter, and for this reason it is often better to increase the order of the spacer rather than the number of layers. First order monitoring curves for the Fabry–Perot filter with no errors, and with reflectance errors of 1% standard deviation are shown in figure 7.7.

In another paper (1973), Macleod investigated the effect of absorption on the inaccuracy of the turning value method. As in the earlier work, a large number of filter profiles were computed, each containing random errors in the layer thicknesses, but in addition absorption was included; the level of absorption in the layers was set at a value such that k/n was 0·001 – this is the order of absorption one expects in practice when dealing with infrared materials. Figure 7.8 shows the results for five such profiles, and from this we see that the errors cause the bandwidth to increase, and that the filters with errors have a higher transmittance than those without, since the errors reduce the effect of absorption in the reflectors on either side of the spacer.

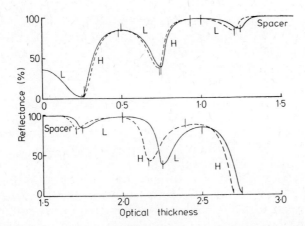

Figure 7.7 First-order monitoring curves for the Fabry—Perot filter design illustrated in figure 7.6. The full line is the case without error. The optical thickness is in units of λ_0, the monitoring wavelength (after Macleod 1972).

Macleod showed that the relative increase in peak transmittance $(\Delta \mathcal{T}_p / \mathcal{T}_p)$ in relation to the relative increase in half-width is bounded by

$$\frac{\Delta \mathcal{T}_p}{\mathcal{T}_p} = \frac{(\mathcal{A}/\mathcal{T})[2 + (2 + \mathcal{A}/\mathcal{T})(\Delta H/H)] \cdot (\Delta H/H)}{[1 + (\Delta H/H)]^2} , \qquad (7.12)$$

when the errors in the reflectors are balanced, and

$$\frac{\Delta \mathcal{T}_p}{\mathcal{T}_p} = 2(\mathcal{A}/\mathcal{T}) \cdot (\Delta H/H) - (1 + 4\mathcal{A}/\mathcal{T})(\Delta H/H)^2 \qquad (7.13)$$

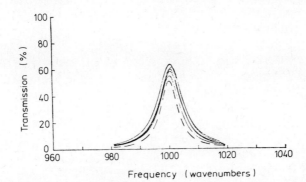

Figure 7.8 A 10-layer Fabry—Perot filter which includes reflectance errors in the turning values of 1% standard deviation and absorption $(K/n = 0.001)$. The broken line is the filter performance without the turning value errors (after Macleod 1973).

156

for the case of unbalanced reflectors. $\mathcal{T}$ and $\mathcal{A}$ represent the transmittance and absorption of the reflector in the absence of error. The overall results of his investigation indicated that for these levels of absorption, the error compensation process will not be seriously affected.

7.5 'Dynamic' errors in monitoring

Macleod and Richmond (1974) continued the error investigation research by first classifying the errors into two types — 'static' and 'dynamic'. The errors we have considered so far in this chapter are static in that they are created when the deposition of a layer is terminated, and remain stable after that time; examples are an overshoot or an undershoot of the true turning value when stopping deposition, or a change in refractive index value of a particular layer. Macleod and Richmond showed that for this latter example, the error propagated through the filter is

$$\left| \left(\frac{\Delta n}{n} \right)_{\text{filter}} \right| \simeq \left| \frac{2\Delta n_f}{n_f} \right| , \qquad (7.14)$$

where n_f is the ideal value of the index of a particular layer, but in practice the value used contains an error Δn_f. ($\Delta n_f/n_f$ is assumed small for the analysis to hold.) The overall effect will usually be small compared to errors caused by changes in layer thickness and can be ignored. (This is also borne out by the work of Pelletier and Giacomo, which was illustrated in figure 7.1.)

Dynamic errors, however, are not stable with time. They can be caused by such factors as temperature changes, or drift in the monitoring system, which can cause changes in the properties of the layers of the filter as time progresses. Macleod and Richmond studied the latter; the temperature problem was investigated by Pelletier *et al* (1974).

Drifts in monitoring can be interpreted as thickness errors, the error for the completed filter being expressed relative to the monitoring wavelength at the end of deposition. To a first approximation, dynamic errors may be treated as though they occurred between deposition of one layer and the next; it is also assumed that the turning values are determined exactly, and that a layer deposited earlier will suddenly change its properties before deposition of a later layer, so although the latter is monitored exactly to a turning value, it will contain a thickness error compensating the dynamic error. The effect of the process on the admittance loci is illustrated in figure 7.9.

If a layer, K, contains a dynamic error, Δd_K, it will produce an error Δd_{K+1} in the thickness of layer $K+1$, and $\Delta n/n$ in n, the admittance of

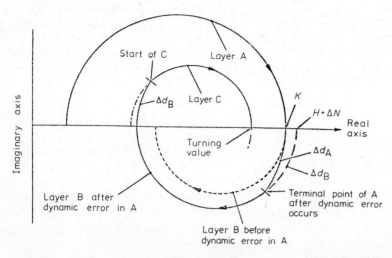

Figure 7.9 The effect of a dynamic thickness error on the admittance loci (after Macleod and Richmond 1974).

the multilayer at termination of the Kth layer in the absence of error, where

$$\Delta d_{K+1} = \frac{n_{K+1}}{n_K} \frac{n_K^2 - n^2}{n_{K+1}^2 - n^2} \Delta d_K = G_K \, \Delta d_K \tag{7.15}$$

and

$$\left(\frac{\Delta n}{n}\right)_{\text{filter}} = (-1)^{S-K} \left(\frac{n_{K+1}}{n_K} - \frac{n_K}{n_{K+1}}\right) G_K \, \Delta^2 d_K = H_K \, \Delta d_K, \tag{7.16}$$

for a filter with S quarter waves, in which we are considering errors in two adjacent layers. More generally, Macleod and Richmond define a dynamic error sensitivity factor Q_{qp} which is a measure of the effect of a dynamic error occurring in layer p during deposition of layer q. This is not so convenient as the sensitivity factor P occurring with static errors, since the filter admittance error is proportional to the square of the thickness error in a particular layer, i.e.

$$\left(\frac{\Delta n}{n}\right)_{\text{filter}} = Q_{qp} \, \epsilon_p^2, \tag{7.17}$$

where

$$\frac{\pi}{2} \epsilon_K = \Delta d_K = \frac{\pi}{2} G_{K-1} G_{K-2} \ldots G_p \epsilon_p, \tag{7.18}$$

so

$$Q_{qp} = \frac{\pi}{2} \sum_{K=p}^{2q-1} H_K (G_{K-1} \ldots G_p)^2, \tag{7.19}$$

158

and if dynamic thickness errors occur in several layers, the expression contains cross product terms. Figure 7.10 shows a plot of the complete set of Q_{qp} values for the multiple cavity filter

$$\text{Glass/HLHL(LHLHLHLHL)}^2\text{LHLH/Air}$$

designed for use in the visible region; L represents cryolite, $n = 1\cdot35$, and H zinc sulphide, $n = 2\cdot35$. These results led Macleod and Richmond to design a monitoring system which allows the most sensitive layers to be monitored separately from the rest of the filter. The layer has to be deposited on the original monitor as well so that the error compensation process is not destroyed. Also, to avoid monitoring directly onto a fresh glass substrate, the separate monitor is precoated with a quarter-wave high-index layer. Table 7.5 shows the results obtained for a number of double half-wave filters centred around 546 nm. These are a clear indicator of the improvement obtainable using this technique, particularly for very narrow band filters, and are a practical verification of the results obtained from the computer simulated production runs of filters containing both random reflectance errors and monitoring wavelength drift.

Preliminary investigations of the effect of using a narrow band filter to select the monitoring wavelength indicate that this may help to eliminate another source of error; further research is being carried out by Macleod and his group in order to quantify the effect.

Pelletier *et al* (1974) modified their computer simulation program to take account of the effects of temperature changes on the accuracy of the

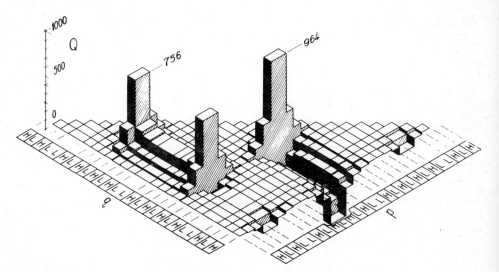

Figure 7.10 A plot of the complete set of values of the dynamic sensitivity factor, Q_{qp}, for the multiple cavity filter Glass/HLHL(LHLHLHLHL)^{2}LHLH/Air (after Macleod and Richmond 1974).

159

Table 7.5 Results obtained using Macleod and Richmond's separate monitoring technique for a number of multiple cavity filters designed for use in the visible region.

Design	Straight through monitoring		With monitor change		Improvement
	Bandwidth	Peak $\mathcal{T}$	Bandwidth	Peak $\mathcal{T}$	
A Glass/(HLH) LL (M) L (M) LL (M)/Air	4·2 per cent 22·5 nm	94	4·2 per cent 22·9 nm	93	–
B Glass/(HLHLH) LL (M) L (M) LL (M) L/Glass	1·5 per cent 8·0 nm	70	1·3 per cent 6·7 nm	90	16
C Glass/(HLHLH) HH (M) L (M) HH (M) L/Glass	0·89 per cent 4·9 nm	80	0·74 per cent 4·0 nm	82	20
D Glass/(HLHLHLHL) HH (M) L (M) HH (M) L/Glass	0·32 per cent 1·8 nm	68	0·27 per cent 1·5 nm	74	17
E Glass/(HLHLHLHL) HHHHH (M) L (M) HHHH (M) L/Glass			0·18 per cent 1·0 nm	75	
F Glass/(HLHLHLHLH) LL (M) L (M) LL (M) L/Glass	0·24 per cent 1·2 nm	82	0·20 per cent 1·1 nm	79	17
G Glass/(HLHLHLHLHL) HH (M) L (M) HH (M) L/Glass	0·18 per cent 1·0 nm	64	0·13 per cent 0·7 nm	65	30
H Glass/(HLHLHLHLHLH) LL (M) L (M) LL (M) L/Glass	Unable to make filter with straight through technique		0·07 per cent 0·4 nm	40	

(M) indicates a repeat of the structure enclosed in the first pair of brackets in each design.

monitoring process. They first considered the case of perfect monitoring (i.e. accurate termination of each layer when $\partial\mathcal{T}/\partial(nd) = 0$) with no errors in layer thickness, but including temperature changes both during and after production of the filter. This depends on the speed of deposition and on the thickness of the deposited films. They approximated by assuming a constant rate of deposition, so that the temperature change, X, is given by

$$X = (\theta_f - \theta_0)/P, \tag{7.20}$$

where P is the number of quarter waves in the filter, and θ_0, θ_f are the temperatures at the beginning and end of deposition. After deposition of the Kth layer, the optical thickness will be such that $(\partial\mathcal{T}/\partial(n_K d_K))\,\theta_K = 0$, and at this point the $K - 1$ previous layers will all differ from quarter waves because of the temperature change. At the end of the deposition process the final temperature is θ_f, but the filter will be used at temperature θ_0, so there is another change $(\theta_f - \theta_0)$ for all layers in the filter. In order to build the temperature changes into the simulation program, temperature coefficients for thickness (α) and refractive index (β) must be known. The coefficients for optical thickness (γ) can be measured: for zinc sulphide and cryolite at 546 nm these were found to be

$$\gamma_H = \frac{1}{n_H d_H}\frac{\partial(n_H d_H)}{\partial\theta} = 3 \times 10^{-5}, \qquad \gamma_L = \frac{1}{n_L d_L}\frac{\partial(n_L d_L)}{\partial\theta} = 3 \times 10^{-5},$$

$$\tag{7.21}$$

and since

$$\gamma_H = \alpha_H + \beta_H, \qquad \gamma_L = \alpha_L + \beta_L,$$

the coefficients for the bulk materials may be used as estimates, namely, $\alpha_H = 1 \times 10^{-5}$, $\beta_H = 2 \times 10^{-5}$, $\alpha_L = 4 \times 10^{-5}$, $\beta_L = -1 \times 10^{-5}$. The results of simulated runs for a Fabry–Perot filter design, taking account of these changes due to temperature, are shown in table 7.6 and figure 7.11. Further theoretical investigation by Roche *et al* (1976) resulted in a slight amendment of the γ values.

Pelletier *et al* (1974) continued their investigation by considering the effect of temperature changes and errors in layer thicknesses, in order to quantify the effect of the former on the error compensation mechanism; they studied the case of an error in a single layer and then that of systematic errors in all layers of the filter. Table 7.7 and figure 7.12 illustrate the results they obtained for a double half-wave filter, which had thickness errors of $\lambda_0/40$ in all layers. It would appear that temperature changes of the order of magnitude they considered would limit the bandwidth of the filter to not less than 0·6 nm; it is therefore important to keep the temperature of the monitoring substrate as constant as possible during deposition. The temperature change will tend to amplify any other errors in the monitoring process, and in particular, it can upset the error compensation mechanism.

Table 7.6 Simulation of the production of the $(HL)^{10}$ $6H$ $(LH)^{10}$ Fabry—Perot filter showing the effect of temperature shift during deposition.

Layer number	Ratio of geometric thickness at end of deposition (80°C) to perfect filter thickness	Ratio of geometric thickness after cooling to 20°C to perfect filter thickness
1 (H)	1·0005	1·00
2 (L)	1·0019	0·9995
3 (H)	1·0005	0·9998
4 (L)	1·0018	0·9994
5 (H)	1·0001	0·9996
6 (L)	1·0016	0·9993
7 (H)	1·00	0·9994
8 (L)	1·0015	0·9991
9 (H)	1·00	0·9993
10 (L)	1·0013	0·9990
11 (6H)	0·9994	0·9988
12 (L)	1·0003	0·9980
13 (H)	0·9975	0·9968
14 (L)	0·9977	0·9953
15 (H)	0·9929	0·9923
16 (L)	0·9894	0·9871
17 (H)	0·9779	0·9774
18 (L)	0·9627	0·9604
19 (H)	0·9289	0·9284
20 (L)	0·8669	0·8648
21 (H)	0·7178	0·7173
Indices		
Substrate (1·52)	1·5209	1·5200
ZnS (2·3662 at 546·1 nm)	2·3690 at 546·1 nm	2·3662 at 546·1 nm
Cryolite (1·3000)	1·2993	1·3000
Pass band		
λ_{max} (546·1 nm)	546·1 nm	545·3 nm
max (0·621)	0·683	0·531
$\Delta\lambda$ (0·27 nm)	0·3 nm	0·43 nm

N.B. There is an error in the original table in the publication in that optical thicknesses were quoted in place of geometrical thicknesses.

7.6 Monitoring systems which employ two or more wavelengths

Pelletier and Giacomo (1972b) agree with Macleod and his co-workers on the importance of using a technique in which the filter is monitored directly; if different monitoring substrates are used, errors due to the different geometrical configurations of the substrates and the source, and surface differences in the substrates themselves will inevitably occur. However, even with direct monitoring, the turning value method can lead to large errors

162

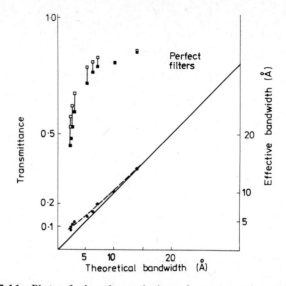

Figure 7.11 Plot of the theoretical performance of narrow band Fabry—Perot filters taking into account temperature shifts during monitoring against error free bandwidth. Full line, bandwidth of perfect filters; broken line, bandwidth of filters with temperature shift errors; open squares, peak transmittance of perfect filters; full squares, peak transmittance of filters with temperature shift errors (after Pelletier *et al* 1974).

Table 7.7 Effect of thickness errors of $\lambda_0/40$ in all layers of the DHW filter $(HL)^3 \ 10H \ (LH)^3 \ (HL)^3 \ 10H \ (LH)^3$ using turning value monitoring with and without temperature shifts during deposition. $\mathscr{T}_{max}$, maximum of transmittance; λ_{max}, corresponding wavelength; $\Delta\lambda$, bandwidth.

Perfect filters obtained including temperature shifts		
Perfect filter	80°C	20°C
$\lambda_{max} = 5461\,\text{Å}$ $\mathscr{T}_{max} = 0.882$ $\Delta\lambda = 10.5\,\text{Å}$	$\lambda_{max} = 5463\,\text{Å}$ $\mathscr{T}_{max} = 0.765$ $\Delta\lambda = 11.3\,\text{Å}$	$\lambda_{max} = 5453\,\text{Å}$ $\mathscr{T}_{max} = 0.810$ $\Delta\lambda = 10.9\,\text{Å}$

Error of $\lambda_0/40$ in all the layers of the filter		
Filter obtained with constant temperature	Filters obtained including temperature shifts 80°C	20°C
$\lambda_{max} = 5463\,\text{Å}$ $\mathscr{T}_{max} = 0.872$ $\Delta\lambda = 18.9\,\text{Å}$	$\lambda_{max} = 5463\,\text{Å}$ $\mathscr{T}_{max} = 0.812$ $\Delta\lambda = 20.3\,\text{Å}$	$\lambda_{max} = 5455\,\text{Å}$ $\mathscr{T}_{max} = 0.796$ $\Delta\lambda = 20.7\,\text{Å}$

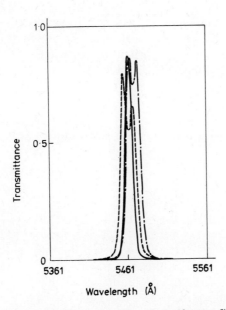

Figure 7.12 Spectral profile of the double half-wave filters described in table 7.7. Full curve, perfect filter; chain curve, filter with errors $\lambda_0/40$ in all layers; broken curve, filter with errors in layer thicknesses and with temperature shift changes during deposition of the layers (after Pelletier *et al* 1974).

in thickness of individual layers, since it is often difficult to locate the exact turning point. It might be better, therefore, to consider the use of a monitoring method in which $\partial \mathcal{T}/\partial(nd)$ is measured directly so that the criterion for terminating deposition is a zero reading. Unfortunately, it is not easy to measure this quantity directly; an alternative method consists of using three monitoring plates upon which are deposited thicknesses $n(d + \Delta d)$, nd, $n(d - \Delta d)$. When nd is an integral number of quarter waves, the transmittance of the first and third films will be equal, so this may be used as the criterion for stopping deposition; with this method, the problems of using separate monitoring substrates are inevitable, and it is not suitable for a filter with a large number of layers. Various workers have suggested the use of two monitoring wavelengths, e.g. Lissberger and Ring (1955). If the two wavelengths λ_1 and λ_2 are chosen so that for the required thickness $\mathcal{T}(\lambda_1) = \mathcal{T}(\lambda_2)$, one may stop evaporation when $|\mathcal{T}(\lambda_1) - \mathcal{T}(\lambda_2)| < \epsilon$, where ϵ is chosen arbitrarily small. Unfortunately, problems can arise if the response of the monitoring system differs for the two wavelengths, and one must take into account the effect of dispersion of refractive index.

Giacomo and Jacquinot (1952) developed a system whereby it was possible to measure $\partial \mathcal{T}/\partial \lambda$ directly — the maximetre system — and it has been developed further by Badoual and Pelletier (1967); $\mathcal{T}(\lambda_0)$ and $(\mathcal{T}^{-1} \, \partial \mathcal{T}/\partial \lambda)_{\lambda_0}$ are measured simultaneously; for each layer of the stack,

λ_0 is chosen to give the highest accuracy. In practice, however, a problem can arise if the bandwidth of the monitoring system is not very much smaller than that of the filter being monitored, since the maximetre reading is a convolution of the signal and instrumental functions; both functions must be symmetrical for the reading to be accurate.

7.7 Filters containing layers with unequal optical thicknesses

Most of the error analysis techniques described in the previous sections relate to filters where the layer thicknesses are all integral multiples of a quarter wave. The monitoring problem becomes more difficult when one attempts to implement designs requiring other values of layer thickness, such as are produced by the automatic design programs, described in chapter 4, or by application of electrical filter design techniques (chapter 3). Pelletier and Giacomo (1972b) have attempted to solve this problem by developing a computer simulation 'control' program, which has to be followed step by step during the evaporation process. This program enables the designer to choose in advance the most suitable monitoring wavelength, λ_K, for each layer. For example, if the maximetre method is used, wavelengths $\lambda_K, \lambda'_K \ldots$ can be found such that the transmittance of the stack (substrate $+ n_1 d_1 + n_2 d_2 + \ldots + n_K d_K$), $\mathcal{T}_K$, is an extremum; the quantity $|\partial(\partial \mathcal{T}/\partial \lambda)/\partial d_i|_{\lambda_K, d_K}$ may be calculated for each wavelength in order to find the wavelength giving highest sensitivity. Then for each layer, the effect of changes in $\mathcal{T}_K$ and $(\partial \mathcal{T}_K/\partial \lambda)_{\lambda_K}$ is known. A similar analysis may be carried out for the turning value method of monitoring, in which case λ_K is chosen so that $(\partial \mathcal{T}_K/\partial(n_K d_K)) = 0$ for each layer. Figure 7.13 shows plots of transmittance against optical thickness for (a) a multilayer with equal optical thicknesses $\lambda_0/4$ monitored at λ_0, and (b) a multilayer with unequal thicknesses monitored at $\lambda_1, \lambda_2, \lambda_3$ etc.

The computer simulation program may also be used to analyse the effects of cumulative errors; this enables the designer to choose the most 'stable' monitoring process for a particular filter, which may be based either on the maximetre system or on the turning value method (Pelletier, private communication 1973). Pelletier *et al* (1973) carried out this exercise for a Fabry–Perot filter and for a multiple cavity design — in both cases, all thicknesses are multiples of $\lambda_0/4$ — and their results indicated that for this type of design the turning value method is more stable because of the error compensation process. Comparative results for the simulation of the multiple cavity filter with a systematic 2% error in each of the layers, using both the maximetre and turning value monitoring are given in figure 7.14 and table 7.8.

Pelletier and Giacomo (1972b) and Pelletier (private communication 1973) have also discussed the possibility of using a fast scanning spectrophotometer to obtain a global picture of the spectral profile of the filter.

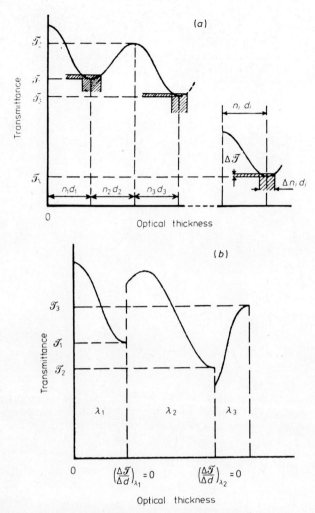

Figure 7.13 Monitoring curves for a multilayer with (*a*) equal optical thicknesses, monitored at λ_0, and (*b*) unequal thicknesses monitored at λ_1, λ_2 and λ_3 (after Pelletier and Giacomo 1972).

This would not be as sensitive a monitoring device as a method which uses only one or two monitoring wavelengths, but it may well prove very stable, and could be most useful for filters designed for broad band applications. The spectral profile can be observed during deposition of a layer by means of an oscilloscope, and compared with the predicted profile; when the two coincide, deposition of the layer is terminated. If K wavelengths are chosen within the range (K would be of the order of 10 if the whole range comprised measurements at 100 wavelengths), then a specifically designed digital electronic unit may be used to calculate a merit function F which is a

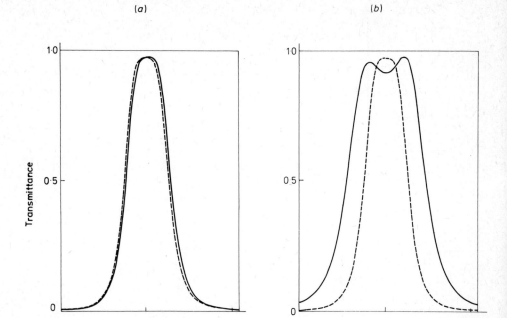

Figure 7.14 Results of the computer simulation of a multiple cavity filter with errors in all layer thicknesses: (*a*) control based on turning value monitoring; (*b*) control based on the maximetre system. The broken lines represent the perfect filter (after Pelletier *et al* 1973).

measure of the distance between $\mathcal{T}_0(\lambda)$, the desired, and $\mathcal{T}_1(\lambda)$, the actual profile

$$F = \sum_{j=1}^{K} w_j \, |\mathcal{T}_0(\lambda_j) - \mathcal{T}_1(\lambda_j)|, \qquad (7.22)$$

where the w_j are appropriately chosen weighting factors. Figure 7.15 shows the evolution of the spectral profile of a filter with several values of thickness of the final layer. As a further refinement, a real time computer attached to the monitoring system might be used to calculate alterations in the design to compensate for errors which have occurred earlier in the deposition process. In this way, a method would be developed whereby the technique for optimising monitoring for a particular layer would at the same time minimise effects of cumulative errors in the layers already deposited. However, a large amount of computer store and many accurate measurements between deposition of successive layers would be needed for such a system to be effective, and this is difficult to achieve at the present time.

Table 7.8 Effect of the monitoring technique used in the simulation of a multiple cavity filter with systematic errors of $\lambda_0/200$ in all layer thicknesses. (H represents $\lambda_0/4$ zinc sulphide, L represents $\lambda_0/4$ cryolite).

Independent errors	Monitoring system based on zeros of $\partial\mathcal{T}/\partial\lambda$	Monitoring system based on zeros of $\partial\mathcal{T}/\partial(nd)$
1·02H	1·111H	1·020H
1·02L	0·985L	1·012L
1·02H	1·026H	1·011H
1·02L	1·015L	1·009L
6·02H	6·002H	6·009H
1·02L	1·033L	0·982L
1·02H	0·862H	0·983H
1·02L	1·115L	0·978L
1·02H	0·697H	0·966H
1·02L	1·298L	1·077L
1·02H	0·505H	1·017H
1·02L	1·539L	1·010L
1·02H	0·190H	1·010H
1·02L	1·900L	1·008L
6·02H	7·115H	6·009H
1·02L	1·890L	0·982L
1·02H	0·755H	0·984H
1·02L	1·217L	0·980L
1·02H	0·636H	0·977H
$\lambda_{peak} = 5499\,\text{Å}$	$\lambda_{peak} = 5462\,\text{Å}$	$\lambda_{peak} = 5464\,\text{Å}$
$\mathcal{T}_{max} = 0\cdot972$	$\mathcal{T}_{max} = 0\cdot979$	$\mathcal{T}_{max} = 0\cdot971$
$\Delta\lambda = 53\cdot1\,\text{Å}$	$\Delta\lambda = 92\cdot6\,\text{Å}$	$\Delta\lambda = 52\cdot6\,\text{Å}$

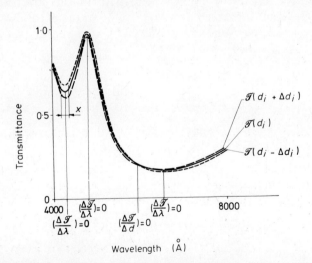

Figure 7.15 Evolution of the spectral profile of a filter as a function of the final layer thickness. X is the absolute value of $\mathcal{T}$ in the zone of maximum sensitivity (after Pelletier and Giacomo 1974).

Appendix 1   A Brief Summary of Optimisation Techniques Useful for a Multilayer Filter Designer

A1.1   Introduction

Nonlinear optimisation is a subject to which much attention has been paid over the last two decades and which has a wide field of possible application in industrial, scientific and commercial problems. Many useful books on the subject have been written, including those by Walsh (1975), Dixon (1972), Murray (1972) and Gill and Murray (1974a), in addition to published proceedings of conferences on the subject, organised by the Institute of Mathematics and its Applications, and others (Fletcher 1969 and Lootsma 1972). Dixon (1976) contains two papers on the use of optimisation techniques in filter design and the interested reader should consult these works for fuller details than can be included here.

Two types of problem can arise: either there are *constraints* to the problem, where the variables involved can only take certain values (e.g. layer thicknesses in a multilayer must be positive quantities) or the problem is *unconstrained*. Methods developed for the former problem are generally more complicated and often use techniques designed for the latter problem. The general constrained optimisation problem can be stated as follows (Lill 1974):

Minimise the *Objective Function*, $F(\mathbf{x})$, where $\mathbf{x}$ is a vector of N independent variables, $(x_1, x_2, \ldots, x_N)^{\mathrm{T}}$ subject to

$$\mathbf{c}(\mathbf{x}) \geqslant \mathbf{0}, \qquad \text{(a vector of inequality constraints)},$$
$$\mathbf{e}(\mathbf{x}) = \mathbf{0}, \qquad \text{(a vector of equality constraints)},$$
$$l_i \leqslant x_i \leqslant u_i, \qquad \text{(lower and upper bounds on the variables)}.$$

Methods designed to solve this problem can also be used to maximise functions since the maximum of $F(\mathbf{x})$ is the minimum of the function $-F(\mathbf{x})$.

A1.2   Methods for unconstrained optimisation

These are generally classified into the techniques requiring evaluation of the objective function only, those requiring evaluation of the first derivative, or *gradient* vector

$$\mathbf{g}(\mathbf{x}) = \left(\frac{\partial F}{\partial x_1}, \frac{\partial F}{\partial x_2}, \ldots, \frac{\partial F}{\partial x_N} \right)^{\mathrm{T}}_{\mathbf{x}} \tag{A1.1}$$

168

and those which require evaluation of the second derivative, or *hessian* matrix **G**, of the objective function

$$G_{ij} = \left(\frac{\partial^2 F}{\partial x_i \partial x_j}\right)_{\mathbf{x}} \qquad \text{(A1.2)}$$

The gradient vector gives the direction of greatest change in F (so that at an extremum, $\mathbf{g}(\mathbf{x}) = \mathbf{0}$), and the hessian matrix describes the curvature of the function at the point $\mathbf{x}$. For an unconstrained minimum of F, **G** is a positive definite matrix i.e. all its eigenvalues are positive.

Many multidimensional optimisation methods employ a linear search technique to find the minimum of $F(\mathbf{x})$ along a particular direction of search. For this purpose, a quadratic or cubic interpolation method, such as the ones described by Powell (1964) or Davidon (1959) is employed. The function is approximated by a quadratic or cubic polynomial whose minimum is used as the next approximation to the function minimum along that direction of search.

One of the simplest methods for unconstrained minimisation which does not employ derivatives is the 'univariate search' method, in which a linear search is performed with respect to one variable at a time. (This idea was used to find an initial approximation in the N^2 scan method of Heavens and Liddell (1968).) Unfortunately, the method becomes very inefficient as the number of variables increases. Rosenbrock (1960) suggested an improvement by rotating the directions of search, while maintaining orthogonality, as part of a 'pattern-search' strategy; Powell (1964) developed a more efficient method by using 'conjugate' directions of search. Two directions **p, q** are said to be conjugate with respect to a matrix **A** when

$$\mathbf{p}^{\mathrm{T}} \mathbf{A} \mathbf{q} = 0 \qquad \text{(A1.3)}$$

If the directions of search are chosen so that they are mutually conjugate with respect to the hessian matrix then the minimum of a quadratic function can be found in at most N linear searches (for a problem with N variables). For non-quadratic objective functions, convergence will usually be fast, although it cannot be guaranteed.

A class of methods which is very popular with engineers, particularly for process control applications, is that based on a 'simplex' or geometrical configuration set up in the parameter space of the design variables. The most frequently used nonlinear simplex method is the one proposed by Nelder and Mead (1965). A configuration of $N + 1$ points is set up and the function evaluated at the vertices of the simplex. At each stage, the worst point is discarded and a new simplex set up by expanding or contracting the current simplex about the most favourable points. Eventually, the simplex should contract onto the function minimum and when its size is within a prescribed tolerance, the minimisation is considered complete. This technique was used by Pelletier *et al* for automatic filter design (1971).

Any method which requires the user to supply a subroutine to calculate analytical derivatives of the function will involve extra work on the part of the user, particularly in the case of filter design problems where the form of objective function is very complicated. However, experience has shown that the algorithms which employ first derivatives are among the best available, and will result in a reduction of the time required to solve the problem and an increase in the size of problem which can be tackled.

The earliest method which employed gradients is that of 'steepest descent', proposed by Cauchy (1847). In this technique, the direction of search at the current point x_K is $-g(x_K)$. Unfortunately, the method is very slow in practice. Fletcher and Reeves (1964) combined the idea of using gradient information with conjugate directions of search and produced a 'conjugate gradient' method which is very efficient and economical on storage for large scale problems, since only three N-dimensional vectors need be stored at each stage.

Second derivative methods are based on a truncated Taylor series approximation to the function. The Newton correction at x_K is given by

$$x_{K+1} = x_K + d_K,$$

where

$$G_K \, d_K = -g_K,$$

(A1.4)

so both the gradient and the hessian matrix must be evaluated. The basic algorithm is usually modified to include a linear search along d_K so that x_{K+1} is the minimum of $F(x)$ along d_K. This method can converge very fast, but has the disadvantage that for filter design work the number of calculations involved per step would be excessive. A more practical approach might be to use one of the 'quasi-Newton' methods, the original one being proposed by Davidon (1959) and Fletcher and Powell (1963). These methods use only function and gradient evaluations; an approximation, H, to the inverse hessian matrix is kept and updated each iteration, and is used with the gradient at the current point x_K to generate conjugate directions

$$d_K = -H_K \, g_K.$$

(A1.5)

These methods are extremely efficient and are widely recommended for use in practice. Stewart (1967) and Gill and Murray (1972) have proposed modifications of the method using numerical derivatives, so that only function values need be supplied by the user.

A1.3   Methods for minimising sums of squares of nonlinear functions

A nonlinear function which has the form of a sum of squares of other functions (sometimes called residuals) is one of the most commonly occurring problems, particularly in design work, where many examples are essentially curve-fitting problems in which the designer attempts to meet a specification by adjusting the values of the design variables or the parameters of the model describing the problem.

Sums of squares problems may either be treated by the general methods described above, or the process may be adapted to exploit the special nature of the function and algorithms developed which are usually more efficient for this type of problem.

We may express such a function as

$$S(\mathbf{x}) = \sum_{k=1}^{M} f_K^2(\mathbf{x}) = \mathbf{f}^T\mathbf{f}, \tag{A1.6}$$

where $M \geqslant N$. The gradient of S may be expressed in terms of the $M \times N$ matrix of first derivatives, or *Jacobian* matrix

$$J_{ij}(\mathbf{x}) = \left(\frac{\partial f_i}{\partial x_j}\right)_{\mathbf{x}} \tag{A1.7}$$

Then

$$\mathbf{g} = 2\mathbf{J}^T\mathbf{f} \tag{A1.8}$$

and the hessian matrix $\mathbf{G}$ is given by

$$\mathbf{G} = 2\mathbf{J}^T\mathbf{J} + 2\sum_{i=1}^{M} f_i\mathbf{K}^{(i)}, \tag{A1.9}$$

where $\mathbf{K}^{(i)}$ is the matrix of second derivatives of f_i. From this last equation it can be seen that if the f_i are small, or if they are approximately linear, the hessian may be approximated by using only the first derivative matrix $\mathbf{J}$, i.e.

$$\mathbf{G} \simeq 2\mathbf{J}^T\mathbf{J}. \tag{A1.10}$$

If this is substituted in Newton's method, we obtain the Gauss–Newton method for nonlinear least squares. Thus

$$\mathbf{J}^T(\mathbf{x}_K)\,\mathbf{J}(\mathbf{x}_K)\,\mathbf{d}_K = -\mathbf{J}^T(\mathbf{x}_K)\,\mathbf{f}(\mathbf{x}_K). \tag{A1.11}$$

Problems can arise if $\mathbf{J}^T\mathbf{J}$ is singular. Marquardt (1963) suggested using a method which combines the Newton direction with the steepest descent direction by introducing a parameter λ so that

$$(\mathbf{J}^T\mathbf{J} + \lambda\mathbf{I})\,\mathbf{d}_K = -\mathbf{J}^T\mathbf{f}, \tag{A1.12}$$

where $\mathbf{I}$ is the unit matrix. (In lens design this is called the 'damped least squares' method.) The method appears very reliable; however, it does involve calculation of the $M \times N$ derivatives of the f_i.

Various methods have also been suggested which use only function values. Barnes (1965) produced a modified secant method which was used by Hansen (1973) in his optical constant determination work; Powell (1965) also developed a method based on the secant method but where the derivatives are approximated along a set of suitably chosen linearly independent directions rather than along coordinate directions. This method has been used in optical design applications by Heavens and Liddell (1968) and Liddell (1974). Peckham (1970) suggested a technique whereby the Jacobian is approximated by differencing the functions over a simplex of at least $N + 1$ points – his method was used in optical constant calculations by Liddell and Staerck (1972). In a more recent method of Powell (1970) the Jacobian is updated every iteration and used to estimate the Gauss and the steepest descent directions. If the Gauss–Newton step does not give a suitable reduction in $S(\mathbf{x})$, a search is made for a reduced minimum along the steepest descent direction and the line joining the predicted minimum to the end point of the Gauss–Newton step. However, this method depends on the variables being evenly scaled and this is sometimes difficult to achieve.

A1.4   Methods for constrained optimisation

Many of the constraints which arise in optical design problems are simple bounds on design variables, or non-negativity restrictions which may be dealt with by means of a simple transformation of variables; for example if one requires $x_i \geqslant 0$, the variable may be transformed to y_i, where

$$x_i = y_i^2 \qquad \text{or} \qquad x_i = \exp(y_i), \qquad (A1.13)$$

or if $u_i \geqslant x_i \geqslant l_i$, one could use

$$x_i = l_i + (u_i - l_i) \sin^2 y_i. \qquad (A1.14)$$

For more complicated constraints there are two types of method which can be applied. The first is the class of transformation methods (penalty or barrier functions (Ryan 1972)) in which the objective function is altered in order to accommodate the constraints, whereas in the second type the method itself is changed so that the search strategy takes account of the constraints. In general, the first type of method is more widely applicable, particularly if a good unconstrained method is readily available, but the most efficient methods such as Rosen's gradient projection method (1960, 1961) or the reduced gradient method of Abadie and Carpentier (1969) belong to the second type.

The basic approach underlying the transformation methods is to change the constrained problem into a sequence of unconstrained problems. A typical penalty function is given by

$$P(\mathbf{x}, r) = F(\mathbf{x}) + \frac{1}{r} \sum_{i \in I} c_i^2(\mathbf{x}), \qquad (A1.15)$$

where I is the set of constraints which are active (i.e. satisfied as equalities) at the solution $\mathbf{x}^*$, and r is called a penalty parameter; under certain prescribed conditions

$$\lim_{r \to 0} \mathbf{x}^*(r) = \mathbf{x}^*, \qquad (A1.16)$$

where $\mathbf{x}^*(r)$ is the minimum of $P(\mathbf{x}, r)$; $P(\mathbf{x}, r)$ may then be minimised by an unconstrained method (usually a quasi–Newton method is recommended). Both Fiacco and McCormick (1968) and Lootsma (1972b) have applied this technique (often abbreviated to SUMT, or Sequential Unconstrained Minimisation Techniques). In this type of transformation a penalty is added to the objective function if the constraint is violated, whereas in the barrier function method, the constraint cannot be violated or the function would become infinite. An example of a barrier function is

$$B(\mathbf{x}, r) = F(\mathbf{x}) + r \sum_{i=1}^{M} [-\ln c_i(\mathbf{x})], \qquad (A1.17)$$

where M is the total number of constraints. This type of method can only be applied to inequality constraints and an initial feasible point (i.e. a value of $\mathbf{x}$ which satisfies the constraints) must be provided by the user. An example of the use of this type of method was given by Carroll (1961). Rosenbrock (1960) also proposed a type of barrier function for use with his unconstrained minimisation technique which has been found to be slow but very reliable for practical problems. This method was used by Seeley *et al* (1973) for the design of low- and high-pass filters. Another constrained optimisation technique which has been applied to filter design by McKeown and Nag (1976) was developed by Biggs (1972) and is based on a penalty function transformation method in which the unconstrained minimisations are approximated by quadratic subproblems.

The simplex method has been modified to take account of constraints; Box (1965) produced a COnstrained siMPLEX (or complex) method and later Dixon (1973) developed an Accelerated Constrained SIMplex (acsim) technique, and like the unconstrained method, these are quite widely used in practice. In both methods, the simplex is constructed in such a way as to take account of the constraints; as a solution is approached, Dixon's method makes use of a quadratic approximation of the function to speed convergence to the solution.

A1.5 Use and availability of optimisation routines in program libraries

Many good algorithms for nonlinear optimisation exist and are available often at little or no cost to the user. The following sources of program listings are particularly recommended (Gill and Murray 1974b):

(1) Numerical Algorithms Group Ltd, NAG Central Office, Oxford (the NAG library);
(2) Division of Computer Science, Atomic Energy Research Establishment, Harwell (the Harwell Subroutine library);
(3) Division of Numerical Analysis and Computing, National Physical Laboratory, Teddington;
(4) Numerical Optimisation Centre, Hatfield Polytechnic;
(5) Applied Mathematics Division, Argonne National Laboratory, Illinois;
(6) George Washington University, Washington DC;
(7) Madison Academic Computing Center, Madison, Wisconsin.

A number of optimisation algorithms have been published in the Computer Journal and the Communications of the ACM, who are now publishing a new journal 'Transactions of Mathematical Software'. Many routines from Harwell and NPL form the basis of the routines in the optimisation chapter of the NAG library and the Argonne MINIPACK package. Both these libraries have contributers who are world experts in the subject; the routines are thoroughly tested and documented and the contents are continuously revised as new and more efficient algorithms become available. The NAG library has been implemented on many different machine ranges; it is already available on most university computers in the UK and is also being marketed to other interested parties.

Appendix 2   Computer Programs

A2.1   Program for calculating reflectance and transmittance of a non-absorbing, non-dispersive film

A2.1.1   Specification

NDRT is a short program written in FORTRAN (the complete listing is given below) for computing the reflectance and transmittance of a multilayer, given the optical constants of the configuration, the range of wavelengths required and the angle of incidence. The materials are assumed to be non-absorbing and non-dispersive.

A2.1.2   Input of data

The data is input by means of a control index card, containing a negative integer value as follows:

(1) *Layer parameters*
    Control index −3,
    Number of layers N (N ⩽ 50),
    Values of refractive indices of the medium of incidence and the substrate,
    Refractive index and phase thickness (in degrees) at the reference wavelength for each layer in the filter;
(2) *Spectral information*
    Control index −4,
    Number of wavelengths M (M ⩽ 50),
    Reference wavelength, initial wavelength and incremental wavelength (REFWAV, WAV (1), WAVINC);
(3) *Angle of incidence*
    Control index −6,
    Angle of incidence in degrees (ANGINC);
(4) *Start of calculation*
    Control index −1;
(5) *Stop execution*
    Control index −2.

Should a control index card contain a value other than −1, −2, −3, −4, or −6, the message DATA ERROR is printed and execution is terminated. A 'format free' type of input may be used in order to minimise punching errors. After the calculation for a particular configuration, range of wavelengths and angle of incidence, control returns to the beginning of the

176

program. The advantage of the control index system is that only changes in data need be input after the first calculation. Execution is terminated when the control index card −2 is encountered. An example of the data required for a three-layer antireflection coating, designed for use at normal incidence, but computed at 10° angle of incidence over a range of 11 wavelengths is shown below, following the listing of the program. The results obtained for this example are given in figure A2.1.

A2.1.3 Output of results
The results are printed as follows:

(1) reference wavelength;
(2) refractive indices of the medium of incidence and the substrate;
(3) a table showing the refractive index and the phase thickness, in degrees, at the reference wavelength for each layer in the filter;
(4) a title: N-layer filter;
(5) angle of incidence;
(6) a table giving values of the average reflectance, p- and s-components of reflectance, average transmittance, and p- and s-components of transmittance against wavelength for each specified wavelength.

A2.1.4 Time
The time taken to run such a program on a modern fast computer is very short. For example, the three-layer filter illustrated below used about 0·4 s cpu time on the Queen Mary College 1904S computer (ICL), which is about four times the time required on a CDC 6600 or twelve times that on a CDC 7600. A 21-layer filter took approximately 1·4 s execution time for calculations over a similar range of wavelengths. The compilation time for the program is about five seconds. Thus this type of program is suitable for use on a small 'in house' computer, whereas the design program described in the next section is more likely to need a larger 'service' computer.

A2.1.5 Listing of program and data

```
      MASTER NDRT
      DIMENSION FREQ(50),WAV(50),R(50),REF(50),PCOMPR(50),SCOMPR(50),
     1TRANS(50),PCOMPT(50),SCOMPT(50),X(50),COSTHJ(50),R1(50)
      LOGICAL TRSUBS
      COMMON
     1/FILM/FREQ,WAV,RAIR,RSUB,R,ANGINC,REF,PCOMPR,SCOMPR,PCOMPT,
     2SCOMPT,TRANS
     4,TRSUBS ,SIGNNS
C     CONTROL INDEX FOR DATA
C        -1 START
C        -2 STOP
C        -3 INDICES AND THICKNESSES OF LAYERS
C        -6 ANGLE OF INCIDENCE
    1 READ(4,2)ID
      ID=-ID
      IF(ID.LT.0.OR.ID.GT.6)GOTO 16
```

```
        GO TO (18,24,3,6,9,13),ID
C       LAYER PARAMETERS
 3      READ(4,4)N
        READ(4,5)RAIR1,RSUB1
        RAIR=RAIR1
        RSUB=RSUB1
        READ(4,5)(R(I),X(I),I=1,N)
        GO TO 1
C       SPECTRAL INFORMATION
 6      READ(4,7)M
        READ(4,8)REFWAV,WAV(1),WAVINC
        FREQ(1)=REFWAV/WAV(1)
        DO 10 I=2,M
        WAV(I)=WAV(I-1)+WAVINC
 10     FREQ(I)=REFWAV/WAV(I)
        GO TO 1
 9      GO TO 16
C       ANGLE OF INCIDENCE
 13     READ(4,15)ANGINC1
        ANGINC=ANGINC1
        GO TO 1
 16     WRITE(12,17)
 17     FORMAT(11H DATA ERROR)
        GO TO 24
C       START OF CALCULATION
 18     CALL RTPSAV(M,N,X)
C OUTPUT OF RESULTS
C    INITIAL OUTPUT
        WRITE(12,44)REFWAV
 44     FORMAT(1H1, 30X, 8HREFWAV =,  F10.4)
        IF(N.EQ.0)WRITE(12,12)RAIR,RSUB
 12     FORMAT(20X,6H RAIR=,F4.2,20X,6H RSUB=,F4.2//20X,17H LAYER PARAMETE
       1RS/20X,6H INDEX,20X,10H THICKNESS/(20X,F5.2,20X,F8.4))
        IF(N.EQ.0)GO TO 1
        IF(N.EQ.0) GO TO 43
        WRITE(12,12)RAIR,RSUB,(R(I),X(I),I=1,N)
        WRITE(12,14)N
 14     FORMAT(I4,13H-LAYER FILTER)
 43     CONTINUE
        WRITE(12,30)ANGINC
 30     FORMAT(20X,24H    ANGLE OF INCIDENCE= ,F6.1,8HDEGREES  )
        WRITE(12,40)(WAV(I),REF(I),PCOMPR(I),SCOMPR(I),TRANS(I),PCOMPT(I),
       1SCOMPT(I),I=1,M)
        GOTO 1
 2      FORMAT(I0)
 4      FORMAT(I0)
 5      FORMAT(2F0.0)
 11     FORMAT(10F0.0)
 7      FORMAT(I0)
 8      FORMAT(3F0.0)
 15     FORMAT(F0.0)
 19     FORMAT(I0)
 40     FORMAT(103H        WAVL.        AVREFL.        PCOMPR.        SCOMP
       1R.        AVTRANS.        PCOMPT.        SCOMPT. /7(4X,F8.5,3X))
 24     STOP
        END
        SUBROUTINE RTPSAV(M,N,X)
        DIMENSION FREQ(50),WAV(50),R(50),REF(50),PCOMPR(50),SCOMPR(50)  ,
       1TRANS(50),PCOMPT(50),SCOMPT(50),X(50),COSTHJ(50),R1(50)
       2,Z(50)
        LOGICAL TRSUBS,SIGNNS
        COMMON
       1/FILM/FREQ,WAV,RAIR,RSUB,R,ANGINC,REF,PCOMPR,SCOMPR,PCOMPT,
       2SCOMPT,TRANS
       3,PHIS,PHIP,TORS,TORP,PHI,TOR
       4,TRSUBS,SIGNNS
```

```
            TRSUBS=.FALSE.
            THETA=0.017453*ANGINC
            SINTH=SIN(THETA)
            COSTH=COS(THETA)
            RAIRST=RAIR*SINTH
            SINTHS=RAIRST/RSUB
            IF(SINTHS.GT.1.)GO TO 255
            COSTHS=SQRT(1.-SINTHS*SINTHS)
            GO TO 256
    255     TRSUBS=.TRUE.
            COSTHS=SQRT(SINTHS*SINTHS-1.)
    256     CONTINUE
C           PHASE THICKNESSES
            IF(N.EQ.0)GO TO 251
            DO 201 J=1,N
            SINTHJ=RAIRST/R(J)
            COSTHJ(J)=SQRT(1.-SINTHJ*SINTHJ)
            Z(J)=X(J)
    201     X(J)=Z(J)*COSTHJ(J)
    251     CONTINUE
            RAIR1=RAIR
            RSUB1=RSUB
C     S-COMPONENT OF POLARISATION
            SIGNNS=.FALSE.
            RAIR=RAIR1*COSTH
            RSUB=RSUB1*COSTHS
            IF(N.EQ.0)GO TO 252
            DO 202 J=1,N
            R1(J)=R(J)
    202     R(J)=R1(J)*COSTHJ(J)
    252     CONTINUE
            CALL REFTCE(M,N,X)
            DO 203 IA=1,M
            SCOMPR(IA)=REF(IA)
    203     SCOMPT(I =TRANS(IA)
C       P-COMPONENT OF POLARISATION
            SIGNNS=.TRUE.
            RAIR=RAIR1/COSTH
            RSUB=RSUB1/COSTHS
            IF(N.EQ.0)GO TO 253
            DO 204 J=1,N
    204     R(J)=R1(J)/COSTHJ(J)
    253     CONTINUE
            CALL REFTCE(M,N,X)
            DO 205 IA=1,M
            PCOMPR(IA)=REF(IA)
            PCOMPT(IA)=TRANS(IA)
            REF(IA)=0.5*(SCOMPR(IA)+PCOMPR(IA))
            TRANS(IA)=0.5*(SCOMPT(IA)+PCOMPT(IA))
    205     CONTINUE
            IF(N.EQ.0)GO TO 254
            DO 206 J=1,N
            X(J)=Z(J)
    206     R(J)=R1(J)
    254     CONTINUE
            RAIR=RAIR1
            RSUB=RSUB1
            RETURN
            END
            SUBROUTINE REFTCE(M,N,X)
            DIMENSION FREQ(50),WAV(50),R(50),REF(50),PCOMPR(50),SCOMPR(50)
           1TRANS(50),PCOMPT(50),SCOMPT(50),X(50),COSTHJ(50),R1(50)
            LOGICAL TRSUBS,SIGNNS
            COMMON
```

```
      1/FILM/FREQ,WAV,RAIR,RSUB,R,ANGINC,REF,PCOMPR,SCOMPR,PCOMPT,
      2SCOMPT,TRANS
      3,PHIS,PHIP,TORS,TORP,PHI,TOR
      4,TRSUBS,SIGNNS
       DO 2 IA=1,M
       IF(N.EQ.0)GO TO 4
       PHI1=0.017453*X(1)*FREQ(IA)
       B11=COS(PHI1)
       B12=SIN(PHI1)/R(1)
       B21=B12*R(1)*R(1)
       B22=B11
       IF(N.EQ.1)GO TO 3
       DO 1 J=2,N
       PHI1=0.017453*X(J)*FREQ(IA)
       C11=COS(PHI1)
       C12=SIN(PHI1)/R(J)
       C21=C12*R(J)*R(J)
       C22=C11
       A11=B11*C11-B12*C21
       A12=B11*C12+B12*C22
       A21=B21*C11+B22*C21
       A22=B22*C22-B21*C12
       B11=A11
       B12=A12
       B21=A21
1      B22=A22
       GO TO 3
4      B11=1.0
       B12=0.0
       B21=0.0
       B22=1.0
3      IF(TRSUBS)GO TO 5
       EMINHR=B11*RAIR-B22*RSUB
       EMINHI=B12*RAIR*RSUB-B21
       EANDHR=B11*RAIR+B22*RSUB
       EANDHI=B12*RAIR*RSUB+B21
       EMINH=EMINHR*EMINHR+EMINHI*EMINHI
       EPLUSH=EANDHR*EANDHR+EANDHI*EANDHI
       REF(IA)=EMINH/EPLUSH
       TRANS(IA)=1.-REF(IA)
       GO TO 2
5      REF(IA)=1.0
       TRANS(IA)=0.0
2      CONTINUE
       RETURN
       END
       FINISH




       -3
       3
       1.00    1.52
       1.38    90.0
       2.1     180.0
       1.7     90.0
       -4
       11
       0.55    0.5   0.01
       -6
       10.0
       -1
       -2
```

```
                    REFWAV =      0.5500
       RAIR=1.00                        RSUB=1.52

       LAYER PARAMETERS
       INDEX                   THICKNESS
       1.38                     90.0000
       2.10                    180.0000
       1.70                     90.0000
3-LAYER FILTER
              ANGLE OF INCIDENCE=    10.0 DEGREES
  WAVL.      AVREFL.    PCOMPR.      SCOMPR.     AVTRANS.    PCOMPT.     SCOMPT.
 0.50000    0.00092    0.00086      0.00097     0.99908    0.99914    0.99903
 0.51000    0.00057    0.00054      0.00061     0.99943    0.99946    0.99939
 0.52000    0.00029    0.00027      0.00031     0.99971    0.99973    0.99969
 0.53000    0.00010    0.00009      0.00011     0.99990    0.99991    0.99989
 0.54000    0.00001    0.00001      0.00002     0.99999    0.99999    0.99998
 0.55000    0.00002    0.00002      0.00002     0.99998    0.99998    0.99998
 0.56000    0.00011    0.00011      0.00012     0.99989    0.99989    0.99988
 0.57000    0.00028    0.00027      0.00030     0.99972    0.99973    0.99970
 0.58000    0.00051    0.00048      0.00054     0.99949    0.99952    0.99946
 0.59000    0.00077    0.00073      0.00082     0.99923    0.99927    0.99918
 0.60000    0.00105    0.00099      0.00111     0.99895    0.99901    0.99889
```

Figure A2.1   Results of NDRT.

A2.2   Specification of the N^2 scan automatic design program NSQ2

NSQ2 is a program based on the least squares method of design developed by Heavens and Liddell; it incorporates the N^2 scanning procedure providing automatically an approximate design which may then be refined. This version of the program assumes that the materials used are non-dispersive and non-absorbir ; other versions have been written to accommodate dispersion and absorp')n, but they require considerably more computer storage and in practice, unless one is dealing with very few layers, it is more economical to use this version of the program to produce a close approximation to the final design and then to use a simple refinement program which includes dispersion and/or absorption. The program has the following facilities:

(1) some layer thicknesses may be fixed;
(2) the minimisation routine may be called more than once;
(3) the thicknesses of the layers may be constrained to lie within certain limits.

A2.2.1   Program structure

MAIN: consists of data input by means of a control index, followed by instructions for the N^2 scanning procedure. The minimum value of the merit function and appropriate thicknesses obtained during the scan are stored; these provide the starting point for the Powell minimisation procedure. Results are output before and after refinement by the Harwell routine VA02A.

CALFUN: The effective thickness and index for each component of polarisation are obtained, using Snell's law, for the specified angle of incidence.

After REFLEC has been called for each component of polarisation, the average of the two components is calculated at each wavelength and the values of the functions

$$f_K(\mathbf{x}) = (R_1(\lambda_K) - R(\mathbf{x}, \lambda_K))\, \omega t(\lambda_K)$$

used in the merit function

$$F(\mathbf{x}) = \sum_{\lambda_K} f_K^2(\mathbf{x})$$

are computed and stored (R_1 and R represent the specified and calculated reflectance at wavelength λ_K.)

REFLEC: In this routine, the matrix multiplications are performed and the value of reflectivity is obtained from the final matrix product.

VA02A: A Harwell library subroutine, written by M J D Powell, for minimising a sum of squares of nonlinear functions of several variables; the routine VD01A, which minimises a function of a single variable by a quadratic interpolation method is called by this routine.

A2.2.2 Input of data

As with the analysis program NDRT described above, each section of data is read in by means of a negative integer, acting as a 'control index'. The data items are as follows:

(1) *Layer parameters*
Control index −3,
Number of layers, N, IXIN, IXMAX, IXINC, (N ≤ 20) (IXIN, IXMAX, IXINC are parameters for the scan; each layer is allowed to assume values of phase thickness ranging from IXIN degrees to IXMAX degrees at intervals of IXINC degrees. These quantities must be integers.)
Values of refractive indices of the medium of incidence and the substrate, RAIR, RSUB,
Refractive index and initial phase thickness (often taken as 90°) of each layer at the reference wavelength, R(I), X(I),
Number of layers whose phase thicknesses are *not* fixed (these thicknesses will be the design variables), layer numbers and limits on phase thickness of these layers, NV, (L(I), A(I), B(I), I = 1, NV);

(2) *Spectral information*
Control index −4,
Number of design wavelengths, M (M ≤ 50),
Reference wavelength for the phase thicknesses, REFWAV,
Wavelength, desired reflectivity and a weighting factor for each design wavelength, WAV(J), GIVREF(J), WT(J);

(3) *Parameters for the minimisation subroutine*
Control index −5,
Absolute accuracy parameters, E(I), I = NV (E(I) is the tolerance on

182

thickness of the Ith layer; the minimisation routine terminates if each design variable changes by less than E(I) during the iteration)
Three parameters controlling steplength, frequency of print out and the maximum number of calls of the subroutine CALFUN allowed in the minimisation subroutine, ESCALE, IPRINT, MAXFUN (normally X(I) will not be changed by a value greater than E(I) × ESCALE in a single step)
(4) *Angle of incidence*
Control index −6
Value of angle of incidence in the medium of incidence, ANGINC
(5) *Start*
Control index −1 starts the calculation for a particular set of data.
(6) *Stop*
Control index −2 terminates the program.

Allowance is made for a data error in the control index card. In this case, the message 'DATA ERROR' is printed and execution is terminated.

A2.2.3 Output of results
The following results are printed:
(1) Reference wavelength
(2) Refractive indices of the medium of incidence and the substrate
(3) A table showing the refractive index and phase thickness at the reference wavelength for each layer in the filter
(4) A title: N-layer filter
(5) Angle of incidence
(6) A table of values showing specified reflectivity, calculated average reflectivity, reflectivity of the s- and p-components of polarisation and the weighting factor for each design wavelength before minimisation by VA02A.
(7) During execution of VA02A, values of the design variables and the values of f_K forming the terms in the sum of squares, together with the value of the sum $F(x)$ are printed every IPRINT iterations.
(8) Tables of the final values of the items listed in (3) and (6) above are printed after the minimisation process has been terminated.

A2.2.4 Time
The time taken to design a 3-layer antireflection coating using 16 design wavelengths and a scan over the range 60° (40°) 180° was 28 s on the 1904S, of which about 7 s was compilation time. The time taken for a 6-layer beam splitter was 75 s and that for a 15-layer filter 562 s; both these examples were also specified at 16 design wavelengths and the same size scan. The complete scan program took 36 s for the 3-layer coating and 927 s for the 6-layer filter; the refinement program took 31 s for the 3-layer example, 54 s for the 6-layer one and 100 s for 15 layers.

References

Abadie J and Carpentier J 1969 *Optimization* ed R Fletcher (New York: Academic Press) p37
Abelès F 1948a *Ann. Phys., Paris* **3** 504
—1948b *C. R. Acad. Sci., Paris* **226** 1808
—1958 *J. Phys. Radium* **19** 327
Abelès F and Thèye M L 1966 *Surface Sci.* **5** 325
Apfel J H 1976 *Appl. Opt.* **15** 2339
—1977 *Appl. Opt.* **16** 1880
Badoual R and Pelletier E 1967 *Proc. 2nd Coll. Thin Films, Budapest* (Gottingen: Vandenhoeck and Ruprecht) pp249–56
Baldini G and Rigaldi L 1970 *J. Opt. Soc. Am.* **60** 495
Banning M 1947 *J. Opt. Soc. Am.* **37** 792
Barnes J G P 1965 *Comput. J.* **8** 66
Baumeister P W 1958 *J. Opt. Soc. Am.* **48** 955
—1962 *J. Opt. Soc. Am.* **52** 1149
—1963 *Notes on Multilayer Optical Filters: Summer course on modern methods of optical design* (Rochester, NY: Institute of Optics)
Baumeister P W and Jenkins F A 1957 *J. Opt. Soc. Am.* **47** 57
Baumeister P W, Jenkins F A and Jeppersen M A 1959 *J. Opt. Soc. Am.* **49** 1188
Baumeister P W and Stone J M 1956 *J. Opt. Soc. Am.* **46** 228
Bennett J M and Booty M J 1966 *Appl. Opt.* **5** 41
—1969 *Appl. Opt.* **8** 2366
Berning P H 1962 *J. Opt. Soc. Am.* **52** 431
Berning P H and Turner A F 1957 *J. Opt. Soc. Am.* **47** 230
Biggs M C 1972 *Numerical Methods for Nonlinear Optimization* ed F A Lootsma (New York: Academic Press) p411
Born M and Wolf E 1959 *Principles of Optics* (Oxford: Pergamon)
Bousquet P 1956 *Opt. Acta* **3** 153
Bousquet P, Fornier A. Kowalczyk R, Pelletier E and Roche P 1972 *Thin Solid Films* **13** 285
Box M J 1965 *Comput. J.* **8** 42
Brune O 1931 *J. Math. Phys.* **10** 191
Buchman W W 1975 *Appl. Opt.* **14** 1220
Carroll C W 1961 *Ops Res.* **9** 169
Cauchy A 1847 *C. R. Acad. Sci., Paris* **25** 536
Chen T C 1970 *Thesis* University of London
Clapham P B 1969 *PhD Thesis* University of London
—1971 *Opt. Acta* **18** 563

184

—1972 *Proc. Int. Conf. Electro Optics, Brighton 1972* (Ind. Sci. Conf. Mngmnt. Corp. Inc.) p277

Costich V 1970 *Appl. Opt.* **9** 866

Cox J T and Hass G 1964 *Physics of Thin Films* vol 2 ed G Hass and R Thun New York: Academic Press) p239

Darlington S 1939 *J. Math. Phys.* **18** 257

Davidon W C 1959 *AEC R&D Rep.* ANL-5990 (rev.)

Delano E 1967 *J. Opt. Soc. Am.* **57** 1529

Delano E and Pegis R J 1969 *Progress in Optics* vol 4 ed E Wolf (Amsterdam: North Holland) p67

Ditchburn R 1963 *Light* (Glasgow: Blackie)

Dixon L C W 1972 *Nonlinear Optimisation* (London: English Universities Press)

—1973 *Comput. Aided Des.* **5** 23

—(ed) 1976 *Optimization in Action* (New York: Academic Press)

Dobrowolski J A 1965 *Appl. Opt.* **4** 937

—1966 Paper presented at the *7th general meeting of the ICO, Paris*

—1970 *Appl. Opt.* **9** 1396

—1973 *Appl. Opt.* **12** 1885

Dobrowolski J A, Hanes G R and Van der Hoeven C J 1968 *Appl. Opt.* **7** 1981

Dobrowolski J A and Lowe D 1978 *Appl. Opt.* **17** 3039

Elsner Z N 1964 *Opt. Spectrosc.* **17** 446

Epstein L I 1952 *J. Opt. Soc. Am.* **42** 806

Ermolaev A M, Minkov M and Vlasov A G 1962 *Opt. Spectrosc.* **13** 259

Fiacco A V and McCormick G P 1968 *Nonlinear Programming: Sequential Unconstrained Minimization Techniques* (Chichester: Wiley)

Fletcher R 1965 *Comput. J.* **8** 33

—(ed) 1969 *Optimization* (New York: Academic Press)

Fletcher R and Powell M J D 1963 *Comput. J.* **6** 163

Fletcher R and Reeves C M 1964 *Comput. J.* **7** 149

Fornier A and Pelletier E 1971 *Seminaire sur le contrôle continu des dépositions sens vide* (Geneva: Battelle) pp21–2

Fujiwara S 1963a *J. Opt. Soc. Am.* **53** 880

—1963b *J. Opt. Soc. Am.* **53** 1317

Giacomo P, Baumeister P W and Jenkins F A 1959 *Proc. Phys. Soc.* **73** 480

Giacomo P and Jacquinot P 1952 *J. Phys. Radium* **13** 59A

Gill P E and Murray W 1974b in *Numerical Methods for Constrained Optimization* ed P E Gill and W Murray (New York: Academic Press) p241

—(eds) 1974a *Numerical Methods for Constrained Optimization* (New York: Academic Press)

—1972 *J. Inst. Math. Appl.* **9** 91

Hadley L N and Dennison D M 1947 *J. Opt. Soc. Am.* **37** 451

Hansen W N 1973 *J. Opt. Soc. Am.* **63** 793

Hass G (ed) 1960– *Physics of Thin Films* vols 1–7 (New York: Academic Press)

Heavens O S 1954 *J. Opt. Soc. Am.* **44** 371
—1955 *Optical Properties of Thin Solid Films* (London: Butterworths)
—1960 *Rep. Prog. Phys.* **23** 1
—1964 *Physics of Thin Films* vol 2 ed G Hass and R Thun (New York: Academic Press) p193
—1970 *Thin Film Physics* (London: Methuen)
Heavens O S and Liddell H M 1965 *Appl. Opt.* **4** 629
—1966 *Appl. Opt.* **5** 373
—1968 *Opt. Acta* **15** 129
Herpin A 1947a *C. R. Acad. Sci., Paris* **225** 182
—1947b *C. R. Acad. Sci., Paris* **225** 17
Jacobsson R 1963 *Opt. Acta* **10** 309
Jacobsson R and Martensson J 1966 *Appl. Opt.* **5** 29
Knittl Z 1967 *Appl. Opt.* **6** 331
—1976 *Optics of Thin Films* (Chichester: Wiley)
Liddell H M 1966 *PhD Thesis* University of London
—1974 *J. Phys. D: Appl. Phys.* **7** 1588
Liddell H M and Fawcett J A Paper presented at the *IPPS Conf. Optical Properties of Thin Films, York 1969*
Liddell H M and Staerck J A 1972 *Proc. Int. Conf. Electro Optics, Brighton 1972* (Ind. Sci. Conf. Mngmnt. Corp. Inc.) p296
Lill S 1974 *Nag Library Document* 760 (Background to (EO4) chapter contents)
Lissberger P H 1959 *J. Opt. Soc. Am.* **49** 121
Lissberger P H and Ring J 1955 *Opt. Acta* **2** 42
Lootsma F A (ed) 1972a *Numerical Methods for Nonlinear Optimization* (New York: Academic Press)
—1972b in *Numerical Methods for Nonlinear Optimization* ed F A Lootsma (New York: Academic Press) p313
MacDonald J 1971 *Metal–Dielectric Multilayers* (Bristol: Adam Hilger)
McKeown J J and Nag A 1976 in *Optimization in Action* ed L C W Dixon (New York: Academic Press) p82
Macleod H A 1969 *Thin-Film Optical Filters* (Bristol: Adam Hilger)
—1972 *Opt. Acta* **19** 1
—1973 *Opt. Acta* **20** 493
Macleod H A and Richmond D 1974 *Opt. Acta* **21** 429
Mahlein H F 1974 *Opt. Acta* **21** 577
Marquardt D W 1963 *J. Soc. Ind. Appl. Math.* **11** 431
Mielenz K D 1959 *J. Res. NBS* **A63** 297
Miller R F and Taylor A J 1971 *J. Phys. D: Appl. Phys.* **4** 1419
Miller R H 1975 *Opt. Spectra* **9** 32
Murray W (ed) 1972 *Numerical Methods for Unconstrained Optimization* (New York: Academic Press)
NBS *Spec. Rep.* **462** (Washington DC: National Bureau of Standards)

186

Nelder J A and Mead R 1965 *Comput. J.* **7** 308
Nestell J E Jr and Christy R W 1972 *Appl. Opt.* **11** 643
Nilsson P O 1968 *Appl. Opt.* **7** 435
Peckham G 1970 *Comput. J.* **13** 418
Pegis R J 1961 *J. Opt. Soc. Am.* **51** 1255
—1963 Presented at *Opt. Soc. Am. Southwest Connecticut section*
Pelletier E and Giacomo P 1972a *Nouv. Rev. Opt. Appl.* **3** 133
—1972b *Le Vide* **157** 1
Pelletier E, Klapisch M and Giacomo P 1971 *Nouv. Rev. Opt. Appl.* **2** 247
Pelletier E, Kowalczyk R and Fornier A 1973 *Opt. Acta* **20** 509
Pelletier E, Roche P and Bertrand L 1974 *Opt. Acta* **21** 927
Pelletier E, Roche P and Vidal B 1976 *Nouv. Rev. Opt. Appl.* **7** 353
Penselin S and Steudel A 1955 *Z. Phys.* **142** 21
Powell C J 1969 *J. Opt. Soc. Am.* **59** 738
Powell M J D 1964 *Comput. J.* **7** 155
—1965 *Comput. J.* **7** 303
—1970 in *Numerical Methods for Nonlinear Algebraic Equations* ed P Rabinowitz (New York: Gordon and Breach) p87
Riblet H 1957 *IRE Trans. Microw. Theor. Tech.* **MTT-5** 36
Richards P I 1948 *Proc. IRE* **36** 217
Ritchie F S 1970 *PhD Thesis* University of Reading
Roche P, Bertrand L and Pelletier E 1976 *Opt. Acta* **23** 433
Rosen J B 1960 *SIAM J. Appl. Math.* **8** 181
—1961 *J. Soc. Ind. Appl. Math.* **9** 514
Rosenbrock H H 1960 *Comput. J.* **3** 175
Ruiz-Urbeita M, Sparrow E M and Eckert E R G 1971a *J. Opt. Soc. Am.* **61** 351
—1971b *J. Opt. Soc. Am.* **61** 1392
Ryan D M 1972 in *Numerical Methods for Constrained Optimization* ed P E Gill and W Murray (New York: Academic Press) p175
Saad (ed) 1968 *The Microwave Engineer's Handbook* (Horizon House Microwave Inc.)
Seeley J S 1961 *Proc. Phys. Soc.* **78** 998
—1965 *Electron. Lett.* **1** 265
Seeley J S, Liddell H M and Chen T C 1973 *Opt. Acta* **20** 641
Seeley J S and Smith S D 1966 *Appl. Opt.* **5** 81
Seidel H and Rosen J 1967 *IEEE Trans. Microw. Theor. Tech.* **MTT-13** 275, 398
Shatilov A V and Tyutikova L P 1963 *Opt. Spectrosc.* **14** 426
Shaw J E and Blevin W R 1964 *J. Opt. Soc. Am.* **54** 334
Smiley V N and Stuart F E 1963 *J. Opt. Soc. Am.* **53** 1078
Smith S D 1958 *J. Opt. Soc. Am.* **48** 43
Smith S D and Seeley J S 1968 *Final Scientific Report USAF contract AF61(052)-833*
Sossi L 1974 *Easti NSV Tead. Akad. Toim. Fuus. Mat.* **23** 229

——1976 *Easti NSV Tead. Akad. Toim. Fuus. Mat.* **25** 171

Stewart G W 1967 *J. Assoc. Comput. Mach.* **14** 72

Thelen A 1971 *J. Opt. Soc. Am.* **61** 365

Thetford A 1969 *Opt. Acta.* **16** 37

Turner A F 1950 *J. Phys. Radium* **11** 444

Turner A F and Baumeister P W 1966 *Appl. Opt.* **5** 69

Van Valkenburg M E 1960 *Introduction to Modern Network Synthesis*
  (Chichester: Wiley)

Vašiček A 1952 *Czech. J. Phys.* **2** 72

——1960 *Optics of Thin Films* (Amsterdam: North Holland)

Veremei V V and Minkov I M 1972 *Opt. Spectrosc.* **33** 640

Walsh G E 1975 *Methods of Optimization* (Chichester: Wiley)

Ward L and Nag A 1970 *J. Phys. D: Appl. Phys.* **3** 462

Ward L, Nag A and Dixon L C W 1969 *J. Phys. D: Appl. Phys.* **2** 301

Weinstein W 1954 *Vacuum* **4** 3

Young L 1961 *J. Opt. Soc. Am.* **51** 967

——1967 *Appl. Opt.* **6** 297

Young L and Cristal E G 1966 *Appl. Opt.* **5** 77

Index

Abelès method for refractive index measurement, 118
absentee layer, 11, 28
absorbing film, (*see also* weakly absorbing films) 6, 119–120, 122–9
  layers, 89, 117
  media, 8
absorption, 26, 42, 80, 126, 130, 133, 154–6, 180
absorption coefficient, 1, 2, 118, 119, 134
achromatic beam splitter, 33, 34, 83, 86, 89, 90, 94, 98
achromatised coatings, 37–40, 44
admittance (*see also* characteristic admittance, equivalent admittance), 10, 25, 55, 151, 156, 157
algorithm for multilayer calculations, 11
alloys, optical constants of, 124
amplitude, 3, 4
amplitude reflection and transmission, 7, 8, 12, 24, 27, 55, 56, 111
analogue computer, 143
analytic methods of design, 1, 30–54
angle of incidence, 2, 11, 12, 102, 104, 117, 120, 133, 175
antireflection coatings, 24, 30, 31, 34–40, 44–8, 52, 59–61, 78, 83, 85, 89, 94, 176, 182
  layer, 63
  of back surface of substrate, 19
approximate design, 78
  methods of filter synthesis, 108
  vector method, 109–11
Argand diagram, 45, 151, 152
automatic design methods, 74, 75, 78–98, 106, 107, 116–7, 169
  programs, 46, 81, 88, 96, 164

back substrate reflection, 19–24, 120
band pass filters, 30, 32, 51–4, 64
bandwidth, 33, 34, 160, 162, 164
barrier function, 172, 173
beam splitter (*see also* achromatic beam splitter, polarising beam splitter, dichroic beam splitter), 29, 30, 33, 74, 94, 104, 106, 182

bi-layer, 50
block diagrams: for program for calculating field intensities, 28
for the thin-film synthesis method of Dobowolski and Lowe, 114
boundary conditions, 4, 5, 9
bounds on variables, 168, 172
Brewster angle, 34
broad band reflectance coatings, low-reflectance, 35–40, 78
  high-reflectance, 26, 28, 30, 31, 46–9, 76–8, 82, 84, 94–7, 143
bulk refractive index, 118, 123
Butterworth function, 63, 102

Central frequency (wavelength), 64
characteristic admittance, 55, 152
  impedance, 55
  matrix, 10, 11, 12, 50, 62, 66, 145, 146
CIE standard observer colour mixture functions, 93
circuit admittance, 66
circuit analogy method (*see also* LC ladder network analogy), 98, 99, 102, 103, 148
circuit prototype, 57
classical (quarter-wave) stack, 14–8, 31, 79, 82, 83, 89, 102, 103, 143, 147
cleaning of substrate, 131
co-evaporation techniques, 2, 75
collimation of source, 22, 23, 120
colour centre absorption, 141
complete scan, 82, 83, 86, 106, 182
complex refractive index, 2, 25
computational procedure for calculating the field intensity distribution, 27
computer refinement, 30
conformal transformation, 25
conjugate directions, 169, 170
consolidation process, 89
constraints on design variables, 87, 134, 168, 172
continued fraction, 111
continuously adjustable reflector, 90
contrast, 95
control index, 12, 28, 176

convergence, 82, 95, 124, 169
convex functions, 74
"couche de passage", 140
cubic interpolation, 169
cumulative errors, 147, 151, 164, 166
curve fitting techniques, 80
curvature of function, 169
cut-off frequency, 99
    rate, 100

damped least squares method, 109, 171
defects of structure, 141
deposition procedures, 131
    rate, 160
design frequency, 66
    parameters, 74
    variables, 74, 78–98, 135, 140, 169, 171
dichroic beam splitter, 33
dielectric coatings, 31, 33, 42, 130, 134
    layers, 62
differential correction, 108
direct monitoring, 161
dispersion formulae, 133–41
    of index, 40, 80, 83, 85, 87, 93, 118, 121, 125, 130, 140, 163, 180
    of phase change, 42, 47, 49
    relation, 127
distributed circuit filters, 61
    network, 55
double halfwave filter, 42–44, 64, 149 150, 158, 160, 163
Drude-Sellmeiers' dispersion formula, 134, 135
dynamic errors in monitoring, 156–61

edge filters, 30, 32, 52, 64
    frequency, 71, 104
    position, 18, 102
effective indices, 12
    interface method (Smith), 21
    phase thickness, 12, 108
eigenvalues, 169
electric field intensity, 25–9
    vector, 2
electrical length, 57
electromagnetic radiation, 2
    waves, 2
electron bombardment, 130, 141
energies, 3, 8
energy reflectance and transmittance, 8
equi-ripple (Tschebysheff) response, 59, 64, 71, 98

equivalent admittance, 151
    index, 50–4, 61, 102, 108, 148
    thickness, 50–4
error analysis, 45, 128, 143–67
    compensation, 144, 145, 147, 149, 151, 156, 158, 160, 166
errors in layer thickness, 47, 71, 98, 142–67
    in methods for determining optical constants, 125–8, 130, 133, 135
    in turning value of reflectance, 151–3
evolutionary design, 78, 87
exact method of filter synthesis, 108, 110–2
exhaustive search, 78, 82, 87
experimental design, 91
external reflection, 128
extraction of design parameters, 70

Fabry–Perot interference filter, 30, 33, 47, 62, 143, 144, 151–5, 160, 162, 164
    interferometer, 40
feasible point, 173
field intensity profile, 28, 29
filter types, 30–4
finesse, 41
finite difference calculation, 76, 145, 147
first-order monitoring, 152, 154, 155
flow diagram: for least squares method, 81
    for Dobrowolski's method, 88
    for method of Pelletier et al, 96
    for Liddell and Staerck's optical constant program, 135, 136
flow of energy, 16
Fourier series, 108–12
    transform 56, 108, 113–6
frequency domain response, 56
Fresnel coefficients (of reflection and transmissions), 5–8, 24, 35, 40, 108, 112

Gaussian distribution, 149
Gauss–Newton method, 171
Gillod–Boutry photocell, 93
glass filters, 93
global optimum, 74, 80
graded index film, 137–41
gradient vector, 168–9
graphical methods, devices, 24, 25, 35–40, 108, 121, 132, 144

halfwidth, 17, 42, 153–5
heating of substrate, 130, 142
Herpin equivalent index, 50–2
    layer, 52, 53
hessian matrix, 169, 171
high-pass filters (*see also* edge filters),
        32, 64, 66, 71, 72, 76, 77, 98
high-power laser systems, 25
high-reflectance band (zone), 15, 16, 51
high-reflecting multilayers (*see also* broad
        band reflectance coatings) 26, 28,
        30, 31, 76–8, 94, 96, 97
homogeneous films, 1

ill-conditioning of equations, 125, 133
illumination, 22
impedance, 55, 56
incident energy, 3
index fixing routine, 89
indirect monitoring, 149
induced transmission filters, 33
infrared filters, 1, 18, 46, 49, 70, 102,
        104, 106, 149, 152, 153
inhomogeneous films, 1, 140, 141
    layer, 108, 113–6
initial design, 75, 81, 84
    iteration, 140
    scan, 81
insertion loss function, 56, 57, 59
intensity reflectance and transmittance,
        13
interface between layers, 10, 12, 25,
        143
interference filter (*see also* Fabry–Perot
        interference filter, narrow band
        filter), 30, 61, 62
    fringes, 24, 90, 122
internal reflection, 128
isoreflectance contours, 151
isotropic film, 1
iteration process (iterative correction),
        68, 71–3, 99, 102

Jacobian matrix, 171

Kard calculator, 25

Laplace transformation, 56
laser damage, 26, 27
    radiation, 26
    source, 27, 29, 38, 102
    systems, reflecting elements of, 25
LC ladder network analogy, 61, 68

least squares method, 69, 78, 86, 94,
        106, 180
library subroutine, 80, 82, 132, 149, 174,
        180, 181
limiting width of multilayer stack, 17, 18,
        46
linear circuit theory, 55
    search techniques, 78, 82, 169
load impedance, 56
low-pass filter (longwave pass) (*see also*
        edge filters), 32, 52, 53, 61, 64, 66,
        69–73, 98, 103, 147, 149
low-reflectance region, 31
Lucas polynomials, 14
lumped constant network, 55

magnetic vector, 2
mass of film, 142
matrix method of calculation, 9
maximally flat (Butterworth) response, 64
maximetre system, 163, 164, 166
maximum number of iterations, 95, 136
    reflectance, 15, 18, 143
Maxwell's equations, 4
mechanical stylus instrument (Talystep),
        131
medium of incidence, 11, 119, 120
merit function techniques, 74–98, 100,
        101, 104, 116, 134, 135, 165
metal–dielectric filters, 33
metal films, 42, 122, 124, 126, 130, 132,
        135
metallic reflector, 31
mica substrate, 23
microwave quarter-wave transformers, 55,
        59
minimisation, 74, 168–73
mismatched stacks, 49, 82, 84
monitor, 142, 158
monitoring curves, 143
    substrates, 145, 149, 151, 158, 160,
        161, 163
    systems, 142, 144, 156, 158, 163,
        165, 166
    wavelengths, 144, 158, 163, 164
monochromatic source, 22
multilayer calculations, 2, 9–13
multilayers, 1, 9
multiple beam interference microscopy,
        90, 140
multiple halfwave (multiple cavity) filters,
        64, 158, 159, 164, 166, 167
    reflections, 7, 24

narrow band filter, 149, 151, 158, 162
neutral density filter, 110
Newton correction, 170
Newton—Raphson method, 123
non-absorbing films, 10, 27
    media, 8
non-isotropic films, 1
non-linear simplex method, 95, 124, 169,
    173
normal distribution, 149, 151
    incidence, 6, 11, 126, 141
notation, 2, 3
numerical inversion, 125, 126
    refinement, 116
N^2 scan, 82, 180

objective function, 124, 168, 169, 172
optical constants, 1, 24, 118—141, 175
    density, 142
    filter, 1
    measurements, 126
    monitoring, 142
    opacity, 13
    parameters, 126
    path, 113
    thickness, 2
optimal design, 70
optimisation techniques, 74, 123, 132,
    168
optimum response, 98

parabolic interpolation, 80
parallel beam of light, 7
parameter space of design variables, 78
pass band, 32, 51
p-component of polarisation, 2, 4, 102—
    6, 120
peak transmittance, 155, 162
penalty functions, 172, 173
period multilayers, 10, 14
phase change on reflection or transmission,
    2, 8, 9, 89, 95, 127, 129, 143
    factors, 4, 113
    thickness, 2, 10, 11
photoelectric detector, 142
photometric methods, 118, 126, 131,
    140
physical thickness, 2, 119, 122, 124
plane wave, 4
polarimetric methods, 118
polarisation, 2, 4, 6, 25, 102—6, 117, 119,
    125
polarising beam splitter, 29, 33
pole and zero plot, 57

positive definite matrix, 169
    going EM wave, 2
    real function, 56
power flow, 3
Poynting vectors, 3, 21
program for calculating optical constants
    of thin films, 122, 130, 141
    for multilayer analysis, 11, 175
    for simulating reflectance during depo-
        sition of a multilayer, 144
    specification, 87, 180
programmable calculator, 25
prototype functions, 63, 64, 67, 74

quadratic functions, 82
    interpolation, 82, 89, 169
quarter-wave layers, 11
    stacks,(see also classical stacks),14, 32
quartz crytsal oscillator, 142
quasi-Newton methods, 170, 173

random errors in reflection, 151, 158
    variations (errors) in layer thickness,
        143, 149—51, 154
rate of evaporation, 142
rational function technique, 57, 59
realisability, 56
reduced gradient method, 172
reference wavelength, 11, 12, 175, 176,
    181, 182
reflectance (reflectivity), 3, 6, 9, 11, 12,
    19, 27, 75, 80, 89, 94, 119, 125—
    7, 142, 175
reflected amplitudes, 7, 8
    energy, 3
    wave, 4, 5
reflection ratio method, 125
reflectometer, 131
refractive index, 1, 2, 11, 12, 75, 118,
    119, 142, 175, 176, 181, 182
    list, 89
    profile, 113, 115
relative bandwidth, 33, 63
    wavenumber, 15
relaxation methods, 75
resistance of film, 142
restart facility, 87
Richard's transformation, 57, 59, 60
ripple (pass band), 100
roughness, 143

sampling theorem for periodic functions,
    111
scattering losses, 131

s-component of polarisation, 2, 4, 102–6, 120
secant method, 126, 171, 172
second derivative methods, 170
semi-conducting materials, 46
sensitivity of design to errors, 142, 147, 148, 154, 157, 158
   of method for determining optical constants, 124, 132, 133
sequential unconstrained minimisation techniques, 173
shearing interferometer, 140
sign convention, 5
Simpson's rule for integration, 78, 129
single film, 1, 6, 7, 118, 119
Smith chart, 24
Snell's law of refraction, 8, 11, 120
sources: coherent, 20–2, 120
   incoherent, 19, 120
spacer, 40–43, 154
specified response, 74, 80, 100, 116
spectrophotometer, use of, 126, 131, 141, 164
split filter (*see also* two effective interface method), 42
splitting between components of polarisation, 17, 102–6
staggered filters, 47–9
static errors, 156
steepest descent method, 80, 170–2
stop band, 32, 51
stopping zone, 16, 32
subroutine (*see also* library subroutine), 28
subsidiary reflectance maxima, 53
   minima, 74, 82
substrate, 11, 19–24, 119, 125, 130
substrate materials, crown glass, 35, 54, 69
   mica, 23
   quartz, 38
   Spectrosil B, 130
successive appproximation (elimination, iteration, relaxation), 47, 75, 87, 88, 108, 115
sum of squared terms, 74, 82, 95, 122, 130, 135, 170–2
symmetrical filters, 50, 53, 63, 68, 87, 147
synthesis, 2, 55, 108–17

tangential fields, 2
tarnishing of glass, 30

temperature change effects, 156, 158
   coefficients, 160
theoretical design, 91
thickness, 1, 2, 12, 75
   measurement, 130, 131, 142
thin-film computer program, 122
   materials, aluminium oxide, 130, 131, 135, 137, 140, 141
      barium fluoride, 39
      cadmium iodide, 129, 130
      cerium dioxide (ceric oxide), 15, 47
      chiolite, 49
      cryolite, 97, 158, 160, 161
      lead fluoride, 39
      lead telluride, 151
      magnesium fluoride, 15, 47, 86, 130, 131
      neodymium fluoride, 130, 138
      neodymium oxide, 130, 141
      silicon, 123
      stibnite, 49
      thorium oxide, 130, 135, 139, 140
      tin oxide, 39
      titanium dioxide, 130, 131
      zinc sulphide, 69, 86, 97, 151, 158, 160, 161
      zirconium oxide, 130
   optics, 1
   physics, 1
time domain response, 56
tolerance, 57, 74, 95, 124, 142, 152
total internal reflection, 12
transformation methods, 172, 173
   of variables, 134
transmittance, 3, 6, 11, 12, 89, 95, 113, 115, 119, 125–7, 175, 176
transmitted energy, 3
   wave, 4
transmission filter, 89
tristimulus colorimetry, 93
   filters, 93, 116
Tschebysheff function, 63, 64, 67, 74, 98, 99, 100, 102, 110
   polynomials, 14, 16, 57, 58, 109
turning point method, 118
   value method (Chen's, 73, 98–102)
      for monitoring, 142, 144, 146, 149–52, 156, 162
      for determining optical constants, 118, 125
two effective interface method, 40–6, 108

ultraviolet, 1, 87, 130

194

undetermined system, 76
uniformity of thickness, 142
units, 3
unity matrix, 10, 11
univariate search, 78, 82, 89, 122, 130, 132, 169

vacuum deposition, 30

variable interference reflector, 89—91
vector amplitudes, 4
    method algorithm, 109
visible region, 1, 18, 46, 83, 107, 134

wave propagation, 4
weakly absorbing films, 129—41
weighting factors (weights), 87, 94, 166